ISBN 978-1-330-04519-0
PIBN 10012049

SCHLIEMANN'S EXCAVATIONS

AN ARCHÆOLOGICAL AND HISTORICAL STUDY

By Dr. C. SCHUCHHARDT

DIRECTOR OF THE KESTNER MUSEUM IN HANOVER

TRANSLATED FROM THE GERMAN BY

EUGÉNIE SELLERS

WITH AN APPENDIX ON THE RECENT DISCOVERIES AT HISSARLIK BY

Dr. SCHLIEMANN AND Dr. DÖRPFELD

AND AN INTRODUCTION BY

WALTER LEAF, Litt.D.

ILLUSTRATED

London
MACMILLAN AND CO.
AND NEW YORK
1891

Dorten setz' ich still mich nieder
Und gedenke alter Zeit,
Alter blühender Geschlechter
Und versunkner Herrlichkeit.

HEINE.

CONTENTS

CHAPTER I

LIFE OF DR. SCHLIEMANN

CHAPTER II

TROY

CHAPTER III

TIRYNS

CHAPTER IV

MYCENÆ

CHAPTER V

MINOR EXCAVATIONS

CHAPTER VI

APPENDIX I

THE RECENT EXCAVATIONS AT HISSARLIK

APPENDIX II

TRANSLATOR'S NOTES

ILLUSTRATIONS

MAPS AND PLANS

TROY

TOPOGRAPHY

THE OLDEST CITY

                                    MYCENÆ

                            GRAVES I AND III

GRAVE II

GRAVE IV

Sophie Schliemann

Printed by F A Brockhaus, Leipzig

PREFACE TO THE GERMAN EDITION

THE task of presenting the results of Schliemann's excavations in a concise form which should make them more accessible to the general public than has been hitherto the case, was entrusted to me in the year 1886, while I was still engaged in Asia Minor with the excavations at Pergamon. I thus had the advantage during that year and most of the following of making the necessary observations on the spot, and by constant personal intercourse with those concerned, I was able to learn much which is not to be found either in remains or in books. I subsequently began to write the book in Athens, I continued it in Berlin and Rome, and finished it in Hanover. These changes of residence occasionally brought with them differences in my point of view, and must be my excuse for the many inequalities I am conscious of in the treatment of my subject.

The undertaking was a difficult one, for the questions which Dr. Schliemann's activity had called up are still undecided, and the picture of that ancient Greek civilisation which he was the first to discover receives every year some important additions through the further excavations of the Greeks. At the same time the task proved pleasant, for the attempt to win from the discoveries some insight into the actual conditions of prehistoric Greece, and to arrive at a clearer conception of what the countries and the people described by Homer were like, could not but appeal to all those who have felt the magic of the old heroic lays. And, in fact, every scholar who wishes to investigate the origins and actual contents of the Homeric poems, or the origins of the Greek people and their civilisation, must nowadays base his researches in the first place on the material afforded by Schliemann's excavations.

b

Since specialists had hitherto only discussed this material with a sort of religious awe, various new points of view naturally suggested themselves to me in the course of the work. I venture to hope that scholars may not find them altogether unworthy of acceptance. On the other hand, there are whole portions of the book—as, for example, the description of the buildings at Tiryns—where all that was needed was to give a *résumé* of the admirable accounts already published.

A selection of suitable illustrations from Dr. Schliemann's books is given, with the addition of a considerable number of new cuts necessary to illustrate fresh views and further discoveries. Some of these are from published works, some from photographs, some from my own sketches in the museums of Athens. The list which follows the Table of Contents gives the source whence each is taken, and will serve to direct those who wish further to study the objects represented.

It only remains for me to express the hope that the book will not merely rouse specialists to a more general appreciation and study of this vast subject, but that it will give the great educated public a clearer conception of the actual and important results of the life-work of a man whom the world has loaded with honours and yet often misunderstood.

CARL SCHUCHHARDT.

Hanover, *November* 1, 1889.

TRANSLATOR'S NOTE

SHORTLY before his lamented death Dr. Schliemann had with the utmost kindness allowed his report of the Hissarlik excavations during the year 1889-90 to be translated and printed as an appendix to the English Edition of Dr. Schuchhardt's work. With equal generosity Dr. Dörpfeld has given his portion of the report for the same purpose, together with his new plan of Hissarlik. As the recent excavations have almost doubled our knowledge of the Trojan Pergamos, the value of this plan and of Dr. Dörpfeld's explanation of it can scarcely be overestimated. The English Edition has been further materially enriched by an Introduction to the whole subject by Mr. Walter Leaf.

I have ventured to alter one or two matters of detail in the course of translation. The statement on p. 21 to the effect that Polemon described the altar of Zeus Herkeios has been corrected, and the account of the Bunárbashi springs on p. 25 has been rectified after consulting the original authorities. The footnotes do not appear in the German Edition. They consist mainly of references to classical authors. References to modern authorities have only been given when, as in the case of the springs, the matter might appear to be one under discussion, or if it seemed important to call attention to some important and easily accessible publication. For the possible convenience of English readers I have referred on p. 76 for the Hissarlik finds, and in Appendix II for the Mycenæan finds, to the cases of the British Museum where objects helping to illustrate the subject may be found. Appendix II also contains a short account of the now famous

Vapheio gold cups, with a reproduction of a drawing of the cups
by Mr. F. Anderson, kindly lent for this edition by Mr. Walter
Leaf, to whom I wish, in conclusion, to express my personal
debt of gratitude, for having relieved me of the whole burden of
correcting the proofs during my absence from England.

EUGÉNIE SELLERS.

BRITISH SCHOOL OF ARCHÆOLOGY,
      ATHENS, *March* 1, 1891.

INTRODUCTION

DR. HENRY SCHLIEMANN died while the following translation was passing through the press. So far as his work is concerned, Dr. Schuchhardt's pages, together with the Appendix describing last season's work at Hissarlik, now give a full and final history. No student of Hellenism can think without deep regret that this should be so; that there is no fresh discovery to be hoped for from the unwearying devotion and unstinted generosity of the famous merchant enthusiast. But the work which he has done is in no way dependent on his individual life; it has been no less than the creation of prehistoric Greek archæology. Dr. Schliemann was essentially "epoch-making" in this branch of study, and it is not for epoch-making men to see the rounding off and completion of their task. That must be the labour of a generation at least. A man who can state to the world a completely new problem may be content to let the final solution of it wait for those that come after him.

An orderly arrangement of the immense amount of material which Schliemann accumulated is the first and essential condition of such a solution. How much it is needed can only be adequately felt by those who have attempted to make it for themselves from the various large and expensive volumes in which it is to be sought. Schliemann's excellent rule of publishing his results at once has one serious disadvantage. Either the whole material must be published twice over, as soon as further exploration and experience have brought new light to bear upon the first crude and imperfect conclusions; or the later deductions must be given separately, apart from a portion at least of the evidence on which they are founded. It is this which makes it a task of serious labour to extract from two such volumes as

Ilios and *Troja* a clear idea of what is really to be learnt from Hissarlik. The difficulty is yet more perplexing when an entire change of view takes place during the publication of a single volume. Many a student of *Tiryns* must have been for a time at sea when he found an elaborate explanation of the citadel walls in the text of the volume absolutely contradicted, without a word of reference forward, in an equally elaborate appendix.

Dr. Schuchhardt has undertaken to bring order into this chaos. He has not merely arranged the facts in intelligible sequence; though it is no small merit that he should have brought into the compass of a single handy volume all that is of first-rate importance in Schliemann's various works. He has gone on to analyse and explain them. His luminous and convincing chapter on the contents of the shaft tombs at Mycenæ is a model investigation, and is hardly likely to require serious correction in the future.

But in its wider aspects Schliemann's problem will long remain unsettled. It presents two questions, intimately connected : What is the true relation of the Mycenæan civilisation to the Homeric poems ? and What is its place in the development of classical Greece ? These questions are touched upon by Dr. Schuchhardt, but not so exhaustively as to forbid a few further suggestions even in the brief compass of a preface.

Dr. Schuchhardt, I think, rates too highly the ingenious but most hazardous speculations of von Wilamowitz-Möllendorf; he follows him even to finding the Peloponnesus itself in the magic land of Thrinakia. And consequently he rates too low, in my opinion, the possibility that the oldest parts of the *Iliad* at least may be actual survivals in their present form from Achaian and pre-Dorian days. But this possibility is one which can be supported by weighty arguments, and must not be left out of sight; it must necessarily affect our view of the relation of the text to the monuments throughout.

It has, moreover, received powerful support from Fick's labours on the Homeric dialect. Fick has shown that the poems were in all probability composed, not in the Ionic dialect, but in what he speaks of as Æolic. Only he seems to err in taking as the original dialect an Æolic which hardly differs from that spoken in the north-west of Asia Minor in the third century B.C. Now we should rather suppose that the original dialect was that of the ancestors of these Asiatic Æolians, the Achaians of the eleventh century. What the form of their speech was we cannot now pretend to say. It must have differed greatly from Fick's Æolic; it was the common parent of Thessalian, Arcadian, and Cyprian, in all of which we see various points of connexion with the Epic language. These affinities do not allow of an even approximate reconstruction of the parent speech; but they do allow us to assume that there was once a common Achaian language spoken by the dwellers in Mycenæ and Tiryns, and over great part of the Greek mainland, and even to detect some of the points in which this speech differed from that common to the Ionian and Dorian tribes respectively. If the *Iliad* was composed in this dialect, and not in its present Ionic form, we no longer need date it after the great migration to Asia Minor; nothing on the linguistic side prevents our referring it to European Greece, and therefore to pre-Dorian days.

If now we assume as a working hypothesis that the poems really do depict, as contemporaries, the Achaian age as they profess, we are at once relieved from grave difficulties. We can understand how it is that they can present with such vivid life a state of manners and customs which must have been utterly unknown to the Ionians of the coast of Asia Minor. The emigrants of the great colonies of Miletus, Ephesus, Smyrna, Colophon, and the rest were eager traders, democratic to the core, ever intent on widening their horizon, and pushing their voyages at early dates to the coasts of the Black Sea, Sicily, Egypt, and the Gulf of Lions. They are the very antipodes of the Homeric Achaians, a race of ancient and aristocratic families, living only on the mainland of Greece proper and in Crete, and knowing, or at least caring, little about so much of the world as lay beyond the Ægean Sea. About commerce the Achaians hardly trouble themselves, leaving trade mostly in the hands of their Phœnician visitors, and living rather on the produce of the flocks and fields which their thralls have in charge. That an Ionian could have reproduced such an age and made a lifelike picture of it is an assumption which strains all probability; for it not only assumes a trained historic imagination, but involves actual archæological study such as is absolutely foreign to the genius of a young and rising nation.

The later portions of the *Iliad* and the *Odyssey* alike may, it is true, have been actually composed in Ionia by Ionian bards. But the continuation of a poem on lines already given is a vastly different task from the first creation of a new world. Working up to the earlier parts of the *Iliad*, a poet of Ionia would have only to avoid inconsistencies with his type, where he found all the scenery drawn in with such strong and broad lines that he could hardly fail to follow them rightly. The task would be altogether more thorny and complex if, instead of merely making his actors talk and move on the old stage, he had to create from his own inner consciousness a fresh plot and fresh scenery. In that case it is hardly conceivable that his work should have shown that remarkable general correspondence with the pre-historic remains which will be found in the following chapters.

Assuming then that the groundwork and foundation of the *Iliad* at least is the picture of a state of civilisation which actually has another and material representative in what Dr. Schliemann has found at Mycenæ and Tiryns, let us see if it is not possible to draw somewhat closer the connexion between the poems and the remains than Dr. Schuchhardt has ventured to do.

In the period known as Mycenæan we can clearly distinguish two great epochs—an earlier, to which the shaft tombs, and a later, to which the bee-hive tombs belong. It is to the former of these that we must ascribe the remains of Tiryns, and about this only that we have gained a very definite idea. That the bee-hive tombs are later than the period of the shaft tombs it is easy to see. The age of the bee-hive tombs, indeed, as we find at Menidi and Amyclæ, passes down into the historical period, and overlaps the age of the early geometrical pottery. Roughly coeval with it are no doubt the walls of Mycenæ and the Lion Gate, where the masonry shows so marked an advance upon that of Tiryns. But we have unfortunately very little in the way of individual finds, to which we can point as demonstrating the culture of the age of the bee-hive tombs in its differences from that of the earlier stage. The "Treasury of Atreus" has long ago been rifled beyond all hope; there is hardly a chance that any of the other bee-hive tombs at Mycenæ can have escaped the same fate. But what little has been found shows that these tombs were connected with a civilisation directly descended from and continuing that of the shaft tombs, only with the introduction of a more marked Semitic influence. Traces of Assyrian workmanship, so markedly absent from the shaft tombs, were found unmistakably in the bee-hive tombs of Attica, probably the latest of the series, and dating from some considerable time after the Dorian invasion. The two gold cups of Vapheio, the most startling discovery of the last two years, betray beyond a doubt their genealogy from the art which created the bull of Tiryns and the hunting scenes of the Mycenæ dagger-blades. There is thus a continuity of development through the unknown number of centuries which extend from the prime of Tiryns to the Dorian invasion. The earlier period of this long age is certainly older than any which can be represented by the Homeric poems, even the oldest of them. Even apart from the evidence of the remains themselves, there is the certain fact that the period presented to us in the *Iliad* is later than the greatness of Tiryns. Legend tells us that Tiryns was older than Mycenæ; the remains confirm the legend, and the silence of the *Iliad* as to Tiryns—a silence hardly broken by a passing mention in the Catalogue—is only explicable on the theory that the rise of Mycenæ had already brought about the decay of her nearest neighbour.

If then we are to find within the compass of the Mycenæan period any epoch corresponding to the age depicted in the *Iliad*, it is clear to demonstration that this age must be that of the bee-hive tombs. And the period which the *Iliad* and *Odyssey* profess to describe is certainly within this compass; for it is a period before the Dorian invasion, which overthrew the Mycenæan power. Either therefore the poems, while professing to describe one period, are in reality describing another, whether real or imaginary; or they describe the age of the builders of the bee-hive tombs.

But it must not be forgotten that there are a few points in which the Homeric poems seem to indicate a departure from the manners and customs of the Mycenæan age. The most important of these is undoubtedly the mode of burial. A few words must be devoted to the consideration of this vital point.

It is now established that the bodies found in the shaft tombs were not burnt on the pyre, but were buried after some imperfect process of mummification. On the other hand, the detailed descriptions of funerals in the *Iliad* and *Odyssey*—those of Patroklos in the 23d, and of Hector in the 24th Book of the

Iliad, and of Elpenor in the 12th *Odyssey*—all make the burning of the body an essential part of the rite.

The contrast is a striking one, but it is easy to lay too much stress upon it. In the first place it must be pointed out that Homeric critics, however widely differing in their views of the poems as a whole, are nearly unanimous in regarding the 23d and 24th Books of the *Iliad* as belonging to the latest additions to the poem; and the *Odyssey* as being decidedly later than the *Iliad*. It is therefore quite conceivable that we have here an instance where later manners have been introduced, bringing about a want of harmony between the older and more recent constituents of the *Iliad*. It might even be supposed that this was done purposely, in order to give the sanction of heroic times to what was still felt as an innovation in funeral rites. But the assumption is not necessary. It may well be that the conditions of sepulture on a campaign were perforce different from those usual in times of peace at home. The mummifying of the body and the carrying of it to the ancestral burying-place in the royal citadel were not operations such as could be easily effected amidst the hurry of marches or the privations of a siege; least of all after the slaughter of a pitched battle. It is there-fore quite conceivable that two methods of sepulture may of necessity have been in use at the same time. And for this assumption the *Iliad* itself gives us positive grounds. One warrior who falls is taken home to be buried; for to a dead son of Zeus means of carriage and of preservation can be supplied, which are not for common men. Sarpedon is cleansed by Apollo, and borne by Death and Sleep to his distant home in Lykia, not that his body may be burnt, but that his kinsfolk and brethren may *preserve* it "with a tomb and gravestone; for such is the due of the dead." The word ταρχύειν is one which is entirely inapplicable to burning on the pyre; it is used with a slight change of form, as ταριχεύειν, by Herodotos (ii. 86), to express the Egyptian process of mummification. In all probability it has a similar sense in Homer, and shows that a part of the *Iliad* regarded such a rite as normal in times of peace. Moreover, it is not proved that cremation did not come into use in the Mycenæan period itself, at the epoch which we have identified as that of the *Iliad* and *Odyssey*; the evidence of the later tombs does not decisively show that the bodies buried in them may not have been cremated on the pyre, and the bones alone laid in the graves. It is thus easy to see how many considerations have to be weighed, and how imperfect our evidence still is, before we can decide that there is a real discrepancy in the mode of sepulture between the poems and the remains of the " bee-hive " tomb period of Mycenæan civilisation.

A few remarks may be added as to the shape of the bee-hive tombs themselves. Dr. Schuchhardt quotes (p. 151) with approval Professor Adler's derivation of the form from a Phrygian prototype. But so definite a reference is too narrow. The conical hut was beyond all doubt the primitive Aryan dwelling-place, and was in no way peculiar to the Phrygians. It survived to historic times in certain religious aspects, as Mr. J. G. Frazer has shown in his admirable and entertaining essay on the Prytaneum and the Temple of Vesta.[1] It was therefore as an inheritance from their remotest ancestors, and not as an importation across the Ægean, that the Princes of Mycenæ took the bee-hive shape of the old royal dwelling and eternalised it in the royal tomb. We are thus led straight to a conjecture as to the circular enclosure which surrounds the oldest shaft tombs of Mycenæ. The tradition will be unbroken if we suppose that this is itself only the ground-plan of a great circular hut. The roof, when the tombs were first dug, must have consisted of a perishable material, no doubt the primitive wattle or thatch. The diameter of the circle, some thirty yards, is not too large for such a roof. It is actually attested in the funeral rites of the Scythians; who, when burying their kings, roofed over the grave with beams and thatched these with reeds.[2] The bee-hive tomb is but the translation of this into stone.

There is another point in which the finds from the shaft tombs do not bear out the evidence of the poems; it is the more worthy of brief consideration, as it is not dwelt upon by Dr. Schuchhardt. The question of the clothing both of men and women in the two poems has recently been placed in a new light by the admirable researches of Dr. Studniczka.[3] He has shown that the *peplos* of the Homeric lady was identical with the garment which we know in the classical age as the Doric chiton, and regard as the type of Greek dress. It was a plain square piece of woollen, or more rarely of linen material, fastened by brooches over the shoulder,

[1] *Journal of Philology*, vol. xiv. p. 145.   [2] Herod. iv. 71.
[3] *Beiträge zur Geschichte der Altgriechischen Tracht*, Vienna, 1886.

and bound round the waist by a girdle. The simplicity of its
form naturally leads to the conclusion that it was a garb which
had survived from extreme antiquity. The Homeric hero, on the
other hand, dressed in the linen chiton, a shaped and sewn
garment of eastern origin, whose name was taken direct from a
Semitic language. But we find no evidence of the existence of
either of these dresses in the various representations of men and
women which have come from the tombs. On the great seal
(Fig. 281), and on the curious fragment of slab-painting (Fig. 288),
which are our sole evidence as to the dress of the Mycenæan
women, we see, not the plain *peplos* with its long sweeping
vertical folds, but a more elaborate garment with series of
horizontal flounces or. tucks. The evidence of the seal might
perhaps be disregarded till we had some better grounds for
attributing it to native workmanship; for it might only represent
the dress of a foreign nation from whom it had been imported.
But the indications of the slab-painting seem too clearly to point
to an identical garb, and it is not likely that this painting was
ever imported from a foreign source. And the negative evidence
of the tombs tends strongly in the same direction; for among all
the numerous finds there is not a single brooch or fibula, though
this was an essential accessory to the Homeric *peplos*. It
appears therefore that the dress of the age of the shaft tombs was
radically different from that of the *Iliad* and *Odyssey*. But even
here we have welcome proof that a change took place in the
Mycenæan fashions during the period of the prevalence of the
bee-hive tombs. For traces of fibulæ have actually been found
in the tombs of the lower city, which are either coeval with or
anterior to the bee-hive tombs. It would seem, therefore, that
the *peplos* is not, after all, so primitive a garment in Greece as its
shape would seem to imply; or at least that it had for a period
been superseded by a more elaborate dress, and was again taken
into fashion when some freak of fancy commanded a return to the
older and plainer garb. Curiously enough we know that exactly
such a return to simplicity and the Doric *peplos* took place in the
historic period, when the more luxurious Ionic chiton had for a
time superseded, with men as with women, the ancient mode.[1]

To a smaller extent the same remark applies to male dress.
We have more information regarding this; for several seals and

---

[1] Herod. v. 87. Studniczka, pp. 1-5.

intaglios from the shaft tomb give us pictures of the Mycenæan man in various stages of activity. The dress in all of them seems to be the same; it consists, both for battle and the chase, so far as can be made out, only of a short pair of drawers or an apron suspended from a girdle. Of course, in a climate like that of Greece, this cannot have been the only dress; a mantle at least must have been worn over it, and cast aside only during violent exertion. But the apron seems quite inconsistent with a chiton of linen; so that here we have a case where Asiatic fashions must have made their way in after the age of the shaft tombs. We may suppose that this change occurred in the epoch of the bee-hive tombs; but we have not in this case any corroborative evidence, for the chiton could not leave behind it any traces like the *peplos*; it was not fastened with any metal work. Indeed the evidence of the Vapheio cups themselves, which give us the best and latest picture of the ancient dress, is adverse; the men are still wearing the apron, not the chiton. This is not in itself conclusive, for it is a familiar fact that art preserves ancient types, in dress as elsewhere, after they have passed out of fashion. Here then we can only recognise the discrepancy, and trust that further discoveries may yet clear it up, as the past has explained so many of our old difficulties.

Once more Dr. Schuchhardt has gone too far in accentuating the difference between the local extension of the Achaians and the actual range of the Mycenæan remains. He speaks almost as though the Homeric Achaians were spread equally over the mainland of Greece, and confined to it. But as a fact, the list of places given at the top of p. 315 exhibits a remarkable coincidence with the geography of the Catalogue of the Ships in the second book of the *Iliad*. Lacedæmon, Argolis, Attica, Bœotia, Thessaly, and Crete are for Homer main seats of the Achaians, as for archæologists they are centres of Mycenæan culture. But the coincidence goes further than this broad correspondence. The Catalogue of the Ships represents the Achaians as extending in a narrow line from Crete through the Sporades to Rhodes, and thus in close touch with Lykia, whose royal house boasts of Greek blood. Now it is surely a noteworthy coincidence that it is precisely this narrow zone which is marked by Mycenæan finds. Of the spots named by Schuchhardt, Cos, Carpathos, Rhodes, and, under the name of

" the Isles Calydnae," Calymnos, all appear in the Catalogue ; and they are the only group of islands in the Archipelago which does so appear. It has often puzzled commentators to find the Sporades thus drawn into the Achaian world, while the historically far more important Cyclades are entirely ignored. The solution to the problem surely is that in Homeric times the Sporades were Achaian, while the Cyclades still remained, as we must suppose, Carian. It is true that finds of Mycenæan ware have been made on two of the Cyclades—on Thera, which lies nearest Crete, and on Syra, the *entrepôt* of the Archipelago. But these isolated cases give us no more right to suppose that these two islands were seats of Mycenæan civilisation than Mr. Petrie's discoveries would allow us to attribute the Fayum to the empire of Agamemnon. They are easily to be explained by importation. So far then from accentuating a difference, this local distribution in the Archipelago is a striking mark of coincidence between Homeric conceptions and the results of archæology.

So when Dr. Schuchhardt goes on to argue (p. 317) that no Mycenæan finds will be made in Western Greece, because all have hitherto been made in the East, he leaps to a conclusion— or rather to a *petitio principii*—against which Schliemann's career should be a sufficient warning. The argument that the Mycenæan civilisation looks towards the East and not towards the West is of course true, as it is of all Greek civilisation ; but it does not forbid us to suppose that there were offshoots in the West in Mycenæan as in historic times. Homeric civilisation also looks towards the East. It would indeed be hard to say where the *Iliad* would lead us to expect Achaian traces in the West, except at Pylos and Ithaca, and perhaps in Ætolia. When sufficient remains of primitive civilisation have been found in these spots to prove that the Mycenæan culture did not extend to them, then and not before shall we be justified in speaking of a discrepancy between the geographical distribution of the Achaians of Homer and the people of the Mycenæan world. At present we are here absolutely without information, and the presumption remains in favour of the correctness of the Homeric record.

This want of agreement, such as it is, cannot for a moment outweigh the positive evidence of the undesigned coincidences between the culture of Mycenæ and Homer. The most important of these is the light which the inlaid metal work throws on Homeric descriptions, such as the shield of Achilles and the panoply of Agamemnon. The coincidence of the arrangements of the palace at Tiryns with the houses of Homer is in its way equally striking, though here some allowances have to be made. We find exactly reproduced the Homeric fore-court, with its colonnades and prothyron, and even its altar; we find the megaron with pillars and hearth and ante-room, and close by the indispensable bathroom. But we find besides a second establishment, a smaller duplicate of the first, and accessible from it only with difficulty. Of such an arrangement there is no trace in Homer. It strongly suggests the view, held by Dr. Dörpfeld and supported by Dr. Schuchhardt, that this second establishment was set apart for the women. If so, it is distinctly in contradiction to Homer, for Homeric manners know nothing of such a separation of the sexes in domestic life as the difficult access from the larger megaron to the smaller would imply. And in the Homeric house of which we know most, the palace of Odysseus, there certainly was in the poet's conception, as Professor Jebb has conclusively shown, an immediate access from the back of the megaron to the chambers in which the women live and work. If Dörpfeld's view is right, we must regard the Tiryns palace as oriental in plan; for it is nothing else than a house with a harem, and implies polygamy. Though the difference is thus one of type, yet the plan of the Tirynthian palace admits of being at once converted into that of a Homeric house by the simple expedient of driving a doorway through the back of the megaron and abolishing the second courtyard with its appurtenances. There is time enough for such a step to have been taken in the long interval between the remains of Tiryns and the bee-hive tombs of Mycenæ; but positive evidence is lacking. There is no trace of a doorway in the megaron at Mycenæ, any more than at Tiryns; but we have as yet no evidence of the existence of a second court.

With regard to the discoveries at Hissarlik, it must in this place suffice to say that the main result as regards the *Iliad* is this: first, that evidence for the historical reality of a siege of Troy by the Achaians is now greatly strengthened; and secondly, that the account of it given in the *Iliad* is at best based upon vague tradition. For the Achaians and the Trojans of Homer

are to all intents and purposes the same people; the trifling
differences between them which can here and there be traced are
as nothing in comparison with the countless points in which they
are represented as agreeing in language, religion, and manners.
But we know for certain that the dwellers upon the hill of
Hissarlik were at a completely different and altogether lower
stage of civilisation than the royal race of Mycenæ. Scarcely
half a dozen objects have been found which show a point of
contact. If, therefore, Homer correctly describes the Achaians,
his Trojans are quite imaginary.

These few introductory remarks will suffice to show how the
field of speculation has been widened by Dr. Schliemann's discoveries. It is, and for a long time will be, open for the cultivation of new hypotheses. Whether these are right or wrong is of
little importance, so long as they are suggestive. But it is a
great and final gain to have attained to a clear and comprehensive
arrangement of the material such as Dr. Schuchhardt has given us.

WALTER LEAF.

February 1891.

CHAPTER I

THE recent death of Dr. Schliemann on December 26 of last year lends at the present time a special melancholy interest to the story of his life. His method of archæological research, however, was so characteristic of the man that any account of his discoveries must always have been prefaced by a brief sketch. Not only was he an enthusiastic admirer of antiquity; he was also a thoroughly practical man of untiring perseverance. Success in business was for him a necessary preliminary to the archæological work which had attracted him from the first. He acquired a fortune, thanks to an energy which neither difficulties nor depressing surroundings could daunt. When at last he could devote himself to the luxury of study, his business habits proved invaluable. The promptitude with which every important discovery was followed up by a book on the subject, did much towards keeping Dr. Schliemann's name before the world, so that by the general public he was regarded as archæology personified.

He has himself given us the leading facts of his biography in *Ilios*, his greatest work.

Heinrich Schliemann, a clergyman's son, was born on January 6, 1822, at New Buckow, in Mecklenburg-Schwerin. In the following year the family removed to the village of Ankershagen, and there, where they remained for eight years, the child's imagination received its first vivid impressions. "Our garden house," says Dr. Schliemann, "was said to be haunted by the ghost of my father's predecessor, and just behind our garden was a pond, called 'das Silberschälchen,' out of which a maiden was believed to rise

B

each midnight, holding a silver bowl. There was also in the village a small hill, surrounded by a ditch, probably a prehistoric burial-place (or so-called 'Hun's Grave'), in which, as the legend ran, a robber-knight in times of old had buried his favourite child in a golden cradle." The chief feature, however, was an old castle, which had once been inhabited by the old knight Henning von Holstein, popularly called Henning Bradenkirl. By the "Wartensberg," close at hand, said tradition, the wicked knight had once lain in wait for the Duke of Mecklenburg. His attempt having failed, the Duke besieged him in his castle, and there they still showed the massive tower, close to which he had buried all his treasures, when escape became hopeless. On the castle-wall stood a relief of Henning Bradenkirl, and in the churchyard was his grave, from which for centuries his left leg, in a black silk stocking, had grown out again and again. All these tales, solemnly vouched for by sexton and grave-digger, were loyally believed by the sensitive child.

Dr. Schliemann proceeds to relate that he often heard his father vividly narrate the story of the destruction of Pompeii and Herculaneum, and the course of the Trojan War. He received at Christmas 1829 a child's history of the world, in which the picture of Troy in flames with its huge walls, and the Skaian Gate with Æneas in flight, bearing his father Anchises ⁻on his shoulders, and leading the boy Ascanius by the hand, made a deep impression upon him, and awoke a passionate desire to visit those regions and see what still remained of their ancient splendour. Finding but little response to his enthusiasm among his playmates, he was attracted all the more towards a sympathetic little friend of his own age, Minna Meincke, who, he says, promised to marry him one day and help him to discover Troy.

When the boy was nine years old, his mother died. As the family numbered seven children, their education became a difficult matter. Heinrich was sent to his uncle, the clergyman at Kalkhorst, and there for a year he was well taught by a divinity student. At Christmas 1832 he could gratify his father by sending him a Latin essay on the chief events of the Trojan War. He was soon afterwards sent to the gymnasium at New Strelitz and put in the third form; but family misfortunes compelled him to give up all hopes of a learned career. Three months later he had to leave the classical school for a commercial one. When he passed out of it in the spring of 1836, at the age of fourteen, he was apprenticed to a small grocer in the village of Fürstenberg. Here his duties consisted in selling across the counter herrings, butter, potato-brandy, milk, salt, coffee, sugar, oil, tallow-candles, etc., grinding potatoes for the distillery, sweeping the shop, and similar congenial occupations.   From early morning till late at night he had to stand in the shop, and could not find a moment in which to cultivate his mind.   Dr. Schliemann remembers a characteristic little event that occurred at this time.   One evening there came to the shop a miller's man, who had been born in better circumstances and educated at a gymnasium, but had come down in the world and taken to drink.   Yet with all this he had not forgotten his Homer.   "That evening," says Dr. Schliemann, "he recited to us about a hundred lines of the poet, observing the rhythmic cadence of the verses.   Although I did not understand a syllable, the melodious sound of the words made a deep impression upon me, and I wept bitter tears over my unhappy fate. Three times over did I get him to repeat to me those divine verses, rewarding his trouble with three glasses of whiskey, which I bought with the few pence that made up my whole wealth, From that moment I never ceased to pray God that by His grace I might yet have the happiness of learning Greek."

For five years and a half Dr. Schliemann dragged on his existence in this situation, till one day he overstrained himself by lifting a cask, spat blood, and had to give up his work.   He walked to Hamburg, and tried to find fresh employment with different grocers there, but in each place his weak chest proved him after a short time unfit for the work.   In despair, he bound himself as a cabin boy, sold his only coat to buy a blanket for the voyage, and set sail for Venezuela, on board the brig *Dorothea*, on November 28, 1841.   Fortune, however, was kinder to him than it seemed.   The ship was wrecked on the Dutch coast.   Its crew, after drifting about for nine hours in a little boat, got safely ashore, and while the others lost everything in the wreck, Dr. Schliemann's chest, with his few belongings, was picked up.   He now felt it his vocation to remain in Holland, and there indeed he was to lay the foundation-stone of all his future success.

His first year was still far from brilliant.   He had gone to Amsterdam and become office-boy in Mr. F. E. Quien's warehouse. In this capacity he had to run all the errands in the town, collect bills, and carry letters to and from the post. But he took advantage of the perfect mental leisure afforded by this employment, to carry on his education. "I never went on my errands, even in the rain," he says, "without having my book in my hand and learning something by heart. I never waited at the post-office without reading, or repeating a passage iu my mind." Thus he learnt English in one half-year and French in the next, and managed to save for intellectual needs the half of his small salary of 800 francs. His method of learning these languages exemplifies his plan of always reaching his goal by the shortest possible way. He did not trouble about grammatical rules or about making translations, but read a great deal aloud, and wrote little exercises which were corrected by the teacher and then learnt by heart. This tended to strengthen his memory, which was quite exceptional. He was in such good training after that year that for each of the languages which he learnt next—Dutch, Spanish, Italian, and Portuguese—he required only six weeks.

Gradually he wearied of the mechanical work of his humble position, and began to neglect it, so that a change seemed desirable both to himself and his employers. On March 1, 1844, he was engaged as corresponding clerk and book-keeper to Messrs. B. H. Schröder and Co. of Amsterdam. He thus entered a firm that could introduce him to the great world of commerce. Here, too, his zeal was fully appreciated and encouraged. Dr. Schliemann always spoke gratefully of his former master as the author of all his later success, and expressed deep respect for the admirable old man who withdrew from business only a few years ago, to enjoy a well-earned rest in Hanover.

Dr. Schliemann now began to study Russian under peculiar conditions. As no teacher of this language was to be found in the town, he learnt by heart the Russian translation of *Télémaque*. So as to have some one to whom he could repeat what he had learnt, he hired a poor Jew, who had every evening to listen to the Russian recitation, of which he did not understand one word. The Jew endured it for four francs a week, but Dr. Schliemann's fellow-lodgers, who also had to hear every word through the thin Dutch partitions, did not feel themselves equally bound to endurance, so the enthusiastic youth had to change his lodgings twice during this educational period. His employers judged his new acquirement more favourably, and sent him at the beginning of 1846 as their agent to St. Petersburg. Dr. Schliemann now came quickly to the front. Within the first year his success was so great that he could think of carrying out the earliest of his childish plans, and marrying Minna Meincke. To his sorrow he found that his first love had married another only a few weeks before. He was idealist enough to feel such an event as " the heaviest blow that could fall upon him," but he was also vigorous enough to throw himself all the more eagerly into his daily duties. In 1847 he founded a mercantile house of his own at St. Petersburg, and still remained agent for Messrs. B. H. Schröder and Co. of Amsterdam, whom he represented for eleven years altogether. He devoted himself almost entirely to the indigo trade, and it was not till later that he temporarily added the tea business to it. He accidentally became an American citizen during a journey to California in 1850. California was made a State on July 4 of that year, and every one who happened to be there at the time became, without further formality, a citizen of the United States.

Dr. Schliemann founded a branch establishment at Moscow in 1852. During the next few years the very difficulties of the Crimean War, which he met in characteristic fashion, were turned by his unfailing ingenuity to the best account, and brought him large profits. Besides this, he met now and then with exceptional good fortune. Thus on October 4, 1850, when goods to the amount of 150,000 thalers, representing his sole capital at that time, were lying stored for him with Messrs. Meyer and Co. at Memel, their great warehouse was destroyed by a fire which laid the whole town in ashes. Dr. Schliemann's goods alone escaped destruction, for, as the warehouse was full, they had been stored to the north of the town in a wooden shed, from which the pre-vailing north wind kept off the flames. These goods were now sold by Dr. Schliemann to great advantage. He invested the profits repeatedly; " did a large business in indigo, dye-woods, and military stores (saltpetre, brimstone, and lead); and as capitalists were afraid to do much business during the Crimean War, he was able to make considerable profits, and to more than double his capital in the course of one year."

So matters went on till 1858, when Dr. Schliemann believed he had made a sufficient fortune and could now devote himself entirely to his favourite study of archæology. He had been studying Greek for two years, since the end of the Crimean War. He had not dared to do this before, for fear he should fall under the spell of Homer and neglect his business, which he could not yet afford to give up. He now made an extensive tour through Sweden, Denmark, Germany, Italy, and Egypt. He had just reached Athens and was on the point of starting for Ithaca, when a lawsuit recalled him to St. Petersburg and detained him there for several years. He therefore temporarily resumed business in that town, and extended it, dealing not only in indigo, but also in cotton and tea. He imported £500,000 worth of goods from May to October 1860. The lawsuit was decided in his favour in December 1863, when he finally wound up his business, to which he never returned.

In the spring of 1864 Dr. Schliemann travelled to Carthage and India, and remained for several months in China and Japan. His first book, *La Chine et le Japon*, was written during the fifty days' voyage from Japan to America. It was published next year in Paris, where Dr. Schliemann now settled, devoting himself chiefly to the study of archæology. He visited for the first time the classical spots which were later to become the sources of his world-wide fame in the summer of 1868. He published an account of these travels in German and French in 1869, under the title of *Ithaca, the Peloponnesus, and Troy*. In this book he first announced the two leading theories which guided him in his later excavations, and which led to his remarkable success. In the first place, the description of the traveller Pausanias (ii. 16, 4), the classical Baedeker, led him to conclude that the graves of the Atreidæ at Mycenæ had lain inside, and not outside, the citadel wall; secondly, he placed Troy on the site of the new historic Ilion, on the hill now called Hissarlik, near the coast. The most distinguished scholars and travellers of the day, if they granted its real existence at all, held it to have stood far inland on the summit of the Balidagh, near Bunárbashi. This book and a treatise written in Greek gained at once for Schliemann his doctor's degree at Rostock. Then he went travelling again, and spent almost the whole of 1869 in the United States.

Next year he began the great work of his life, the excavation of Troy. The first sod was turned on Hissarlik in April 1870. It was only a preliminary cutting, to decide how deep was the accumulation of *débris* on the hill. When the first ancient wall came to light, at a depth of sixteen feet, it was clear that extensive operations would be necessary before the ancient city could be laid bare. Permission had first to be obtained from the Turkish Government, but, owing to the disturbed state of foreign affairs at that time, it was long delayed. The permission only arrived in September 1871. On the 27th of the month Dr. Schliemann set off for the Dardanelles, with his young wife Sophia, a Greek, whom he had married two years before in Athens. As usual, all sorts of preliminary difficulties with the local authorities had to be got over; the excavations could not be begun till October 11; and even then they bore at first but little fruit, for the arrangements were found to be insufficient to meet the requirements, which grew from week to week. Eighty workmen had to be employed in order to make any progress with the huge trench which was opened on the north side of the hill. Pickaxes and wooden spades were the only available implements; and there were but eight wheelbarrows to cart away the rubbish, all the rest being carried in baskets to the edge of the slope. Added to this, Dr. Schliemann and his wife had to put up with miserable quarters in the neighbouring village of Tschiblak, where the houses are little better than cowsheds. Consequently, when the work ceased for the winter on November 24, there was nothing to show for it except a Hellenistic building in the upper layer of ruins—to judge from several inscriptions found on the spot, it had probably been the Bouleuterion, or senate-house of New Ilion;—and still lower, at a depth of 33 feet, several walls of houses made of rough brick, and numerous stone implements.

After the experience gained from these first difficulties, Dr. Schliemann sent for a great number of English wheelbarrows, pickaxes, and spades, and resumed the work much more thoroughly in March 1872. To begin with, he had secured the co-operation of an engineer; he also engaged three overseers to direct the different groups of workmen, who always numbered between 100 and 150; and finally he made arrangements for a suitable dwelling, getting a wooden house of three rooms, with a store-house and kitchen adjoining, built on the spot. The excavations were carried on by digging out a platform 233 feet wide, from north to south, in the hill. As it appeared, however, that this cutting did not nearly reach the original level, a large trench was dug within it. All the walls in the upper strata which crossed this cutting were ruthlessly cleared away, so that the lowest and last stratum, which must be the real Troy, might be brought to light. The excavations were carried on well into the hot summer, and only stopped on August 14. In spite of this, they had led to no satisfactory result. Owing to the enormous depth that had to be reached, the work had to be confined almost entirely to the broad trench. In it, indeed, many separate walls were laid bare, but the connection between them, if any existed, remained doubtful. Among the single finds, the finest was the metope from a Greek temple, representing the rising Helios, sculptured in high relief.

In the following year Dr. Schliemann with too much zeal returned to Hissarlik on February 1, and had therefore to endure six weeks of bitter cold. The wind, which at that season blows up from the Hellespont, is no less severe than in our northern climate. Through the chinks in the thin wooden shed the north wind blew so hard that, in spite of a constant fire, the water in the room was frozen. The cold was just bearable during the day, while they were busy with the excavations, "but of an evening," says Dr. Schliemann, "we had nothing to keep us warm except our enthusiasm for the great work of discovering Troy."

This year, however, brought the first real success. The town walls appeared more and more distinctly. To the south-west, too, a great gate was uncovered, and quite close to it, over the foundation of the town wall, was found the famous "great treasure," consisting of countless golden ornaments and many silver and copper vessels, weapons, etc. It was about mid-day when Dr. Schliemann observed the first signs of the treasure, and during the workmen's dinner-hour he lifted and concealed the whole mass, with the assistance of his wife, whose shawl served as a basket. He thus managed to keep together the whole find, of which, by agreement, the half should have been given over to the Turkish Government.

After this third campaign, Dr. Schliemann described the results of his excavations in the work *Trojan Antiquities.* It was published in German with an atlas of 218 maps in 1874, and a French translation by M. Rangabé appeared at the same time. The book did much to shake the deep-rooted Troy-Bunárbashi theory. The abundance of pottery and orna-

ents with their peculiar forms indicated that a very old and
ot unimportant settlement must have stood upon · Hissarlik.
he town walls also, although only partially laid bare, might,
ven then have awakened confidence. But they did not receive
istice, largely because of the defective illustrations, and were
assed with the insignificant walls within the town. No doubt
ie masonry of small quarry-stones and clay was that which
eople had up to now only associated with periods of decline,
nd would not accept as the strongly fortified and lofty fortress
scribed to Poseidon. Moreover, Dr. Schliemann was rash in
aming his gold relics " Priam's Treasure "; the largest building
iscovered " Priam's Palace "; and the entrance, " the Scæan Gate."
hese three names were enough to make most people refer every
assertion in the book to the realm of fancy, and but few scholars
aid any serious attention to what they considered to be wild
heories. Writers in newspapers and comic prints saw their
·pportunity, and archæology has since had to regret the ill repute
nto which the " science of the spade " thus fell. The final con-
lusion of sober thinkers was that even if a primeval settlement
lid exist on Hissarlik, its ruins did not correspond to the great
eriod depicted by Homer. Hissarlik could scarcely have been
he capital of the land; and therefore, until further excavations
hould take place, Bunárbashi, defended by such acute and varied
arguments, must still be accepted as Troy.

The next four years were very busy ones for Dr. Schliemann,
ind well illustrate his restless love of enterprise. If baffled in
iny one plan, he always had two new ones to fall back on. In
February 1874, while he was busy with a trial excavation at
Mycenæ, the Turkish Government, believing itself to have been
unfairly treated at the division of the last Trojan spoils, began
a lawsuit against him at Athens. He had to return there, and
was detained for a year with the proceedings, which ended in
his having to pay 10,000 francs compensation. Instead of
10,000 francs, Schliemann sent 50,000 to the Ministry at
Constantinople, as a contribution towards the funds of the
Imperial museum. He hoped by this to win over the offended
authorities, and to be allowed soon to resume his Trojan excavations. From that time onwards, however, he had a difficult
position in Turkey. He went himself to Constantinople in 1875,
but although he was fairly well received, and influential friends

interceded for him, the negotiations for a new firman were very much delayed. When at last he obtained it, in April 1876, and set off for Troy, impatient to resume labours from which much was now expected, he only met with new disappointments. The governor of the Troad, Ibrahim Pacha, detained him for two months at the town of Dardanelles, under the pretext that the firman still required confirmation. When he at last allowed him to begin, he sent with him to Hissarlik a commissioner, who did all in his power to annoy him. Under such circumstances, Dr. Schliemann gave up the excavations and wrote from Athens a violent article to the *Times*, to show how the attitude of the Pacha conflicted with the interests of the civilised world. In consequence of this, Ibrahim was removed in October to another province. Meanwhile, however, Dr. Schliemann had again begun to work at Mycenæ in July, and was so successful in the very first months, that he thought no more of Troy for the present. If the Trojan treasures had seemed a remarkable reward of his labours, no wonder that his delight knew no bounds when, from the kings' graves in the fortress of Mycenæ, he dug up such masses of gold as even he, the millionaire, had perhaps never before seen upon one spot. Nearly all the ornaments worn by the dead, diadems, masks, breastplates, bracelets, earrings, were worked in solid gold, and some of the goblets and tankards weighed as much as 4 lbs. By an article of the Greek constitution, everything found in the country must remain there and become the property of the Government, so these treasures were taken to Athens. They are exhibited in the great hall of the Polytechnicon, and form one of the most interesting and imposing collections in the world.

The excavations at Mycenæ went on to the end of 1876. In 1877 Dr. Schliemann published the results in his book *Mycenæ*. An English edition appeared simultaneously in London and New York, and in 1878 a French one was issued in Paris. The preface was written by Mr. Gladstone, whose keen interest in Homeric studies is well known. Then new negotiations began about a firman for Troy. So as to waste no time, Dr. Schliemann started on a journey to Ithaca. He had already paid a flying visit to this island in 1868. No ruins of any importance had ever been observed here, and even the site of the ancient capital was unknown. But the experience gained at Troy as to the primitive state of Greek building now enabled Dr. Schliemann to fix this site on Mount Aëtos, where he discovered the ruins of about 190 houses of Cyclopean masonry surrounded by primeval walls, along with the palace of the kings situated on the very summit of the hill, and enclosed by a double line of fortification walls.

On his return Dr. Schliemann was able to set out for Troy towards the end of September. Fresh success but also fresh disappointment awaited him. The district all around was now considered unsafe. Shortly before, some Circassians had attacked a farmhouse and tried to pillage it. A fight ensued between them and the villagers who hastened to the rescue, and two men on each side were killed. Dr. Schliemann had therefore to accustom himself to the escort of ten *gensdarmes*, who remained with him at Troy during the whole of the excavations. The new Turkish commissioner, who also lived on the citadel, was a pleasant enough companion, but he carried the key of the storehouse where the treasures were kept. The excavations extended principally over the area in which the gold ornaments had previously been found. The so-called palace of Priam was completely uncovered, and near it a few more small treasures were found. On November 26 the work stopped. This time two-thirds of the treasure discovered went to Constantinople, while Dr. Schliemann retained one-third.

Operations were resumed at the end of February 1879. This campaign was specially encouraging and productive in various ways, for Professor Rudolf Virchow joined it from March onwards. The illustrious Professor not only helped Dr. Schliemann at Hissarlik, where his quick eye observed many new points, but he also explored the whole of the Troad with him up to the very summit of Ida. He made geological, botanical, and meteorological observations everywhere; his subsequent essays and lectures afford interesting evidence of his studies. A French scholar, M. Emile Burnouf, also made a prolonged stay at Hissarlik. He was sent by M. Jules Ferry, who was at that time Minister of Public Instruction, and who recognised this rare and important opportunity for study. M. Burnouf also placed his talents at Dr. Schliemann's disposal; and the plans he drew of the excavations deserve special recognition. The chief work this year was to uncover the town walls as far as possible. Close by, on the plain of the Skamander, fourteen so-called heroic tumuli were excavated, at great cost and trouble, but with such scanty results that Dr. Schliemann came to the conclusion that they must be cenotaphs, or empty tombs, put up later in memory of the dead and not erected for actual burial.

After this campaign, which ended with the year 1879, Dr. Schliemann collected all the results of his excavations at Troy in his great work, *Ilios*. It was written in English, and was at once translated into German, so that both editions appeared simultaneously at the end of 1880. For the first time, the whole material was laid before the public with good illustrations, which brought out clearly the great antiquity of the discoveries. Professor Virchow's investigations, giving several new confirmations of the Troy-Hissarlik theory, and his enthusiastic preface to the book, did not fail to make a great impression. Still, however, there remained the difficulty of the insignificance of the house walls within the citadel, and the so-called " Palace of Priam " was still the largest building to be seen. It was now more cautiously named " the city chieftain's house," while the gold find was from 1873 onwards simply called " the great treasure."

After his eighteen months of literary work, Dr. Schliemann returned with increased energy to his excavations. At Orchomenos, in 1880 and 1881, he excavated the so-called treasury of Minyas, a great bee-hive tomb exactly like those of Mycenæ. He then made another tour through the Troad, both of which undertakings were described in two short articles—" Orchomenos " and " A Journey through the Troad."

On March 1, 1882, Dr. Schliemann resumed work at Hissarlik. This time he had the co-operation of Dr. W. Dörpfeld, now chief secretary to the German Archæological Institute at Athens, who, for several years previous to his work with Dr. Schliemann, had taken a leading part in the German excavations at Olympia. They now gained important results by uncovering several great complex buildings in the most important stratum, the second from the native rock. Dr. Schliemann and Dr. Dörpfeld at that time held that the extensive buildings with vestibules in front, and a great round hearth in the centre, were temples. Two years later, however, the ground-plan of the palace at Tiryns was discovered almost intact. It had the same long central hall, with a vestibule and a great round hearth, and thus it was proved that the analogous buildings in Troy were not temples, but the chief apartments of the king's palace. The same apartment, with exactly the same ground-plan, has recently been also found at Mycenæ, in the centre of the palace. Consequently, it is now perfectly certain, even if it was not so in 1882, that Dr. Schliemann has discovered the Pergamos of Troy in the chief stratum of Hissarlik. This city, like Tiryns and Mycenæ, belongs to that same great and flourishing period of Græco-Asiatic culture which is obviously pre-Homeric. We can unhesitatingly recognise in it the Troy whose memory survived in the poems of Homer.

The devout and childlike faith with which Dr. Schliemann, in spite of all ridicule, clung to an actual historic foundation for the Homeric poems and the Trojan War, has been victorious over all the acuteness and erudition expended on the opposite side. This result certainly tends to justify the way in which he excavated at Troy. The ruthless removal of the upper strata, the cutting through interesting foundations of Greek temples and fortress-walls, naturally awoke indignant regrets. It has often been said that he ought at least to have cleared them away layer by layer, so that each one might have been surveyed separately, before giving place to the next. But people forget that the strata do not lie neatly sandwiched one above the other. The settlers who inhabited the town at different periods did not each in turn level the surface, but generally built on the *débris* as they lay. Where a large building had fallen down, the new one built upon it stood several yards higher than another which had been built on open ground. Moreover the different layers of Dr. Schliemann's cities are by no means entirely separated from each other by complete breaks between the settlements. Newer houses are often right in the midst of older ruins. Under such conditions, how is one layer to be separated from another? The topmost one, certainly, the Hellenistic town, stands on a new and carefully levelled foundation. It might easily have been uncovered by itself. Supposing this town, with the ground-plan of its temples, markets, towers, and gates, had been laid bare, Dr. Schliemann would hardly have ventured to destroy what at that epoch would have been the only known plan of a Hellenistic town on the mere chance of verifying his conjecture that there was something below. He was assuredly wise in going promptly to work on the north trench, for which he has been so much blamed, and thus to make regrets of no avail.

Most of the Trojan treasures are now in the " Völker Museum " at Berlin. The few gold ornaments which two of Dr. Schliemann's workmen concealed in 1873, as well as two-thirds of the finds of 1882, went to Constantinople; and Dr. Schliemann has kept a large collection of pottery in his house at Athens. Everything else, including the "Great Treasure," belongs to that splendid collection which he presented to his country in 1881. He had the satisfaction of receiving several letters from the old Emperor William, in gracious acknowledgment of this gift. His Majesty, by an edict of January 24, 1881, decreed "that the above-named collection shall be consigned to the charge of the Prussian Government, and afterwards preserved in the Ethnographical Museum at Berlin, now in course of construction, in as many special rooms as are necessary for exhibiting it to advantage; and also that the rooms set apart for this purpose shall always bear the donor's name." The "Schliemann Collection" has year by year received additions from the travels and minor excavations of the great discoverer, who has also bequeathed to it that portion of the Trojan relics which are still in Athens. In return Dr. Schliemann received from the city of Berlin the honorary citizenship of the German capital, a gift which has been bestowed on scarcely any one else, except Bismarck and Moltke.

The work of the succeeding years is soon told. A new book on the new excavations was promptly written and entitled *Troja*. It appeared, with a preface by Professor Sayce, at the end of 1884, in English and German. As no French translation of *Ilios* had yet appeared, this work was revised and enlarged in accordance with the new discoveries, and in this form it was published in Paris in 1885, under the title of *Ilios, Ville et Pays des Troyens*.

Dr. Schliemann made a small excavation at Marathon in February 1884. The hill, which Pausanias describes as the grave of the 192 Athenians killed in the battle of 490 B.C., was opened and found to belong to a much earlier period than the Persian War. From March till June 1884 Dr. Schliemann worked at Tiryns. Here he made a splendid discovery, which threw light on all sides. He came on the foundations of a palace in excellent preservation, dating from the heroic age. As usual, he wrote a description of it immediately, but as he entrusted Dr. Dörpfeld with further excavations for the following spring, the book was kept back till November 1885, when it appeared with Dr. Dörpfeld's additions and an excellent preface by Professor F. Adler. French and English editions appeared at the same time in Paris, London, and New York. In this work the chapters on architecture are written entirely by Dr. Dörpfeld, so that for this section we have a specialist's admirable presentation of his own subject.

Dr. Schliemann's researches always found special recognition in England. He was made a D.C.L. of the University of Oxford and Honorary Fellow of Queen's College in 1883. After the excavations at Tiryns, the large gold medal of the Royal Institute of British Architects was awarded to him.

Dr. Schliemann next began excavations at different other places. Their results, however, were not sufficiently encouraging to lead him to undertake more extensive operations. Two winters, 1886-87 and 1887-88, he spent in Egypt, the latter in company with Professor Virchow. From that journey he sent a number of coffers, together with some very ancient vases of great interest, and a fine collection of Egyptian stuffs and embroideries, as a present to the Ethnological Museum in Berlin. Since the spring of 1887 he had had several animated negotiations in Crete, where he wished to uncover the fortress hill of the old city of Gnossos. Judging from the preliminary excavations, it seems to cover a royal palace like that of Tiryns. The excessive demands of the landlords unfortunately hindered the realisation of the plan. In the spring of 1888 he worked for a short time at Cythera, where he discovered the original temple of the Uranian Aphrodite in the chapel of Hagios Cosmas. In the same year he made investigations at "sandy Pylos" and on the island of Sphacteria, where he laid bare the old fortifications, which, according to Thucydides (iv. 31), were discovered and made use of by the Spartans in 425 B.C.

Dr. Schliemann generally spent the intervals of rest at Athens. His palatial house in the *Rue de l'Université* reminds us at every point of the world in which its owner lived and moved. In the mosaic floors the chief specimens of the Trojan vases and urns are represented. Along the wall run friezes with classical landscapes and pictures from the Greek epic, with appropriate Homeric quotations. The visitor was admitted by the porter Bellerophon and conducted by the footman Telamon to the master, who was generally found reading one of the Greek classics, and stopping at intervals to complain of the number of Stock Exchange lists brought by the morning post from Paris, London, and Berlin. These used to lie piled up on a chair by his side, and had an incongruous appearance among the other surroundings. Dr. Schliemann was no longer engaged in business, but the management of his great fortune, and the ownership of the several houses which he let in Paris, Berlin, and Athens, obliged him to keep up his relations with the world of commerce.

Even the flying visits which tourists always made a point of paying him gave a glimpse of his family life. Dr. Schliemann was not like Goethe, who only now and then made a momentary appearance at the grating of his hall-door. With unwearying courtesy he ushered visitors several times a day into his drawing-room. There they found Mrs. Schliemann (*née* Kastroménos of Athens), a kind and gentle hostess, with her daughter Andromache, who has just reached womanhood, and her son Agamemnon, a boy of twelve. It was only within this circle that the warmth and tenderness of Dr. Schliemann's character came out. These traits explained not only his eager adherence and trustful loyalty to mythical tradition, but also the charity of his judgment towards opponents, which became every year more remarkable. He thus formed an exception to the general rule, that, with advancing age, men become more obstinate in their opinions. We prefix to the book a likeness of Dr. Schliemann from a photograph taken a few years ago. A portrait of Mrs. Schliemann is also given, wearing the Trojan ornaments which can grace no head so well as hers.[1]

[1] In the German edition Dr. Schuchhardt had added : "Dr. Schliemann is now in his sixty-ninth year, but his activity and love of enterprise show no signs of decay. We may still look to him for many additions to science, and we hope to thank him for disclosing the heroic age of Greece in the periods of its prime and of its decadence, which may perhaps be found in Crete, the land of Minos." Unhappily these hopes have not been verified. The great explorer died suddenly at Naples on December 26, 1890, from the effects of cold after an operation for deafness. A few days later Dr. Dörpfeld, the illustrious archæologist and friend, who has shared all Dr. Schliemann's later labours, escorted the remains back to Athens. In accordance with a wish he had expressed, Dr. Schliemann was buried in the Greek cemetery south of the Ilissos. His body lies in the land he loved so well ; but the example of noble ambition and patient research which he set before the world will long abide as a living spirit, not only among archæologists, but among all who anywhere in the civilised world have caught something of his devotion and enthusiasm for classical learning and antiquity.

ἀνδρῶν γὰρ ἐπιφανῶν πᾶσα γῆ τάφος. (TRANS.)

1. History and Topography

AT the time when Dr. Schliemann began his excavations in Troy, the Homeric poems—then the main source of our knowledge of prehistoric Greece—had already been subjected to keen and searching criticism by F. A. Wolf, Wilhelm Müller, and Lachmann, and the results of this criticism were known not only to specialists, but to the educated public in general. The main contention was, that the *Iliad* and the *Odyssey* were really a collection of songs composed at different times, and of very unequal value, and that, like the German *Niebelungen Lied*, they could be resolved into shorter lays, each celebrating the deeds of individual heroes. The more famous of these heroes, Achilles for example, like Siegfried, had, it was maintained, their ultimate origin in mythological personages, once worshipped as divine.

English scholars, it is true, in the face of the Wolfian doctrine, maintained intact their peculiar Homeric orthodoxy. They made, indeed, a few outward concessions to the spirit of reformation, especially by ceding the notion of a single supreme head in the realm of epic poetry, but they remained faithful on the whole to the old catholic belief. Grote considered that the *Odyssey*, though not the *Iliad*, was originally one complete whole : he further placed Troy exactly on the spot where Dr. Schliemann afterwards excavated it.[1] In Germany, however, the conviction daily gained ground that it was impossible to decide how much in the ancient Epos was truth and how much poetic fiction. Every influential scholar and traveller—and among them we find the names of Moltke, Welcker, Kiepert, and Curtius—favoured

[1] Grote, *Hist. of Greece*, vol. ii. ch. xxi., and vol. i. ch. xv. p. 312.

C

the view that disregards the leading traits of the Homeric picture, and bids us recognise the ancient capital of the Troad in a small mountain fastness near Bunárbashi, situated at a considerable distance from the sea. This, they held, had been transformed by the imaginative descriptions of a Homer into a royal city, capital of a broad domain.

The question is now decided for ever. On the hill of Hissarlik Dr. Schliemann has uncovered the ancient palaces of Troy, has laid bare its colossal fortifications, and brought to light its treasures of gold and silver. Moreover, in the country round about, his unwearying exertions have proved the accuracy of many details, which show a coincidence, astonishing even to the most credulous, between the picture unfolded in Homer and the one preserved to this day. In order to be able rightly to estimate the significance of these results, we must first take a rapid survey of what ancient tradition has handed down to us concerning Troy and the Trojan plain.

Our knowledge of the "Ilios" of the Trojan War is solely derived from the Homeric poems. The Greeks of historic times themselves knew nothing beyond what these poems tell us. Their assertions about remote antiquity either have Homer for their source or are pure inventions. In Homer Troy is a wealthy capital, situated in the neighbourhood of the Hellespont, and facing the little island of Tenedos.[1] Its horizon is bounded on the one side by Samothrake, the high snow-capped peak whence Poseidon watched the battle,[2] on the other by wooded "many-fountained" Ida, the seat of Zeus.[3] The Trojan princes dwelt originally farther inland on Mount Ida; later on they came down from this lofty position, and founded the present citadel "upon the plain."[4] So wonderful are the walls and towers of this citadel, that their building was ascribed to no mortal hand but to Poseidon and Apollo.[5] On the summit of the Acropolis were situated the palaces—the palace of Priam,[6] and next to it those of Hector and of Paris.[7] There also Zeus was worshipped,[8] and Athena[9] and Apollo[10] had their temples. The only exit from the city mentioned in the poems is the Skaian Gate, through which the road led to the battle-field on the plain.

[1] *Il.* xiii. 33.   [2] *Il.* xiii. 11-14.   [3] *Il.* viii. 47, etc.   [4] *Il.* xx. 216.
[5] *Il.* vii. 452.   [6] *Il.* vi. 242.   [7] *Il.* vi. 370, 313.   [8] *Il.* xxii. 169-172.
[9] *Il.* vi. 88.   [10] *Il.* v. 445, and vii. 20.

The Greeks are encamped near to their landing-place, along the coast of the Hellespont.[1] A number of passages in the poems prove that the distance from the camp to Troy was not great. As a rule, every night after the battle the Trojans go back to their city, the Greeks to their camp. Messengers go early from the city to the station of the ships, and are back before sunrise.[2] In one and the same day the battle often surges to and fro along the whole distance. Priam journeys during the night to the hut of Achilles, to ask for the body of his son, and when his sorrowful quest is ended, and he has once more tasted meat and drink, he enjoys in his enemy's hut the sleep so long denied to him, and yet is back in Troy before break of day.[3]

Between the city and the Greek camp flows the Skamander, the chief river of the country. It rises on Mount Ida, and its size is such that it can only be forded at one spot. This river plays an important part on the battle-field. To a certain extent it marks the boundary between the Greek and the Trojan region. When the Greeks pass it, the Trojans give way, and turn back in flight to the city. On the other hand, a great success of the Trojans is marked by the fact that Hector and his army pass the night on the enemy's side of the river, on a "swelling of the plain" ($\theta\rho\omega\sigma\mu\grave{o}\varsigma$ $\pi\epsilon\delta\acute{\iota}o\iota o$), and have the necessaries for the evening meal, meat, flour, etc., brought to them from the city.[4] On this evening Agamemnon anxiously sees from his camp the watch-fires of the Trojans, and hears the sound of their flutes and pipes.[5] When Priam is driving to the Greek camp, and Hermes is commanded to provide a safe escort, he only joins the king at the moment when the latter has halted in the middle of the ford to water his horses; here it is that the real danger begins, and to this point only Hermes escorts the old man back on his homeward journey.[6]

The Simoeis is often mentioned in connection with the Skamander; its course is nowhere clearly indicated, and only one passage in the *Iliad* affords any clue. The conclusion arrived at may well be correct, as it is due to a scholar who denies all connection between the Homeric description and the actual features of the Trojan plain, and who maintains that Homer created "an ideal stage for his ideal drama." Yet it is

---

[1] *Il.* xiv. 31.   [2] *Il.* vii. 381, and 421-423.   [3] *Il.* xxiv. 695.
[4] *Il.* viii. 505.   [5] *Il.* x. 11-13.   [6] *Il.* xxiv. 353, 694.

completely satisfactory to the opposite party, as it places the Simoeis in the only region where its course could lie, according to the present state of the plain. The facts of the case are as follows. Hera and Athena leave their car at the junction of the Skamander and the Simoeis, and hasten on foot to the field of battle.[1] R. Hercher,[2] commenting on this passage, says: "It is self-evident that the goddesses must leave their car at a place where the battle is not yet raging; this is moreover confirmed by the fact that the two proceed without hindrance to the battle-field. But in the *Iliad* the side of the plain which is free of fighting is generally the left. Ares, for instance, when removed from the battle, sits 'on the battle's left.'[3] It follows that the poet has made the goddesses halt on the left, *i.e.* on the north side of the plain." He must therefore have imagined the Simoeis as flowing on the north side of the city. We shall see further on that on this side a small river still runs, which we may consider is the ancient Simoeis.

In front of the Skaian Gate, close to the great "waggon track," rise two springs, one cold and one warm, to which the Trojan women and maidens were wont to come for water, "and to wash bright raiment, in the old times of peace."[4] Now, however, these self-same springs must witness the catastrophe of all the murderous fight; for hard by Hector falls before his unconquerable foe.

Such are the features gathered from Homer which go to make up the picture of the city and its surroundings. With the lament over the body of the Trojan hero the *Iliad* closes. The *Odyssey* gives us only a few hints concerning the destruction of Troy. The event was first celebrated by the poets of the following period in the so-called Epic cycle. The cyclic poems themselves are lost; we only possess prose extracts from them, which tell of the stratagem of the wooden horse, the feigned departure of the Greeks, the sudden attack, and the burning of the city, the slaughter of the heroes, and the leading away of the women into captivity. After this comes a long break in tradition.

It is not till the time of the Persian wars that Ilion all at once reappears. Hellanikos held it to be identical with the Homeric city. His successor Herodotos in his account of the expedition

---

[1] *Il.* v. 774.   [2] R. Hercher, *Ueber die Homerische Ebene von Troja*, pp. 61-63.
[3] *Il.* v. 355.   [4] *Il.* xxii. 147.

of Xerxes against Greece writes: "When the king reached
Skamander he went up to the citadel of Priam, having desired
to see it, and having seen it and learnt by inquiry of all those
matters severally, he sacrificed a thousand heifers to the Athena
of Ilion, and the Magians poured libations in honour of the
heroes." [1] From this time on we frequently hear of the city. In
the Peloponnesian war the Spartan admiral Mindaros watched
from Ilion the sea-fight between Dorieus and the Athenians.[2]
Alexander the Great went up to the citadel as Xerxes had done
before; he made sacrifice to Athena and offered libations to the
heroes; he also sacrificed to Priam on the altar of Zeus
Herkeios; he hung up his armour in the temple of Athena, and
took away with him in exchange some ancient sacred weapons,
reputed relics of the Trojan War.[3] He moreover planned to
enlarge the city substantially by giving it new walls. This
project, however, was not carried out till the time of Lysimachos,
who conquered North-western Asia Minor in 301 B.C. Lysimachos settled the inhabitants of various neighbouring towns in
Ilion, and surrounded the city with a wall 40 stadia (5 miles) in
circumference.[4]

Thus the ancient name of Ilion had once more a definite
significance. The inhabitants of Ilion maintained that the city
of Priam had never been completely destroyed, and looked upon
their own city as its direct successor. They pointed to the
identical altar of Zeus Herkeios, on which Priam had been
slain; [5] and the learned traveller Polemon described the very
stone on which Palamedes had taught the Greeks to play at
dice.[6] The Romans took especial pride in this resurrection of
Ilion. They regarded themselves as sprung from Æneas, who
alone escaping from the universal destruction, had migrated to
Italy, and hence they held Ilion to be the cradle of their race.
Ennius sang of the enthusiasm with which the Roman armies
greeted this, the reputed home of their ancestors, when in the
year 191 B.C. they first trod Asiatic soil. At that time the
whole of the neighbouring region, and the coast from Tenedos
to Dardanos, were assigned to the Ilian territory. [7]

But the fuller and more joyous the confidence, the more

---

[1] Herodot. vii. 43.   Translation, G. C. Macaulay, vol. ii. (p. 148).
[2] Xen. *Hell.* i. 1, 4.   [3] Arrian, 1. 12. 7.   [4] Strabo, xiii. 26.   [5] Arrian, i. 11.
[6] Polemon Iliensis.   Müller, *Frag. Hist.* ii. 124.   [7] Livy, xxxviii. 39.

certainly was it to be embittered by the gall of scepticism. In
the midst of the rejoicings over the continuance of the old
races of heroes — while Trojans, Ilians, and Romans were
enthusiastically fraternising,[1] came the Alexandrian age with its
whole train of pedantic erudition and assumption of superior
critical knowledge. *Skepsis* was the ominous name of the birth-
place appointed for the man who was to deny the continuity of
Ilion, and who consequently was to dispute every connection
between the Ilians and the Romans. The ancient Ilion, Demetrios
explained, could not have existed on the site of the present Ilion
(*i.e.* the Hissarlik discovered by Dr. Schliemann), chiefly on two
grounds. In the first place, the plain stretching from it to the
sea only came into existence through a later alluvial deposit of
the Skamander, and would therefore in the days of Homer have
been far too small to be the scene of the combats described. In
the second place, the pursuit of Hector by Achilles thrice round
the walls of the city could not have taken place on the site of
the New Ilion; for the New Ilion is not situated on an isolated
hill, but on the spur of a long mountain ridge, so that at one
point the runners would have had to climb up a considerable incline. He would rather recognise old Ilion in the
"village of the Ilians" (Ἰλιέων κώμη). According to the
measurements Demetrios gives, this is 30 stadia from New Ilion,
10 from the hill of Kallikolone, and 5 from the Simoeis. It will
therefore be found to coincide with the site now called Hanaï-
tepeh, opposite Bunárbashi. No ancient ruins could be discovered
there, but this did not, he maintained, invalidate his assertion;
for the stones would be used for the building of New Ilion,
and the greater part of them would be carted away to Sigeum.

At first these difficulties of detail disturbed no one. The
Romans continued to make Ilion the centre of their interest.
The destruction of the city by Fimbria during the Mithridatic
wars[2] was atoned for by Cæsar, who rebuilt and richly endowed it.
Cæsar, and Augustus after him, contemplated transferring the
imperial capital to the Hellespont. Only Strabo is completely
under the spell of the adverse criticism of Demetrios, and in our
own age, so Alexandrian in its temper, it is the testimony of
Strabo which has rekindled the old controversy.

The site of the *later* Ilion has never been disputed. On the

---

[1] Livy, xxxvii. 37.   [2] Appian, i. 364.

hill of Hissarlik, even before Dr. Schliemann's excavations, part
of its Hellenistic fortifications were visible, and on the north
slope the semicircle of an unmistakable theatre was clearly
preserved.   In addition we have the statement of Skylax, that
the city was 25 stadia (about 3 miles) distant from the sea, a
measurement which exactly suits the site of Hissarlik.   But
with regard to the Homeric Troy, two alternatives had to be
taken into consideration.   Either we must accept the universal
belief of the ancients as to its identity with New Ilion, or doubts
similar to those which disturbed Demetrios must lead us to seek
another site for it.   Most scholars have accepted this second
alternative, and have almost unanimously identified the ruins on
the Balidagh, half an hour above Bunárbashi, with the ancient
Troy.   Dr. Schliemann held to ancient tradition, and excavated
at New Ilion.   His first labours there, in 1871-79, were not
likely to convert many of his opponents.   Great fortification walls
and gates were laid bare, but what Dr. Schliemann declared to
be the palace was in reality only an assemblage of petty dwelling-
houses with small rooms and thin walls, very unlike the picture
we had formed of the Homeric royal palaces.   In 1882 it
became possible to recognise in the second stratum from the
bottom the strong walls of extensive buildings, which were afterwards proved, through the closely analogous structures of Tiryns
and of Mycenæ, to have been the principal chambers of a palace.

The double question now arises—how came it that even
the ablest men were so completely misled in this matter; and
further, what is the relation between the existing facts and the
features of the landscape as gathered from the Homeric descriptions?   The view of the Alexandrian Demetrios that the plain
between Ilion and the sea is a later alluvial deposit has clearly
been suggested by a passage in Herodotos, who says that the
plain was formerly a bay.[1]   This, however, is a geological statement made without reference to history.   Herodotos was far
from thinking the plain lay under water in Homeric times, for he
himself believed in the identity of the old and the new Ilion;
otherwise how could he have recounted without a word of criticism
the visit of Xerxes to Priam's citadel and its new inhabitants?
Recently Professor Virchow has examined the plain geologically, and
has dug in different places to a depth of several metres, but he

[1] Herod. ii. 11.

has nowhere found traces of a marine formation. Every statement of the *Iliad* is based on the supposition that the camp of
the Greeks lay immediately on the coast of the Hellespont;
accordingly the plain must already have covered about the same
area at that time. In the second century A.D. Skylax gives 25
stadia as the distance between Ilion and the sea, a measurement
which is still quite correct according to the present conditions.
Therefore, if the plain has not appreciably increased from the
time of Skylax down to ours, that is in a period of nearly 2000
years, it can scarcely have come into existence altogether in the
preceding period of 1000 years.

The second argument of Demetrios, that Achilles and Hector
could not have run three times round the site of New Ilion,
raises the question of how much in Homer is fact, and how much
is poetic fiction. When Achilles slays whole hosts of Trojans,
and fills the waters of Skamander with the slain, when Priam is
represented as having fifty sons and twelve daughters, when the
Trojan War lasts ten years, and Odysseus employs ten further
years on his homeward journey, we have the workings of the
same poetic fancy which enables Samson to slaughter a thousand
Philistines with the jawbone of an ass, and which places moral
sentiments in the mouth of Balaam's ass. It matters little
whether the running of the heroes would be more difficult
because they would have to climb up the ridge which joins the
mound of the citadel to the neighbouring heights. There is no
more exaggeration in the threefold pursuit than there is in the
prowess of Diomede, when he easily hurls a stone which two
other men could scarcely have raised. However, if stress need
be laid on the question, then we must remember that the last
excavations prove this ridge to have been originally 39 feet
lower than it is now. During its continuous occupation the
plateau of the citadel has not only gained in height, but also in
breadth. A portion of the old *débris* was cleared away to the
sides, and so the level of the ridge has gradually risen towards
the level of the citadel mound.

If the objections which Demetrios raises against the identification of the old with the new Ilion are thus illusory, his positive
assertions are easily disposed of; for the village of the Ilians in the
Hanaï-tepeh fulfils none of the topographical conditions, either in its
great distance from the sea or in any other particular. Besides, the

excavations have shown it to be an insignificant prehistoric settlement, perhaps merely a homestead. Modern writers who support the criticism of Demetrios have as a rule recognised the weakness of his positive statements. They have accordingly attempted to transfer the renown of the ancient Troy to another site, which, it must be owned, was favoured by remarkable coincidences.

At the end of last century Le Chevalier maintained that he had discovered near Bunárbashi a cold and a warm spring, rising exactly as Homer describes them at the foot of the citadel.[1] The springs in question consist partly of a group of sources called by the Turks *Kirk gös, i.e.* the forty eyes, which are close to the village of Bunárbashi; and, secondly, of a warm spring, not far off, which was afterwards visited by Dr. E. D. Clarke[2] and others. Although this site by no means answered exactly to the Homeric description, yet it was argued that since no spring was known near Hissarlik, Homer, when he furnished Troy with the famous springs, must have had in his mind the singular natural phenomenon at Bunárbashi. In favour of these springs, the weighty reasons against identifying the Balidagh fortress with the Homeric Ilion were overlooked. It is best to state at once that in 1882 Dr. Schliemann discovered the much-disputed site of the springs and washing-troughs in a very ancient rock channel at the foot of Hissarlik, near to the gate which may fairly be identified with the Skaian. Existing traces show that there must have been basins at the outlet of this channel as late as Roman times. But even before this final proof, the broad characteristics of the Homeric landscape, which absolutely contradict the notion of a Troy situated near Bunárbashi, should not have been made secondary to the minor question of the springs.

The fortress on the Balidagh is not in any sense " built upon the plain," like the Troy of Homer. Its hill is almost 500 feet high, and is prolonged into the plain by groups of hillocks which the traveller must laboriously climb, only to find himself far back among the mountains. On such a spot the battle could never have been described as surging continuously from the plain up to the city walls. Moreover, the springs of

---

[1] J. B. Le Chevalier, *Voyage de la Troade* (Paris 1802), ch. iv. p. 191 *seq.*

[2] E. D. Clarke, *Travels in various countries of Europe, Asia, and Africa* (4th ed., London 1817), p. 141.

Bunárbashi are half an hour distant at the foot of the hill spurs, and cannot be seen from the citadel.

In 1835 Moltke wrote concerning his visit to the Balidagh: "Scholars are not altogether agreed about the exact site of Troy, but we, who are no scholars, are simply guided by our military instinct to the spot where in olden times, as well as now, men would have built, when their object was to found an inaccessible fortress." This point of view has misled many people. For the low mound of Hissarlik is apparently utterly unsuited for an "inaccessible fortress," rising as it does only to a height of 50 to 65 feet. But the Homeric Troy was above all things a maritime city, a characteristic which comes out clearly in the story of the rape of Helen. To its highly favoured situation on the straits between two seas the city owed the power and the wealth sung of in the Homeric poems. It resembles almost all the other cities proved by recent excavations to belong to the same wealthy civilisation. Tiryns, Orchomenos, Athens, are only so far removed from the sea as was necessary to avoid the immediate dangers of piracy, and in each case the inhabitants preferred to settle on a low hill and to surround it with high walls, rather than seek in the mountains the natural protection of rocks and precipices. Besides, the incidents of the *Iliad* referred to above imply a much shorter distance from Troy to the sea than is the case at Bunár-bashi. And last, since the fastness falls away precipitously on three sides, the pursuit of Hector by Achilles, which is after all conceivable at Hissarlik, becomes here altogether impossible.

With regard to the actual ruins on the Balidagh, they are simply the remains of a small circuit wall. In one place indeed, the south-east corner, the masonry, as in the prehistoric circuit wall at Hissarlik, consists of a scarp of small stones; but the remainder belongs at the earliest to the fourth or fifth century B.C. The surface of the rock within the walls is covered with a very thin layer of *débris*, which proves it to have been inhabited only during a short time; and, in spite of the various excavations carried on by Hahn in 1864, and later by Dr. Schliemann, no traces of a prehistoric settlement have been discovered in this *débris*. We probably have here one of those small fortresses forsaken at an early period, such as are found scattered everywhere about the Troad. The existence of such a fortress precisely on this spot is easy to account for. The Skamander flows here from

the mountains into the plain, and, since the ruins of a second small
fortress are visible just opposite, on the other side of the river, it
is plain that the two formed the key of the Skamander gorge.

We may therefore consider the Bunárbashi theory as finally
disposed of, and accept with the greater readiness and confidence
the tidings of the real Troy that come from Hissarlik. Here for
the first time we shall obtain a standard by which to examine
the legendary and poetical picture of Troy ; and at least in this
instance we shall be able to discover how closely the oldest poetry
of the Greeks adhered to reality.   —

The distance from Hissarlik to the west coast is $3\frac{1}{4}$ miles,
to the Hellespont $3\frac{3}{4}$ miles. It is therefore so short that the
occasional advance of the battle from the ships right up to the
city walls, the swift return of the heralds before sunrise, and
Priam's night journey, receive a full and obvious explanation.
Right in the midst, between the city and the west coast, flows
the Skamander, now called Menderé. Even in the hot months
it usually has a stream 2 feet deep and 20 broad, and it only
dries up in years of extraordinary drought, when its bed becomes
a series of isolated puddles. But in the spring, when sudden rains
fall and the snow melts on Ida, the river becomes a roaring torrent,
and rolls down masses of rock and trunks of trees, often flooding
the whole plain. Some such occurrence gave rise, no doubt, to the
Homeric description of the fight of Achilles with the river.

At the northern base of the citadel flows a smaller stream, the
Dumbrek-su, which joins the Skamander where it falls into the
sea, and forms a delta with its many mouths. In it we may
recognise the Simoeis, a river occasionally mentioned in the *Iliad*.

The station of the Greek ships was on the Hellespont, as several
passages in the *Iliad* prove. It was only natural that the poet
should place it here at the mouth of the Skamander, from which
point the road ran according to the course of the river, while at the
same time it formed the most direct way to Troy. The ships
lay there thickly packed together, "and filled up the wide mouth
of all the shore that the headlands held between them." The two
"headlands" can only be Cape Sigeum and Cape Rhœteum ;
Strabo, in the first century B.C., was of this opinion. Although
it is the firm opinion of geologists that the plain of the Skamander
cannot have been very different at the time of the Trojan War from
what it is now, yet the river must have thrust its mouth some-

what farther into the Hellespont, so that 3000 years ago there was a bay where now there is a sandy promontory.

At present the Skamander discharges itself close under Cape Sigeum, i.e. to the west of the bay inclosed by the two promontories. If this fact holds good for antiquity also, then the ships which crowded the bay must have lain east of the river, on the same side as Troy, and thus one of the chief conditions of the Homeric battle-field would be violated. But this difficulty also has now disappeared. Professor Rudolph Virchow has shown that the Kalifatli-Asmak, which flows nearer to Hissarlik than the present Skamander, represents the former course of this river. The bed of the Asmak is so broad and deep that it can only be filled by a considerable and powerful current of water; and it is formed of a syenitic sand which is brought down by the Skamander only, partly direct from a particular spot in the mountain range (near Ewjiler), partly from its upper tributaries, which rise on the north-east of the Chigridagh. Farther to the north it is continued by the Intepe-Asmak, which has the same peculiarities, and which may therefore be considered the ancient mouth of the Skamander.

It must be admitted, however, that this does not prove the Skamander to have flowed along that bed precisely at the time of the Trojan War. But the site of the city on Hissarlik, like that of countless ancient cities, was evidently planned to be at the confluence of two rivers in order to receive protection from their streams. For this reason alone it is probable that when Troy was founded the Skamander flowed close under the city walls, and that during the period of its prosperity great care was taken that the river should not deviate from this course. Accordingly, if the Homeric Skamander flowed along the bed of the Kalifatli-Asmak and was discharged through the mouth of the Intepe-Asmak, then the Greeks can only have been encamped on the west side, and must have crossed the river in order to reach the city. The Simoeis, which nowadays is really an independent stream, would then have united with the Skamander close under Troy; and the confluence of the two rivers, where Hera and Athena leave their chariots, is therefore not an invention of the poet.

So, too, the most recent excavations afford an equally satisfactory explanation of the much-disputed θρωσμὸς πεδίοιο or "swelling of the plain," whence the Trojans, when they have pressed exceptionally far, begin a fresh onset; here also they once bivouack, in order to remain nearer to the Greeks, and to prevent their launching their ships and departing during the night. This "swelling," which clearly must have lain in the middle of the plain between Troy and Cape Rhœteum, had for all that been looked for in vain. Dr. Schliemann, when excavating in 1882, used frequently to ride down to bathe in the sea on a white horse. His fellow-workers on the citadel observed that the white horse, which could be seen at a great distance, regularly disappeared at a particular spot in the plain; it was apparently hidden from sight by the ground just behind, and reappeared again as it approached the seashore. Dr. Schliemann has not recorded this observation in his book, but has kindly communicated it by word of mouth; yet the little anecdote proves more vividly than any measurements the presence of a "swelling" of the ground. If we, moreover, consider that in the last 3000 years the Skamander must have considerably raised the level of the plain (Dr. Schliemann and Professor Virchow compute the average increase to be about 10 feet, Dr. Dörpfeld 3 feet 3 inches), and that the "swelling" must therefore have been far more prominent in early times, the question of the Homeric θρωσμός is satisfactorily set at rest.

The last important point in the Homeric topography is the site of the cold and warm springs where the Trojan women came for water and washed their raiment. Only 300 paces from the southern base of the citadel Dr. Schliemann has discovered a channel cut in the soft limestone rock. It is 5 feet 6 inches in height, and 10 feet broad. It pierces the rising hill in a straight line for a distance of 60 feet; about mid-way there is a round hole at the top, to admit of light and air, and at the end the channel divides into three branches, of which the most northern preserves the breadth of the single channel, while the other two are so narrow that a man can only just get into them. When these three branches were cleared out for a distance of some 33 feet more, a spring of good drinking water was found at the end of each. On the floor of the channel was discovered a water conduit extending from the broad north branch to where the channel ends in the open air. This conduit is formed, just like the Cyclopean conduits of Tiryns and Mycenæ, of unhewn stones, apparently put together without any binding material. But the stones must have been originally bonded with clay mortar like the blocks of the walls of Tiryns; these were once believed to have been loosely piled one upon the other, but Dr. Dörpfeld has shown that they lay in a bedding of clay. In Roman times an earthenware pipe leading to some partially preserved washing-troughs was laid above the conduit.

This whole disposition of the site corresponds exactly to the one presupposed in the *Iliad*. The excavations resulted in the

1.—CHANNEL CUT IN THE ROCK NEAR HISSARLIK.

discovery of no less than three gates on Hissarlik, all approximately turned towards the south. Whichever of these may be the Skaian Gate, or even if, as Dr. Dörpfeld and Dr. Schliemann maintain, this gate is still unfound and must be sought in the lower city to the south-west of those three, the springs will at any rate be in its immediate vicinity, and the great road must have passed quite close to them. But where is the warm spring sung of by Homer? Unfortunately excavations have been discontinued in the neighbourhood of the shaft, so that it might possibly still be found there. Strabo, however, as early as the first century B.C., did not see this spring. Perhaps it dried up at an early date, or perhaps, when its outlet was filled up, it forced itself into another channel which has not yet been discovered. Perhaps also—and this seems the more probable—its supposed existence at this spot is after all due to a confusion. The actual springs of the Skamander, which are situated in the range of Ida, at the foot of the peak of Gargaros, have exactly the peculiarities which Homer describes. E. D. Clarke [1] discovered them in 1801, and Barker Webb [2] visited them in 1819. Dr. Schliemann and Professor Virchow tested and confirmed their assertions in 1879. The springs flow from two rocky cavities a few minutes distant from one another, and immediately unite to form the brook of the Skamander. At an air temperature of 57° Fahrenheit one spring showed 47° Fahrenheit, the other 60° Fahrenheit (Virchow). It is therefore easy to suppose that the springs at the foot of the southern slope of the Trojan citadel, which are called the "springs of the Skamander," to distinguish them from the streamlets on the north side which flow towards the Simoeis, were adorned in later poetry with the properties of the real springs of the Skamander. However that may be, we can at any rate recognise in the ancient site rediscovered by Dr. Schliemann an important and tangible basis for the Homeric description.

After this we may feel certain that other peculiar features, such as the several burial-mounds which are mentioned, could have been pointed to in the Trojan plain in the days of the Homeric singer. But we cannot be required to point out every individual barrow at the present day. The description is often too vague, or has become vague through the fate of the poems; often also the site has been completely destroyed. For instance, the tomb of Aisyetes, from which the bold Trojan spies observe the camp of the Greeks,[3] cannot be distinguished from the many tumuli in the neighbourhood of the sea; the mound of Ilos,[4] which must have been close to the ford of the Skamander, must long ago have been washed away by the rapid winter floods.

If we group together all these several features, the picture we finally obtain agrees far more closely with the Homeric landscape than the most zealous advocates of the Troy-Hissarlik theory dared at first to assume, for the material to their hand has been enriched

---

[1] *Travels in various countries of Europe, Asia, and Africa*, p. 160. Clarke's measurements were 34° Fahrenheit and 69° Fahrenheit.

[2] P. Barker Webb, *Topographie de la Troade*, p. 46. His measurements were 43° Fahrenheit and 70° Fahrenheit.

[3] *Il.* ii. 791-794.   [4] *Il.* xxiv. 349-351.

by many a convincing detail. The Skamander and Simoeis flow
under the walls of the town, and the first separates the town from
the Greek camp. In the middle of the plain is the "swelling"
on which the Trojans stood so alarmingly near to the Achæans;
close in front of the city gate are the springs where war made
havoc of the idyllic scenes of peace. Thus much all must own,
the story received its fixed outlines from singers who lived in the
Trojan country, and were familiar with its every aspect of cloud
and wind, with the sea and the mountains and the islands, and
with every minute topographical circumstance of the royal capital.
We know now that the Epic poems have not come down to us
in their original form, but that they were welded together into
larger wholes by later singers, and finally worked up into the *Iliad*
as we have it now. But in the work of compilation the original
homelike picture has been preserved, and even the late patchwork,
which is clearly recognisable and which binds together the original
independent portions, scarcely disturbs this unity of impression.
The *Iliad* is as yet far removed from the fantastic transformations
of reality indulged in by the poet of the *Odyssey*, where dangerous
rocks become Scyllas with ravenous jaws, and whirlpools monsters
which suck in and vomit back their prey. So too Thrinakia, or
the "pitchfork-land," which is in reality the Peloponnesus, the home
of Circe, ever recedes into further distance, till it is placed on the
farthest confines of the known world, and is lost in a magic mist.
In the *Odyssey* we have the first free workings of that individual
fancy which was to suggest to the lyric and dramatic poets transformations of legendary matter as audacious as those which our
own age has seen emanating from the bold brain of Richard
Wagner. The beauty of the *Iliad* is of a tale told simply, yet
with a close reality, faithful always—like the flowery turf—to the
outline of the soil from which it sprang. The *Odyssey* shoots up
more boldly from its native earth, delighting in the luxuriance of
ᵗangled bough and thicket, while lyric poetry and the drama are
stately trees, so high and splendid, that as we look up we wonder
a clod of common earth could foster a beauty so majestic.

2. *General Survey of the Excavations at Hissarlik*

Hissarlik is not, as is often supposed, the name of the modern
village nearest to the ancient Troy, but that of the actual site of

the ruins. The word means "citadel," and is very often used
by the Turks to indicate the site of ancient cities.

The higher eastern range of mountains is continued into the
delta formed by the Menderé and the Dumbrek-su (Skamander
and Simoeis) by a chain of hills of about the same height. Shortly

2.—HISSARLIK AS SEEN FROM KOUM-KIOI.

before they end a slight depression occurs, and the piece thus cut
off is the mound of Hissarlik.

The plateau of the citadel is shaped like an oval stretching
from east to west. The building of the successive cities kept
adding to the height and breadth of this plateau, for the new
settlers always built their houses on the *débris* left by their predecessors, part of which lay where it fell, while part had been
swept away to the sides.

Thus we find that the oldest city which has come to light in
the excavations at Hissarlik is only 115 feet above the sea, and
150 feet broad, while the citadel of the second, the Homeric
city, lies several feet higher, and its walls inclose a space 320
feet wide. The full height of the hill at the beginning of the
excavations was 162 feet. In a similar manner the depression
which separated the Acropolis from the adjoining ridge became
as insignificant as it now appears through the gradual enlargement
of the ancient city. The researches of the year 1882 have shown
that its original level was from 33 feet to 39 feet lower than
the present level, and that its increased height is due to successive
layers of *débris* coming from the city.

The first years of the excavations had laid bare an inextric-

D

able labyrinth of walls on the Acropolis.   Dr. Schliemann, judging from their construction and from the pottery he found, tried to distinguish seven periods, but he did not succeed in showing in its entirety any one of the seven strata, each of which was supposed to represent a city.   This would have necessitated the carrying away, or rather the destruction, of one stratum after the other ; and we must feel grateful to Dr. Schliemann for not having adopted such radical means, for the remote period of antiquity here disclosed was so new to investigators that they might very likely have failed to distinguish the essential from the worthless, and the palace of Priam might have been irretrievably swept down the hill.   The building which Dr. Schliemann with wise reserve called at the time " the city chieftain's house " is no larger than the ante-chamber of the real palace, which was afterwards discovered ; its divisions form rooms of the most modest size, and the thin walls are built in the simplest manner of quarry-stones and clay-mortar.

The German excavations at Olympia, which followed close on the first Trojan excavations, were the first to give some insight into the oldest method of building on Greek soil.   The Hermes of Praxiteles was found imbedded in a thick layer of clay in the Heraion, the oldest temple of the festal precinct.   At first it was thought that this mass of clay had been washed down from the neighbouring hill of Kronos, but it soon became apparent that it was formed by the disintegration of the cella walls, which had consisted of large clay bricks.   The stone substructure of the walls ceases at the height of 3 feet 3 inches, and these clay bricks were employed for the superstructure.   The door-posts and entablature were of wood, the columns of the peristyle of the cella had also originally been of wood,[1] but as restorations became necessary they were replaced one by one by stone columns.   This interesting discovery is due, like so much else in Greek archæology, to the keen insight of Dr. Dörpfeld.   It was a happy inspiration that led Dr. Schliemann to associate Dr. Dörpfeld with himself when excavations were resumed at Troy in 1882.   Now light was also thrown on the citadel of Priam.   Among the large and small walls of the different epochs were found important traces of a homogeneous period of clay-brick construction.   With the exception of the late Græco-Roman buildings, the most stately

[1] Cf. Paus. v. 16, 1.

structures on the Acropolis consisted of this material, and all lay in one and the same stratum, *i.e.* the second from the bottom. It was further proved that the stone scarp of the huge fortification walls was only a substructure; upon it rose a wall also built of clay bricks, which, however, was here much stronger. It now became possible confidently to sweep away the later hovels, and to restore more and more clearly the picture of Troy in its prime. This picture is the culminating point of our interest in Troy, and will therefore take the chief place in the following description.

Among the seven superimposed cities of Dr. Schliemann the first and the second can be clearly separated. The first lies on the virgin rock. On its ruins a new level was formed, whose altitude above the old level varies from $11\frac{1}{2}$ to 20 feet, according to the undulations of the latter. On it are the buildings belonging to the second settlement, the golden era of the citadel; and these are constructed, as already mentioned, with clay bricks.

This golden era seems to have been of long duration. In the city walls and gates, and also in the buildings in the interior of the citadel belonging to this period, repeated alterations have been made, which were carried out without affecting the city level. The city finally came to an end in a great conflagration. Dr. Schliemann at first assigned the great mass of burnt *débris* which bore witness to the catastrophe to the third settlement, and accordingly in his book *Ilios* he describes it as "the burnt," *i.e.* the Homeric city. But the later excavations proved that the *débris*, since it consisted entirely of clay bricks, must belong to the second city. As the foundations of the third settlement often reached to nearly the level of the second, the previous error was very natural.

The third, fourth, fifth, and sixth settlements of Dr. Schliemann can be clearly distinguished from the preceding second city, and from the subsequent "seventh" city, *i.e.* the Græco-Roman Ilion; but the four together form a mass which can scarcely be divided into separate layers. It consists merely of mean dwelling-houses, constructed of quarry-stones and clay, and from the different heights at which they lie above the level of the second city, no safe conclusion whatever can be drawn as to the space of time which divides them from it. Dr. Schliemann himself says that the third settlers did not take the trouble to make a new level,

but let the *débris* of the second city lie as they found it; one
erected his house on the high heap of ruins formed by the fall of
the palace, while another built on the comparatively empty space
in front of it, where the fifth or sixth rebuilding would only
approximately reach the height which the former set of buildings
attained from the first. Moreover, as neither the masonry of the
houses nor the find of utensils or pottery enables us to group into
periods the settlements which followed on the second occupation,
we shall have to regard the third, fourth, fifth, and sixth cities as
representing one continuous village settlement, which began soon
after the destruction of the second city and possibly spread over
several centuries. It never seems to have risen beyond the condition of a mere village, and only now and again shows a new
element.

The citadel offers a different aspect only in its last stratum,
during the period of its resurrection in Hellenistic and Roman
times. This epoch is characterised by a new strong circuit wall,
and by the solid ashlar masonry of its big public buildings.

Thus all the buildings preserved on the citadel, and the
separate finds made at the time of their discovery, may be divided
into the following periods: first the oldest city, then the second
city—the Homeric Troy,—next, the village settlements which
represent an impoverished continuation of the second city, and
finally the Græco-Roman Ilion.

3. The Oldest City

The remains of the first city are only known to us through
the big north trench which Dr. Schliemann had already made across
the city in 1872-73. In all other places the ground of the
second city has not been broken through, so that this most important layer may be left undisturbed. The trench, which is
about 50 feet broad, disclosed a row of walls approximately
parallel, the most northern and southern of which are clearly
characterised as fortification walls by their greater solidity and
their scarped exterior. They are about 8 feet thick; their core is
of rough limestone revetted with somewhat bigger stones of the
same material. The distance between the two, *i.e.* the breadth of
the citadel, is only 150 feet. At a distance of 26 feet within
the southern line of wall lies a second similar fortification wall,

evidently the remains of an older and narrower circuit. In the intervening space we see several house walls from 2 to 3 feet thick; they are constructed of small stones bonded with clay, and in some places they still preserve the old coating of clay. Neither baked nor unbaked bricks are found in this settlement. Its level has an inclination of 6 feet 6 inches from south to north.

Although the utensils of the first settlement often correspond entirely in kind and in shape to those of the second, yet the following characteristics are peculiar to the first. Metal is still very rare; the axes, knives, saws are uniformly of stone. Among the vases those of black baked clay preponderate, and instead of the regular handles, most of them have perforated projections through which a string was passed to hold or hang the vase by. The vases in the shape of a human face, so common in the second and third settlements, are not found here. The potter's wheel is already known, but it is more rarely employed than by the subsequent inhabitants.

A few examples will serve to illustrate these main points more closely. No metal objects were found in the first city, except a few bronze knife - blades of the

3.—BRONZE KNIFE-BLADE (size 1 : 2).

shape shown in Fig. 3, a thick ring, and several dozen pins, from 4 to 4½ inches long, some of which have a round head, others a head in the form of a spiral (Figs. 4, 5, 6). These may be spindles or hairpins, probably the former when the head is pierced with a hole. They can hardly be brooches, for *fibulæ* or "safety-pins," to use a modern expression, and all pins evidently used for purposes of

4, 5, 6.—BRONZE HAIR-PINS (size 1 : 3).

dress, are unknown in the oldest settlements on classical soil. The pins of the Mycenæ graves are very similar to the Trojan ones, but their size and thickness, and the rich, sometimes even figured decorations of their heads, prove without a doubt that they were intended as ornaments for the hair. We must evidently suppose that the oldest inhabitants of all these cities wore sewn garments, of the kind afterwards considered as peculiarly Asiatic; a style of dress for which pins would naturally not be needed.

The stone implements are, as is usually the case in the oldest

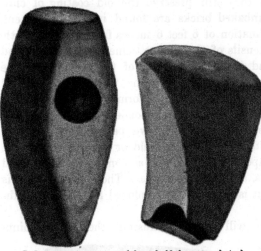

periods, chiefly of jade, greenstone, and serpentine, some also of hematite and porphyry. The two axes in Figs. 7 and 8 are of the last named material. In the excavations of the year 1882 eight stone axes or chisels (celts), five of which were of greenstone and three of jade,

7, 8.—TWO STONE AXES (about half the natural size).

were found in the *débris* of the first city. According to Mr. Calvert, greenstone is frequently found in the interior of the Troad, in the valley of the Rhodios. In Troy only smaller tools, to be regarded as chisels or celts rather than axes, are made of jade. It is the toughest of all stones. With the exception of New Zealand and of South America, which cannot be taken into account as supplying materials for antiquity, jade has hitherto only been found in Central Asia, and in small quantities in Silesia, Switzerland, and Styria. Up to this time we only knew of implements of green jade. Dr. Schliemann found the first chisel of white jade $6\frac{1}{2}$ feet beneath the topmost level of the hill of Hissarlik, *i.e.* in the third stratum. Yellowish, greyish, and greenish white jade appears to be common in Turkestan, but the pure white is only to be found in China. Thus the material of the implements

9.—CELT OF GREEN JADE (natural size).

discovered affords us interesting hints of a trade route leading to Central Asia existing as early as the oldest period of the city.

Figs. 10–13 are stone knives from the oldest strata of the city. Those which are toothed only on one side, like Figs. 12 and 13, had their smooth side fixed into a handle of wood or bone, and cemented with pitch, remains of which are still to be seen in some instances. Since the edge of the blade can never be so sharp in stone as in metal,

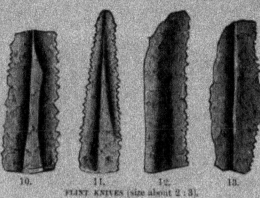

FLINT KNIVES (size about 2 : 3).

these ancient knives have teeth like a saw to facilitate the cutting.

Almost all the pottery of the first city is of a lustrous black; a very few fragments of red, brown, and yellow ware have also been found. The vase in Fig. 14 is one of the best preserved; it was probably used for cooking. It is of a dull black colour,

14.—BLACK EARTHENWARE VASE (size 1 : 4).

and has on each side those projections pierced by two long, vertical, tubular holes which are characteristic of the vessels of the first period. It is not yet quite clear how the black colour was obtained. Professor Virchow imagined that the vessels were merely exposed in closed chambers to a fire of smoke, the soot of which completely permeated the clay. But Dr. Hostmann of Celle, an expert in these matters, maintains that the smooth black coating could never be produced by a smoke fire. He supposes that the vessels were soaked in a thin coating of liquid pine resin, to which a little oil may have been added, and that after cooling they were exposed in such a way to the action of fire that the resinous layer became carbonised.

The vertical holes in place of a handle, so common in the Hissarlik pottery, are elsewhere very rare. Even in the mounds of the plain of the Skamander they are not found. The British Museum possesses three such vases from Nimroud and one from Babylon. Cyprus, Eleusis, France, Hungary, Meck-

15.—BLACK EARTHENWARE DISH (size about 1 : 4).

lenburg, and the Emilia have likewise each yielded one specimen.

The horizontal tubular piercing, on the other hand, as shown in the cup Fig. 15 (a shape which occurs in twenty-five other instances), is much more common, and is fully illustrated by the specimens at the Museum of Schwerin. This shape is also found in the Hanaï-tepeh, about three miles to the east of Hissarlik.

16.—BLACK JUG (size about 1 : 4).   17.—BLACK CUP (size 1 : 4).

Vases with handles of the usual shape are rare in the first city; Fig. 16 shows the only perfectly preserved jug with a handle. It is further remarkable for its thin clay sides, $\frac{1}{8}$ inch thick, of which only $\frac{1}{24}$ inch is baked. It is one of the lightest earthenware vases found in the older settlements of Troy. It has been made on the potter's wheel, another proof of its advanced workmanship.

The peculiar black cup of Fig. 17, with a high hollow foot, has only one handle, carried across from one rim to the other. The clay is thick and only slightly baked. Many fragments of this shape have been found in the first settlement; it seems to have been the usual one for cups. It disappears in the following strata.

As a rule, ornamentation is only found on the interior of the cups. It is quite simple, and uniformly reproduces the patterns given in Figs. 18-21. These are composed of zigzag lines, or of straight strokes and points. The lines are scratched into the clay, and then filled in with white chalk, so that they detach themselves charmingly on the

18.   19.

20.   21.

black ground. Occasionally the potter has made a clumsy attempt at representing the human face, as, for example, in the fragment Fig. 22. The eyes are perfectly round, but the pupil is marked; the nose is suggested by a simple stroke, the mouth does not appear. In another fragment, Fig. 23, the shape of the eyes comes nearer to nature, and the eyebrows have not been forgotten. This last fragment so clearly shows the effort towards using the human face as an ornament, that it is useless to argue, from the faulty

22.—FRAGMENT FROM THE LIP OF A CUP
(size about 1 : 2).

representation of the nose and the total absence of the mouth in the first example, that it was intended for an owl-face.

Spinning-whorls have been found in great quantities, both in the first and in the second stratum. They resemble the

23.—FRAGMENT FROM THE LIP OF A CUP (size about 1 : 2).

24.—WOMAN SPINNING (from a Roman relief).

whorls common to every classical period and site. Their use was to weight the wooden spindle fastened to the end of the yarn, and thus to facilitate twisting the latter into thread. Fig. 24 shows a woman spinning, with the distaff usual in antiquity; the yarn is drawn from the distaff; when it is so long that the

25-27.—TERRA-COTTA SPINNING-WHORLS (size 1 : 2).

spindle with its whorl nearly touches the ground, the thread is wound round the spindle, made fast in a notch, and the process begins anew.[1] The Trojan whorls are decorated with the same simple patterns as the cups, and the incisions are always filled in with chalk. Figs. 25-27 show some of the most common shapes.

[1] Cf. Catullus, lxv. 312-315.

4. *The Buildings of the second City, the Homeric Troy*

The layer of *débris* of the first city is about 8 feet deep. It is succeeded by a layer of earth of an average depth of 1 foot 9 inches, which proves that the site had been left deserted and not built upon for a long time. On the top of this layer of soil came the great layer of *débris*, by means of which the new settlers levelled and enlarged the plateau. The increase in elevation thus produced is only 1 foot 8 inches on the south side, but on the north side it reaches up to 10 feet, so that the ground level of the second city lies from 11 to 20 feet above the level of the first city. This solid layer of earth and *débris* explains the foundations sunk to a depth of 8 feet which the new settlers laid for the greater security of their buildings.

The most imposing erection of the new period is the great citadel wall, which is in good preservation, especially on the south side. The northern line of wall fell a sacrifice to the excavations carried on in the seventies, when the important and the unimportant were not as yet distinguished. Along the preserved portion the line of wall is double. Both lines are precisely similar in construction, but as the outer line blocks up the entrance of the great gate NF, which belongs to the inner line, and makes it useless, it must be the later of the two. This is confirmed by the fact that while the upper structure of the outer wall still rises in places to a height of 6 feet 6 inches, the inner wall is nowhere preserved above the ground level of the city. It was probably purposely levelled to facilitate an enlargement of the city.

The intervening space is filled up, not with *débris* but with earth, so that the first wall cannot have fallen down and been lying a long time in ruins when the second one was built, but the two merely marked two stages in a continuous development. On this is based the assumption of two epochs for the second city, representing a long period of prosperity, which manifested itself in great building activity, and which could only have fallen to the lot of the city once in that remote time.

The circuit walls consist of a stone substructure scarped on the outside at an angle of 45°, with a vertical face to the inside. The top surface is 13 feet wide, and keeps an uniform level, while the depth varies according to the exigencies of the soil. In the east it is only 3 to 5 feet, everywhere else more; the core of the wall consists of small quarry-stones bonded with clay; the outer scarp is revetted with big stones as much as 18 inches long, by 10 inches high (see Fig. 28).

On this substructure was erected a vertical wall of clay bricks, 11 feet to 13 feet in thickness. On the eastern portion of the outer course this wall is still standing to a height of about 8 feet. Judging from its thickness, its original height must have been at least 13 feet. Absolutely no vestige of this clay-brick wall can be made out on the older inner course; but it must have existed here also, for the big scarped wall alone, with its low inclination and broad joints between the stones, would have been easy to climb over. The bricks of which the upper wall is built are $3\frac{1}{2}$ inches high, and their superficies is about 9 inches by 18 inches; they are sun-dried, and they not only contain a quantity of straw, purposely introduced, but also many small potsherds and shells, a proof that the clay was not subjected to any levigation, but was employed for the fabrication of the bricks just as it was found. A finer, lighter coloured clay, mixed likewise with straw or hay, has been used as cement, and has been put on from $\frac{2}{5}$ inch to $\frac{3}{5}$ inch deep in the horizontal as well as in the vertical joints.

In order to insure the solidity of the wall, several strong beams, measuring 1 foot square, were laid along it. The only traces left of these are the holes in which they were fixed;

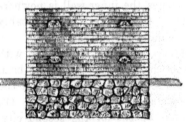

29.—SECTION OF THE TOWER GM ON THE EAST SIDE OF THE ACROPOLIS.

accordingly, Dr. Dörpfeld thought at first that these holes were channels through which the heat of a fire lit on the outside was conducted, with the object of baking the bricks after the wall had been built. Indeed there are unmistakable traces of a fire coming from the channels: the ring of bricks immediately round the channels is quite permeated by the heat, and has a light colour; then comes a black ring which has received its colour from the smoke, farther on the bricks are dark red, and still farther the red gets fainter and fainter. But to bake a colossal wall in this way would, to say the

least, strike one as strange. Moreover, when the brick buildings of Tiryns and Mycenæ were disclosed, it became apparent that bricks were employed unbaked, and that when the reverse appears to be the case, the baking is due to the great conflagration by which each of these cities was in turn destroyed. Thus, Dr.

Dörpfeld now explains the condition of the Trojan walls as caused at the time of the destruction of the city, by the burning of the beams imbedded among the bricks.

Both sides of the wall have a clay coating $2\frac{1}{4}$ inch thick.

The course of the circuit walls resembles an almost equilateral polygon. The sides are something above 165 feet long, and the angles are regularly fortified with bastions which project some 6 feet 6 inches. Owing to the scantiness of the remains, the construction of these towers cannot now be determined.

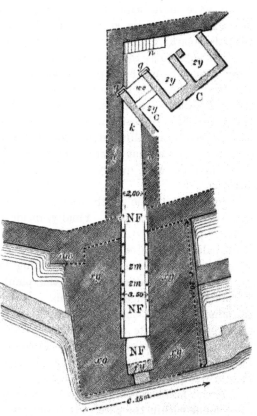

30.—GROUND-PLAN OF THE SOUTHERN GATE NF (scale 1 : 500).

The greater number of them were probably square.

Of the gates situated on the south side, the central one is the oldest. Its ground-plan is that of a colossal tower 130 feet long, by 59 feet broad, and projecting 59 feet beyond the citadel wall. Through it the road to the citadel passes, and as the projecting part of the tower reached to the foot of the Acropolis hill, the road was protected the whole way from there to the interior of the citadel. This road through the gate is 11 feet 6 inches broad, and has a gradual ascent of 13 feet. Its lateral walls at the lower end are thus extremely high, and are composed of larger stones than the walls higher up. But even so, this construction cemented merely with clay could scarcely have been safe if strong wooden posts had not been fixed against the walls at intervals of 6 feet 6 inches to 8 feet. From the marks left in the wall, they were 8 inches thick, and were sunk into the ground to a depth of 20 inches. Considerable remains of these posts have been found in a carbonised condition. The walls themselves were covered with a coating of clay, still preserved in parts. In the northern portion (*i* on the plan) the right wall seems in spite of all to have fallen down, or to have been near falling down, for it has received a facing, the posts of which stand at intervals of 2 feet, the intervening spaces being filled up with quarry-stones. This facing is also coated with clay.

Still farther to the north, where it is no longer supported by posts, the wall is scarped. Finally, inside the citadel the road bends to the right. At this spot a ramp to the left leads up to the palace; the direction of the road to the right cannot be clearly made out, as an important building belonging to the later period of the second city (C on the plan) covers it just here and prevented any deep excavation. It is likewise difficult to determine accurately the exact disposition of the actual entrance of the gateway at its southern end. Judging from the sudden narrowing and broadening of the road at that spot, it seems likely that the gate had two portals. The whole road through the gate was paved with beaten clay.

There is another point of special interest connected with the arrangement within the gate. It is obvious that the big wooden buttresses of the walls could not fully serve their purpose unless they were connected at the top by horizontal beams crossing the road. We can scarcely imagine that these beams stood out singly against the blue sky. Doubtless they supported a complete ceiling, and the existence of such a ceiling has been proved by the great mass of charred spars and of clay *débris* which lay heaped up on the road. The upper structure of this gateway formed the continuous flat roof of a gigantic tower. Probably this is how we should picture to ourselves " the great tower of

Ilios," so often mentioned in Homer, which is identical with the
Skaian Gate.   When Iris fetches Helen from her chamber, to
show her the fight between Menelaus and Paris, we are told that
they came " straightway to the place of the Scæan gates.   And
they that were with Priam and Panthoos . . . being elders of the
people, sat *on* [1] the Scæan gates." [2]

On another occasion, when Hector cannot find Andromache
in the house, and he is told that she has gone to the great tower
of Ilios, he makes his way to the Skaian gates and finds her there.[3]

The main difference between the two smaller gateways, FM
and OX, and the one
just described, is that
in their case the whole
of the approach from
the foot of the hill
was not protected and
roofed in, but only
that portion of it
which actually passed
through the fortifica-
tion wall.   A massive
ramp about 26 feet
broad and built of
roughly hewn rocks,
paved with large slabs
of stone, ascended at
an angle of 20° to the
south - western   gate
FM (Fig. 31).   The
ramp may be seen in
the middle of Fig. 28.
In   the   gate   itself,
judging   from   the

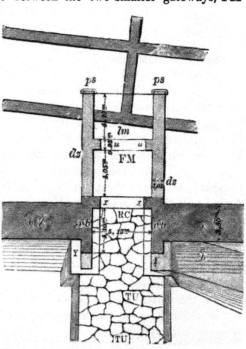

31.—GROUND-PLAN OF THE SOUTH-WEST GATE (scale 1:333).

different scale of the masonry, and assuming the larger to be the
older, we can distinguish between the original plan and its later
enlargement.   At first the side walls only projected slightly over
the ramp (Y Y), and the portal was formed by two quadrangular projections (*x x*), to which the folding gates were attached.   Later the

---

[1] The Greek word is ἐπὶ, translated by Messrs. Lang, Leaf, and Myers "at."
  [2] *Il.* iii. 145 *seq.*   [3] *Il.* vi. 386 *seq.*

lateral walls were slightly prolonged to the front, and were made
twice their original length at the back, where a second portal (*u u*)
exactly similar to the first (*x x*) was constructed. The inner
faces of the side walls (*ps ps*) were strengthened by wooden
pillars (parastades, antæ), the well-wrought stone bases of which
are still *in situ*. These pillars show, what might otherwise have
been taken for granted, that this gate also had a roof.

The third gate (OX), which lies east, close to the great tower,
has an exactly similar construction. We find here the same
double portal and lateral walls projecting beyond the gate proper,
and the masonry is the same. Only all the dimensions are somewhat larger; the inner breadth of the gate is 24 feet 6 inches
instead of 16 feet 10 inches, and the walls are 6 feet 6 inches
to 8 feet thick instead of 4 feet.

After this survey of the fortifications with their walls and
gates, we penetrate into the interior of the citadel. Here in
the very centre, surpassing everything else by its superior size,
lies the building which, after the analogous discoveries made at
Tiryns in 1884, we can have no hesitation in calling the palace.
In Tiryns we pass from the great gateway into the outer courtyard of the citadel, then through a farther gate into the inner
courtyard of the palace, in front of the men's apartments.
Within it is the altar of Zeus Herkeios, and on two of its sides
are colonnades. Precisely similar, although more closely packed
and less rich in detail, is the disposition of the interior of the
citadel at Troy. The south-east gate OX is the one which
leads direct to the palace. Behind it is an empty space, the
court of the citadel. Through the gate C we reach the courtyard of the palace, and have the chief apartments of the palace
(A and B) in front of us; to the right and to the left is the way
to the inferior apartments.

The first courtyard measures 50 feet between the outer and
the inner gate. The inner gate C is much dilapidated, because
at this spot the buildings of the third settlement were only 8
inches above the level of the second. The chief, and at the same
time the best-preserved, portion is the one on the west. Between
two lateral walls, 3 feet 3 inches thick and 10 feet 3 inches
apart, is a cross partition almost entirely taken up by a great
door. The threshold, consisting of a block of limestone 8 feet
8 inches in length and 3 feet 11 inches in breadth, is still *in situ*,

and is completed by a step on its south-east side. The ends of the lateral walls were faced on the north-west, at a distance of 8 feet from the gate, by wooden antæ similar to those of the great south-west gate; these antæ were apparently formed by the juxtaposition of four posts. Their two massive stone bases are still preserved; they have a carefully worked groove into which the jambs were fixed. East of this gateway two small chambers open to the north can be made out; they evidently correspond to the colonnade which surrounds the inner courtyard at Tiryns. Beyond this everything is destroyed. The floor of all the divisions of this gate consists of a clay layer, which also covered the great door-sill, and the exposed portions of the antæ bases.

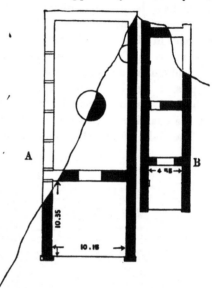

As this building cuts across the road leading from the great south gate, the road must have already been filled up when the gate C was built.

After an intervening

32.—GROUND-PLAN OF THE PALACE WITH COURTYARD AND GATE.

space of scarcely 33 feet, comes the palace. The building A consists of an entrance hall, about 33 feet square, with another hall behind it, 66 feet deep. In the centre of the latter are clay remains, only $2\frac{3}{4}$ inches high, of a large round hearth about 13 feet in diameter. This is the hearth which Homer tells us is situated in the innermost part of the house and marks its most sacred spot. Odysseus swears "now be Zeus my witness before any god, and the hospitable board and the hearth of noble Odysseus whereunto I am come."[1]

[1] *Od.* xiv. 158, 159.

And Nausicaa, when she describes to the stranger the way to her mother, says, " She sits at the hearth in the light of the fire weaving yarn of sea-purple stain, a wonder to behold.   Her chair is leaned against a pillar and her maidens sit behind her." [1]   No pillars have been found round the Trojan hearth, but in Tiryns their bases are still visible.   The megaron in Tiryns differs from the one in Troy in having two ante-chambers.   The smaller building B in Troy also has two chambers, and though in 1882 Dr. Schliemann and Dr. Dörpfeld considered both A and B to be temples, it yet had occurred to them to compare this building with the house of Paris, of which Homer says that they " made him his chamber and hall and *vestibule*." [2]

The walls of the chief apartment A, which we may now un-

33.—BRICK WALL OF THE PALACE, FACED WITH ANTÆ, CONSISTING OF
SIX WOODEN JAMBS.

hesitatingly regard as the megaron or men's apartment, are 4 feet 9 inches thick, and, like the fortification walls, consist of a stone substructure 8 feet deep, overlaid with stone slabs, which support a wall of clay bricks.   Over every four courses of bricks, on both faces of the wall, lay wooden longitudinal beams, connected together at intervals of 13 feet by cross-beams.

The left lateral wall and the back wall of the megaron were unfortunately completely destroyed in 1872-73 to cut the great north trench ; but the cross-beams recurring at regular intervals

---

[1] *Od.* vi. 305-307.

[2] *Il.* vi. 316.   The Greek word is αὐλήν—translated "courtyard" by Messrs. Lang, Leaf, and Myers.

enable us to establish its probable depth. As the lateral wall does not end with the fifth cross-beam, it must have been continued at least 13 feet farther. But with the addition of these last 13 feet the length of the hall stands to its breadth in the proportion of 2 : 1 ; it is therefore highly probable that the back wall actually corresponded to the lost sixth beam.

The bricks are $4\frac{3}{4}$ inches high, and have a superficies of 18×27. With this proportion of 2 : 3 the wall could be bonded with regular alternation in the vertical joints. Thus two bricks laid end to end, or three side by side, alternately formed the thickness of the wall.

The antæ were formed of six wooden jambs, which again stood on well-wrought stone bases. Between the antæ we must imagine two wooden columns, as the span of 33 feet seems too wide for a single roof beam. However, no traces of these columns are visible.

The purpose of the semicircular projection in the farthest corner of the megaron is unknown.

Like all the houses in the oldest settlement at Troy, the building had a horizontal roof constructed of beams, planks, and clay. This is made evident not only by the entire absence of any tiles, but also by the existence in the interior of a layer of clay 1 foot thick, mixed with calcined rafters and some large well-preserved pieces of wood.

The second chief building B is considerably smaller and shorter than the first ; and its walls are only 4 feet 1 inch thick. The foundations are only 20 inches deep, and are not overlaid with stone slabs ; the wooden beams only come in every sixth course of bricks, but on the other hand the cross-beams come closer together than in A. The building is 15 feet broad. From the vestibule, which is 20 feet long, a doorway 6 feet 6 inches wide, situated in the centre of the cross-wall, leads into a second apartment, 24 feet long. A smaller door in the left corner of the next cross-wall leads into the last room, which is 29 feet 3 inches long. The faces of the door were probably dressed with boards, and the antæ were constructed in the same way as in A.

In the fortress of Tiryns the women's apartments come next to the men's in size and shape. Thus at Troy also we may venture to call the second building the women's megaron, with its vestibule and ante-room. The remaining rooms of the palace, the ground-plan of which is still so clear at Tiryns, are at Troy in such a ruined condition that a complete chamber can only rarely be made out. At the most a few traces of the floor claim our attention. Some of these exhibit a plain surface of beaten clay, others a pavement composed either of clay and very small pebbles or of pebbles alone, others again slabs of green slate.

The ruthless destruction of the city is not to be ascribed so much to the later settlers as to the great conflagration in which it perished. In the great buildings lay masses of vitrified brick *débris* and calcined wooden beams, and in places where the fire had found food in the quantity of wood-work,—for instance, near the parastades and doors,—great portions of the brick walls have been completely melted and transformed into a sort of spongy vitreous substance.

The second settlement, and apparently even the first, were not, like all the following settlements with the exception of the Æolic and Hellenistic Ilion, confined to the plateau of the citadel, but comprised on the south-west and east an extensive lower city. At the north-east corner of the citadel the piece of wall BC has come to light in a trench: it is only about half_as thick as the circuit walls above, and runs from these in an easterly direction. Its masonry differs from that of the citadel walls, and, like the circumvallations of Tiryns and Mycenæ, consists of great unwrought blocks, the interstices of which are filled up with smaller stones; moreover, this wall is not scarped, but is built vertically. It can scarcely be anything else but the circum-vallation of that part of the city which lay outside the citadel.[1] No portion of its further course can, however, be pointed to, and no walls of either small or large buildings have been discovered; but the rock shows in several places traces of the bedding of the stones, and every trench dug in the lower city has yielded countless potsherds, similar to those of the first and second city. Dr. Schliemann and Dr. Dörpfeld are therefore doubtless correct in supposing that, during the subsequent occupations of the citadel, the lower city was deserted, and afforded building

---

[1] BC has been proved by last year's excavations (1890) to be a great ramp, which, like the ramp at Tiryns, ascended to the citadel. The steps leading to the ramp have also been discovered. See Appendix I and *Berl. Philolog. Wochenschr.*, June 28. 1890.—(Tr.)

material for the little houses on the hill; moreover that Archæ-
anax of Mitylene, who, according to Strabo,[1] built the walls of
Sigeum with the stones of Troy, removed these stones, and thus
caused the lower city to disappear almost entirely.

The existence of this lower city explains many features in
the Homeric picture. Obviously the poet cannot have imagined
his "broad-wayed Ilios" as confined to the narrow space on the
citadel mound. Moreover, the Skaian Gate, up to which the battle
often surges from the plain, can only be sought in the outer walls,
i.e. in the lower city, and consequently no vestige of it can any
longer be pointed out. It must have been situated on the west
side, between the springs and the citadel, so that our choice is
restricted within a narrow space.

5. The Separate Finds

The separate finds of the second city also prove it to have
belonged to the golden era of the citadel. A quantity of gold and
silver objects are of special interest. Most of these belong to a
single find, the celebrated "great treasure" discovered by Dr.
Schliemann in May 1873, buried deep in the fortification wall
near the gate with the ramp (FM). On this discovery he writes
as follows :—"While following up the circuit wall, and bringing
more and more of it to light, I struck, at a point slightly
north-west of the gate, on a large copper article of the most
remarkable form, which attracted my attention all the more
as I thought I saw gold glimmering behind it. On the top was a
layer of reddish and brown calcined ruins from 4 to 5 feet thick
as hard as stone, and above this again the wall of fortification (5
feet broad and 20 feet high), which must have been erected shortly
after the destruction of Troy. In order to secure the treasure
from my workmen and save it for archæology, it was necessary
to lose no time; so, although it was not yet the hour for breakfast,
I immediately had the *paidos* (interval for rest) called, and while
the men were eating and resting I cut out the treasure with a
large knife. This involved risk, as the fortification wall, beneath
which I had to dig, threatened every moment to fall on my head.
And indeed I should not have succeeded in getting possession of
the treasure without the help of my wife, who stood at my side,

[1] Strabo, xiii. p. 38.

ready to pack the things I cut out in her shawl, and to carry
them away. As I found all these articles together, packed into
one another in the form of a rectangular mass, it seems certain
that they were placed inside a wooden chest." [1]

The nature of the place where the find was made could
not afterwards be established, because that portion of earth and
wall was entirely removed to facilitate further search. But the
" reddish and brown calcined fragments " Dr. Schliemann describes
seem to be the burnt bricks of the second city, and the wall built
upon these a restoration of the fortification carried on at a later
period. Dr. Dörpfeld makes the admirable suggestion that, just
as in the walls of Tiryns there are whole galleries and casemates,
so in the Trojan walls several places were constructed where
objects of value could on occasion be stored.

The adjoining illustration (Fig. 34) shows the whole treasure
arranged together. The objects in the topmost row are all
women's ornaments, and lay together in the biggest of the
silver jars, which stands on the right of the third row. This
circumstance again shows that we have here the contents of
a treasury, and not of any grave that might have possibly
been constructed on the Acropolis at a later date. In a
grave the corpses would, as at Mycenæ, have been adorned
with the ornaments, which in that case would have been
found scattered. The most magnificent articles taken from the
silver jar are two big diadems, formed by a number of small
chains, which in the middle are about the depth of the forehead,
but are considerably longer at the sides, where they hung down
in front of the ears. In one of the diadems (Fig. 36) the chains
are composed of small heart-shaped leaves strung together with
fine wire; the short chains terminate in little pendants which
imitate two spear-shaped leaves growing together on one stem;
the long ones end in pendants closely resembling the " idols,"
which will be described later on; they may, however, be imitated
from a flower, possibly the campanula. If so, the small upper
portion would represent the calyx, the big under portion broadening at its base the corolla. In the other diadem (Fig. 35) the
chains are composed of double rings, with a spear-shaped leaf,
after every three or four rings. They are uniformly terminated
by campanula-shaped pendants, which are here ornamented down

[1] *Ilios*, pp. 40, 41.

85.—GOLD DIADEM (size 1 : 3).

discovered, five are shaped like the bracelet in Fig. 37 ; the sixth
is simply a wire welded into a circle.

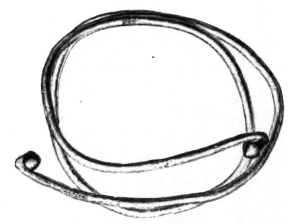

37.—GOLD BRACELET (natural size).

Figs. 38-40 show the most common shape of earrings ; some
thirty pairs of these were found in the silver jug. The double
ear ornament (Fig. 41) is specially interesting ; a pin fixed to a
hollow head fits into a sheath provided with a similar head. In
many of these objects the skill with which the Trojans soldered

38.   39.   40.   41.

GOLD EARRINGS (size 2 : 3).

gold with gold is astonishing. In this kind of work tiny grains
are fixed into holes, which seem to have been bored with the
point of a pin.

On the second shelf from the top (see Fig. 34) are six
remarkable flat bars of silver resembling large knife-blades.
Their surface dimensions, as shown in Figs. 42-44 (which give
three sizes), vary considerably ; but as the smaller bars are thicker
than the bigger ones, their weight only varies from 6 oz. to
$6\frac{1}{10}$ oz. Dr. Schliemann has therefore conjectured that these

were used for purposes of exchange, and that we probably have
here the Homeric talent.   They look more like pendants meant
to hang from the girdle, but as
none of them have any holes by
which they could be suspended,
the explanation given by Dr.
Schliemann cannot for the present be replaced by a more satisfactory one.

42-44.—FLAT BARS OF SILVER
(size about 1 : 3).

Next in order on the same
shelf are two silver vases with
covers like caps, and with vertical tubular holes at the sides
instead of handles. These holes,
which, as already stated, appear
instead of handles in the vases
of the two oldest Trojan layers,
prove that the treasure belongs
to the same period as the vases,
i.e. to the second stratum, and
not, as some have maintained, to a much later period.   The vases
resemble in shape the Egyptian *canopi*.   Next come three cups,
of which the two largest are of
gold, the smaller of *electrum* (one
part of silver to four of gold).
Beyond these stands a spherical
golden bottle, and last is a two-
handled oval cup, which is also
given separately in Fig. 47.   The
shape of the cup is that of a
broad boat. The body of the vase
is beaten out of one piece, the
hollow handles are rolled out of
separate plates and soldered on
to the body.   At one end it has
a spout 2¾ inches broad, at the
other, one 1¾ inch broad.

45, 46.—SILVER VASES (size 1 : 4).

On the third shelf from the top are four silver vases, the
largest of which has a handle.   The only shape analogous to these
jars is found among Egyptian pottery.   In the midst of these

four vases lies a copper object, which Dr. Schliemann has correctly identified as the hasp of the treasure-coffer.   To the left is a silver vase, to the right a small cup of the same metal which has stuck to the hasp.

On the shelf beneath are copper daggers, spear-heads, and battle-axes.   The daggers are of

47.—GOLDEN CUP (weight 600 grammes).

the same shape as the silver dagger given later (Fig. 63); they have a broad leaf-like blade, with a thick round tang, which ran through the handle from end to end and was bent round it at the bottom.   Three examples of the spear-heads are shown in Figs. 48-50.   They are fairly flat, and differ from the spear-

heads of almost all other prehistoric finds in not being fixed over the spear-shaft by means of a socket (the usual method of fixing in the case of the Homeric spear),[1] but in being fixed into it by means of a tang. In these tangs one may still, as a rule, discover the hole destined to hold the rivet.   Only Cyprus is known to have yielded similar spear-heads; they are in the British Museum and in the Louvre.

Two battle-axes are shown in Figs. 51, 52.   They are shaped like a chisel, and agree

48-50.—SPEAR-HEADS (size 1 : 5).

in this particular with the simple battle-axes of other finds.

Dr. Schliemann has had the metal of these weapons analysed, with the interesting result that they are almost entirely composed of pure copper.   In 0·286 gramme of metal analysed,

[1] *Il.* xvii. 297.

0·274 gramme was found to be copper, and only 0·011 gramme to be tin.

The last objects of the treasure are seen quite at the bottom

51, 52.—BATTLE-AXES (size 1 : 3).

of the picture; on the left a copper pot, in the centre a copper cup, and on the right a large flat cup, likewise of copper, with a boss in the centre, and shaped exactly like the later Greek sacrificial cups. We perhaps have here the vessel for everyday use whose time-honoured shape was afterwards preserved only for religious purposes. With this cup we come to an end of the great treasure.

The shapes of the principal ornaments found in it—the great diadems, for instance—are completely without analogy in the other finds on Greek soil. They remind one of Egyptian necklaces, and of many barbaric ornaments in ancient and modern times. It is therefore the more surprising that the smaller gold-finds, which took place principally in the year 1878 on various spots between the south-west gate and the palace, carry us right into the great system of Mycenæan shapes, where the spiral and the rosette reign supreme. The earring of Fig. 55 is made up of chains and pendants similar to those of the great treasure, but the bar that holds them is adorned with three graceful rosettes. Fig. 56 shows a bracelet, and Fig. 53 one of several ornaments where spirals form almost the whole decoration. These last were strung together in great numbers by means of a thread passed through the spine, and were worn as chains round the neck. Exactly the same kind of ornaments is found again in Mycenæ. In each case the decoration is made of fine wire, and soldered on to the object. Further, the round discs of gold-leaf (only three of these, similar to the one in Fig. 54, have been found in Troy) immediately call to mind the countless similar discs used as dress trimmings in Mycenæ. Still more charming are the two hair-pins (Figs. 57, 58). In one a rectangular plate decorated

with spirals is surmounted by six tiny jugs, each with two handles;
in the other a rosette with a boss in the centre is supported by
two spirals, and surmounted by two other spirals. Finally, the

53.—GOLD ORNAMENT
(size 2 : 4).

54.—DISC OF GOLD PLATE (size 1 : 2).   55.—GOLDEN EAR-PENDANT (size 3 : 4).

56.—LARGE BRACELET (size 7 : 8).

eagle in Fig. 59 is thoroughly in keeping with Mycenæan art.
It consists of two small plates held together by gold rivets.
Seen from above it resembles a dove, but in profile the crooked
beak clearly betrays the less gentle bird.

The few ornaments last mentioned (Figs. 54-59) are the

only objects which overstep the narrow limits of Trojan pro-
duction. It would seem as though the city had tried for a short

period to share the
great culture that
spread over the lands
of the Mediterranean
in the second millen-
nium B.C., and had then
sunk or been forced
back into its old
poverty of forms and
clumsy technique.
Unfortunately Dr.
Schliemann, spite of
his careful watch over
the gold finds, could
not prevent a quantity
of these being made
away with by some
workmen in the year
1873. The Turkish

57, 58.—GOLD HAIR-PINS (size 3 : 4).

police afterwards recovered a portion of these objects in the
house of a peasant in Yenischehr, but several pieces had already
been melted down and turned into modern ornaments.

59.—GOLD EAGLE (size 3 : 4).

Among the objects found in other metal the small lead "idol"
(Fig. 60) is very remarkable. It represents a nude female figure
with long curls over her ears, and arms crossed on the breast;

the strongly accentuated feminine characteristics mark it as the Asiatic Aphrodite. Similar figures of this deity in terra-cotta have been found in the tombs of Mesopotamia and Cyprus, and stone ones in the Cyclades. The swastika or hooked cross on the lower part of the body so repeatedly found in all prehistoric sites, and among the ornaments of later date, is Asiatic in origin. It seems to be the symbol of some very ancient divinity.

60.—LEAD FIGURE
(twice the original size).

Fig. 61 shows a copper knife, bent at one end into a round head. The opposite end served to fix the blade into a handle. Fig. 62 shows what advanced workmanship we may expect to find in many of these handles; it represents a crouching animal carved in ivory. The triangular end behind has a slit to receive the blade and a hole to rivet it through. Oddly enough, in the Kestner Museum at Hanover a bronze handle of the same shape may be seen; it probably comes from the Necropolis of Corneto in Etruria.

The annexed silver dagger (Fig. 63) was, like the bronze daggers, fixed into its hilt by a tang passing through the hilt and bent round its end. Besides Troy, this method of fixing the handle in the hilt has up to now only been found in the oldest Necropoleis of Cyprus.

The shape of the Trojan arrowheads from the oldest layers, with the exception of one example which is barbed, is simply that of a pointed peg, a shape which previous to this had only been found in a few instances in Hungary.

Spear-points, toothed daggers, chisels, and axes are found in

great numbers, and the numerous moulds of mica slate found
along with them prove that they were manufactured on the
spot. Fig. 65 shows one of the best-preserved moulds.

Among the most interesting objects found are the terra-cotta

61.—COPPER KNIFE-BLADE (actual size).

vases, and, above all, the vases imitating the human face. These,
as they develop, come to resemble the human form more and
more, and thus afford us another proof of that striving to infuse
life into dead material which is the final aim of artistic endeavour.
The advance is especially clear in this case. Instead of being
scratched on the clay, the nose and eyes are moulded on; soon
also two ears are added, the cover appears as a hat or conical cap,
and the projections, serving originally only as supports to balance

62.—IVORY HANDLE (actual size).

the vase or to hold the string used to carry it by, take the form
of the female breast; and finally the semblance of life is carried
so far that the vessel receives arms, and, moreover, those arms are
made to carry another vessel (Figs. 66-68).

The desire for imitation is not confined to the human form,
but manifests itself in vases of grotesque animal shapes. Fig. 69
shows a vase in the shape of a pig, Fig. 70 resembles a mole, and
Fig. 71 a hippopotamus. We must not imagine that the Trojans
wished to represent the owl-headed Athena (if ever such a
divinity existed) in those vases. There is no one instance that
can force us to recognise in it an owl-face instead of a primitive
attempt at the human face; on the other hand, there are several
which, owing to the clearly-marked mouth (see Fig. 72), can be
meant for nothing but the human countenance. Moreover, the

people would hardly have copied at random the holy image of
their tutelary goddess for the decoration of
saucepans or waterpots.

Some vase shapes are specially interesting
because they are found again in the oldest
Necropoleis of Cyprus, and nowhere else besides.
Such are the slim vases with long bill-like neck
(the so-called German *Schnabelkanne*, Fig. 73), so
frequent in Troy, and the vessels made up of
several vases fastened together, as in Fig. 74.

Fig. 75 shows a kind of cup common in the
second city ; Dr. Schliemann considers it to be
the " double cup " (δέπας ἀμφικύπελλον) so often
mentioned in Homer. The meaning of ἀμφικύπελλον has long been disputed ; in opposition
to the many ingenious explanations given of a
double bowl, etc., Dr. Schliemann's theory that
it must be understood to mean " two-handled "
is the simplest and probably the most correct.
The Trojan cup would be exactly suited for
guests sitting in a circle at their meal. It
cannot stand, and it must therefore be emptied
at one draught, or else be passed round, and
this would be much facilitated by the two big
handles, one of which would be held by the
giver and the other by the receiver of the
cup.

After learning from the vases made in
imitation of the human face that ordinary
utensils often assumed a living form, we may
suspect the flat stones hitherto interpreted as " idols " to have had some
everyday use. They vary in size
from large to small, they are always
notched on both sides, and generally
have a nose and eyes scratched on
their upper portion ; in some cases
also the stumps of arms have been
added. The attributes of the living

64.—BRONZE
ARROW-HEAD
(nat. size).

63.—SILVER DAGGER
(actual size).

form do not seem to have been peculiar to them from the

first, but appeared by slow degrees as the natural development of their original shape. It is probable that the simplest of these stones, of which Fig. 76 gives an example, served as spools for thread. They are usually flat ovals notched on either side, without any trace of the human countenance. About ten stones of this kind are known. The more developed forms may have been evolved from these; for if once the notch happened not to be quite in the middle, it would be tempting to turn the smaller segment into a primitive head, and to let the rest represent the trunk of the human body. The instance given in Fig. 77 comes nearest to the pendants hanging on the bigger gold diadem (Fig. 36). Both it and the one repeated in Fig. 78, where locks of hair on the brow and neck-bands are represented,

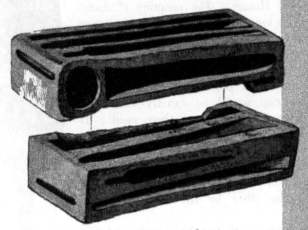

65.—MOULD OF MICA SLATE (size 1 : 4).

and finally the large stone in Fig. 79 with its stumps of arms, can quite well be explained in this manner. The more developed forms, which might possibly be idols, consist of a different material. Fig. 80 shows a figure of bone, which comes nearer to the human form, as the upper and lower parts of the body are in juster proportion. Fig. 81 gives the front and the back view of a small terra-cotta figure, in which we may clearly distinguish the raised arms and the hair combed down over the back of the neck. It must be owned that these later examples might very well be idols.

There has been much discussion about the Trojan seals, on

66.—TERRA-COTTA VASE (size 1 : 4).

67.—TERRA-COTTA VASE (size 1 : 3).

68.—TERRA-COTTA VASE (size 1 : 2).

which Professor Sayce wanted to recognise Hittite writing.
On none of them, however, can anything beyond mere decoration be made out. For instance, the example given in Fig. 82

69.—TERRA-COTTA VASE (size 1 : 3).

70.—TERRA-COTTA VASE (size 1 : 4).

71.—TERRA-COTTA VASE (size 2 : 3).

72.—FRAGMENT OF A VASE (size 4 : 5).

seems at first sight to have characters inscribed on its surface,
but on closer examination they are only lines and circles in
regular alternation. And the marks on the example which forms

the basis of Professor Sayce's theory (Fig. 83) can be explained in just the same way. However, he thought that he could read here the word *renta*, the meaning of which he is unable to tell us. There can be no doubt that we have here three angles with their points to one another, and separated by a plain line ; only some of the lines have run together, and have thus made the ornamentation obscure.

After this experience we should hesitate before making

future attempts at deciphering. Quite lately, however, in the Schliemann Museum at Berlin, the following marks have been discovered on a spinning-whorl.

They were immediately considered by Professor Sayce and his followers to be sure proofs of writing, and were read *vu sa lo po zo ma ko.* Nevertheless, until we learn what sort of language this is, and what the sounds mean, we may well continue to doubt whether the Trojans had a written alphabet.

73.—JUG WITH LONG NECK (size 1 : 5).   74.—CLUSTER OF THREE CUPS (size 1 : 4).

Two more objects of daily use may be mentioned. One is a triangular piece of baked clay, with a multitude of small holes on its upper surface (Fig. 84); bristles were evidently fixed into these holes, and the object must have been a brush. The other is a great hook, also of baked clay, which served an

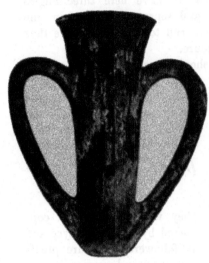

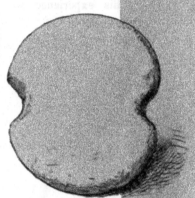

75.—TERRA-COTTA CUP (size 1 : 4).   76.—STONE SPOOL.

77.—STONE OBJECT (size 2 : 3).   78.—STONE OBJECT (actual size).

79.—STONE OBJECT (size 1 : 3).

80.—OBJECT OF IVORY
(actual size).

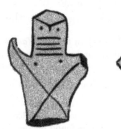

81.—UPPER PORTION OF A TERRA-COTTA FIGURINE (size 1 : 2).

equally realistic purpose; by means of its plate pierced with three holes it could be fixed on to a wall, and served as a peg for hanging clothes or utensils.

A convincing proof that the second city did not gradually decay, but was suddenly destroyed in a great conflagration, is

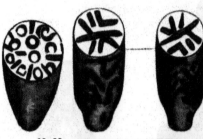

82, 83.—TERRA-COTTA CYLINDERS   84.—TERRA-COTTA BRUSH HANDLE
(size 1 : 2 and 1 : 3).   (size 1 : 2).

afforded by the skeleton of a young girl which was found buried in a stone house "in an almost erect position, and only just slightly bent backwards" under "yellow and brownish wood cinders," i.e. under the ruins of the upper part of the building. Close by were found several ornaments: a pin of electrum with rounded head, two earrings, and a finger ring. The last-named objects were merely bent pieces of thick gold wire.[1]

6. The Third Settlement

The people who, after the destruction of the second city, settled on the citadel utilised any available remains; for instance, they kept the city walls, only restoring them for a little distance on the west in a very inferior style of masonry. As entrances they kept the site of the S.W. and the S.E. gates of the preceding settlements, and apparently made use also of the walls of these gates as far as they remained, but the ground level

[1] For comparison with Hissarlik pottery see in *the first Vase Room* of the British Museum, cases 1-4. "Vases from primitive tombs in the Greek islands."
a. Shelf 3 (cases 1 and 2). Vases with tubular holes for string handles.
  „ 2 („). }
  „ 3 (cases 3 and 4). } Pottery with incised lines filled in with chalk.
b. Knives and other objects of obsidian, in the left-hand bottom corner of case 1.
c. A series of very primitive human figures of stone and alabaster (the earliest are spools according to Dr. Schuchhardt) will be found on the north side of case A, and at the bottom of cases 1 and 2.

was raised about 5 feet, and at the time of a later restoration
of the gate it was increased by another 5 feet.

Within the walls, as already noticed, the *débris* of the buildings which had fallen down was not removed, and thus the level
on which the new houses were erected was very unequal.   The
houses themselves were carelessly constructed ; the walls were not
even at right angles, and were built of quarry-stones or small clay
bricks, often eked out by the half-burnt material of the ruined
city.   The largest of these houses is that situated between the
palace and the west wall (D in the plan) : it is the one which
Dr. Schliemann in the seventies held to be "the house of the city
chieftain."   The walls of this building are 25½ inches thick, and
it is 24 feet 6 inches broad by 49 feet long.   The inhabitants
confined themselves to the citadel during almost the whole period
of these village settlements ; only a few houses which Dr. Schliemann claims for his fifth town, and which therefore belonged to
the latter end of the period of these settlements, project beyond
the old fortification walls.

"In this last Trojan campaign," writes Dr. Schliemann, " we
have had ample opportunity to convince ourselves by gradually
excavating layer by layer from above that the third settlers could
only have been very poor, for we found but little in their houses," [1]
and what was found rarely differs in shape or technique from the
objects of the preceding periods.   We find the same vases shaped

85.—CUP OR LADLE (size 1 : 4).   86.—CUP (size 1 : 4).

like the human face, the same slim *Schnabelkanne* and two-handled
cups, the same bronze and stone implements, the same " idols "
and spinning-whorls.   Only a new style of grey pottery, found
close under the Hellenistic city, and specially affecting the shapes
given in Figs. 85, 86, seems to prove that for a short time a new

[1] *Troja,* p. 182.

element was introduced either in the population itself or in their
commercial relations. Dr. Schliemann has called these vases
Lydian, on account of their resemblance to Italic and especially to
Etruscan shapes, because, according to Herodotos, the Etruscans
were colonists from Lydia.[1] The same pottery occurs again in
several heroic tumuli and other places in the plain of the
Skamander, and probably belongs here also to a somewhat later
epoch following on the golden era of Troy.

Evidently most of the graves found at Hissarlik belong likewise to this period. Dr. Schliemann has found two skeletons of
warriors, buried with their spears and probably with their helmets
as well. There were also a quantity of urns containing ashes.
At the time when the citadel was crowded with buildings, it could
not have been used as a burial-place; the two urns which were
found on the virgin level of the first city form an exception,
parallel to that of the small graves discovered during the last
excavations on the Acropolis at Athens. On the other hand, it
would not be surprising to find burial taking place on the citadel
in the intervals of time when it was either forsaken or only
scantily built upon. The finds show that cremation of the dead
was universal among the Trojans, for with the exception of those
two skeletons which were imbedded in the layer of the second
city, Dr. Schliemann only found urns containing quite fine ashes;
once a tooth was found in an urn, once also a skull, which was
perfect except for the under jaw. Professor Virchow has thoroughly
analysed this skull, together with those of the skeletons mentioned
above, and finds that in spite of strongly marked differences in
the breadth of the head and the shape of the chin, all these skulls
" present in a striking manner the appearance of the bones of a
race in an advanced state of civilisation." "Nothing of the
savage," he continues, "nothing massive in the formation of the
bones, no particularly strong development in the attachments
of the muscles and tendons, can be observed. All the parts
have a smooth, fine, and almost slender appearance." Therefore
we may safely "infer that the ancient owners of these heads
belonged to a settled people, who were acquainted with the arts
of peace, and who, through intercourse with distant races, were
more exposed to being mixed in blood."[2]

---

[1] Herodot. i. ch. 94.   [2] *Ilios*, p. 510.

7. The Grœco-Roman Ilion

A description of Greek, and still more of Roman ruins has little to do with the ideas which we connect with excavations by Dr. Schliemann. We are accustomed to associate his name with one well-defined period of antiquity, the Greek heroic age; and this association rises naturally from the individuality of the man, and his absolute devotion to that romantic world of legend. In Troy he has troubled himself but little about the uppermost stratum, or the seventh city, according to his reckoning. Whatever was left of this stratum was carefully examined and surveyed for the first time in 1882, by Dr. Schliemann's architects. Accordingly, our description of these remains will only be a short one, especially as the Hellenistic and Roman Ilion shows in its buildings, monuments, and utensils characteristics with which we are familiar in many other cities of the time.

87.—PAINTED FRAGMENT FROM A VASE (size 1 : 2).

Several fragments of vases prove that long before the visit of Xerxes recounted by Herodotos there was once more a settlement on the citadel. The fragment in Fig. 87 gives the upper part of a female winged figure, painted in black on a light red ground. The pointed nose and the big almond-shaped eyes, drawn *en face* in spite of the profile position, betray the archaic Greek manner. The hair seems to be braided in a long tail, which flows back from the head in a double wave, and ends in a tuft divided into two spirals. The back hair falls loose on the neck, and a lock curls in front of the ear.

A more regular cast of feature is to be seen in a second winged figure (Fig. 88) from the interior of a cup. It is drawn in brown

on a light yellow ground. The shape of the eye is still quite archaic, but the chin and neck are correctly rendered. The hair flows in full waves down the neck, and is bound by two fillets, the lower one of which is continued by an end falling between the ears. Both these fragments are of the sixth century B.C. They belong to the style of pottery hitherto, from its provenience,

88.—PAINTED FRAGMENT (actual size). called Rhodian, which appears to have been extensively manufactured on the whole coast of Asia Minor at that time, or at any rate to have been largely imported. The finds from Asia Minor have up to now been very scanty; yet we already know of these vases in the Troad, in Æolis (Kyme, Larissa), and in Ionia (Clazomenæ).

The accounts of the visits of Xerxes and of Alexander to Troy show that Athena was at that time still worshipped there as tutelary goddess, as she had been in the Homeric age. The coins of the city (Fig. 89) show on one side Athena standing

89.—COIN OF ILION (TETRADRACHM), actual size.

holding her lance on her right shoulder, and her distaff in her left hand, which is outstretched. On the other side is the head of the goddess with a crested helmet wreathed with laurel. We may therefore consider the largest temple of the citadel, of which numerous remains have been found, to be the Temple of Athena.

90.—CAPITAL, FRIEZE, AND CORNICE FROM THE TEMPLE OF ATHENA (scale 1 : 5).

her left hand a fallen warrior by the hair, while she raises her right hand aloft to deal him the death-blow. Her opponent, evidently the giant Enkelados, is wounded, and strives in vain with his right hand to free himself from the grip of the goddess; his left arm holds his shield, on which he is propping himself up. The treatment is interesting on account of its resemblance to the same scene on the Pergamene Gigantomachia. Remarkable similarities of technique have also been observed between these metopes and the sculptured slabs of the great altar at Pergamon; even their marble seems to be the same. The Ilian temple probably, therefore, belongs to the same period as the Pergamene altar, and was possibly dedicated by the Attalid kings themselves,

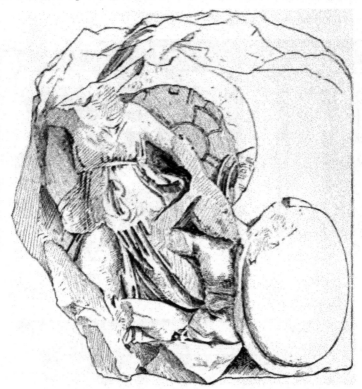

91.—METOPE FROM THE TEMPLE OF ATHENA (scale 1 : 8).

who, as we know, cherished Ilion as the ancestral home of their most influential friends, the Romans.

In addition to these remains of the chief temple, columns and fragments of the architrave of a smaller and apparently somewhat older Doric temple have come to light. Most important are whole stretches of the fortifications of Lysimachos; they formed a small circuit round the plateau of the citadel, and a larger circuit, the traces of which can be made out almost everywhere, round the extensive lower city. The walls exhibit regular courses of ashlar masonry, excellently jointed. On the northern slope lay the theatre, but the excavations undertaken here have yielded nothing remarkable; the building seems to have been erected in Roman times. To Roman times also belongs the last building which we shall mention—a gate on the south-east of the citadel (L on the plan). Behind a vestibule raised on three steps, three doors cut in the cross wall and framed by Corinthian semi-columns formed the gate proper. On the southern outer side of the gate stood four Doric columns, the corner ones facing the antæ of the vestibule; on the interior side there were probably two similar columns between the antæ of the inner portico.

The numerous inscriptions found at Ilion cover a period extending from the fourth century B.C. down to late Roman times. They afford varied information on the relations of Ilion to the neighbouring States; they tell of royal donations, of private dedications and honours, and seem to proclaim unanimously, what is confirmed by various writers, that the old fortress of Priam had become once more the flourishing capital of the Troad.

8. The Tumuli in the Plain of the Skamander

Next to the actual citadel Dr. Schliemann devoted his chief attention to the tumuli, which are so numerous in the Trojan plain, especially on the coasts of the Hellespont and of the Ægean Sea. Of the five tumuli situated close together on Cape Rhœteum, the largest, now called In-tepeh, was even in antiquity famed as the tomb of Ajax. When Hadrian [1] visited Troy the sea had already washed away a portion of this mound, so that, it is said, the mighty limbs of the hero were laid bare. The Emperor shed tears of emotion, and buried the bones under a new and stately barrow, over which he erected a temple and a statue of Ajax.[2] Remains of the building may still be seen on In-tepeh.

On Cape Sigeum were several other mounds; the first and biggest of these is the so-called grave of Achilles, the next that of Patroklos. Farther along the coast, on the heights, there is another row of similar mounds. Among these the Ujek-tepeh and the Beschik-tepeh reach the stately height of 50 feet and

[1] Paus. i. 35, 3.   [2] Lucan, *Phars.* ix. 961.979.

80 feet respectively.   These and some others, sixteen in all, were
excavated by Dr. Schliemann, but in none of them did he discover

92.—TUMULUS OF IN-TEPEH, SO-CALLED TOMB OF AJAX.

any traces of burial.   He therefore considers all these hillocks to be
cenotaphs, erected in honour of the dead, without containing
their bones.   Most of them have yielded nothing beyond potsherds,

93.—TUMULUS OF UJEK-TEPEH, SEEN FROM THE SKAMANDER

like those of the second city and those of Dr. Schliemann's Lydian
settlements, though possibly somewhat coarser.   Only in the so-

called tomb of Protesilaos on the European side of the Hellespont was pottery found of the kind peculiar to the first city; fragments of lustrous black cups with horizontal tubular handles, and also with vertical tubular handles, along with stone axes, saws, and other objects. Masonry was only found in two mounds; a small square tower-like chamber 14 feet high and 12 feet wide, in the so-called tomb of Priam on the Balidagh, close to the ruins of Bunárbashi, which was once held to be Troy, and another similar but considerably larger tower, 15 feet square by 40 feet high, in the Ujek-tepeh. It is built of well-wrought stone slabs, and rests on a round, massive foundation of carefully jointed polygonal stones. Dr. Schliemann considered this mound to be the tumulus erected by Caracalla[1] in honour of his friend Festus, who died during the Emperor Trajan's journey. Some of the fragments of terra-cotta found in this tumulus can, he says, be assigned to the fifth and sixth centuries B.C., but the greater quantity are late Roman. Of the three tumuli on Bunárbashi, two bear the name of "tomb of Priam"; one of them was excavated by Mr. Calvert in the fifties; the excavation of the other was entrusted by Dr. Schliemann to Dr. Dörpfeld in 1882. Mr. Calvert does not say to what period the fragments of pottery belong. The building inside consisted, it seems, of large irregular stones, roughly worked on the outward surfaces only, and put together without cement; the space in the interior was filled in with small loose stones. The discoverer holds that this structure either served to strengthen the mound, or else that it was the base of a statue or the foundation of an altar.

In the excavation of the second hill in 1882 nothing was found beyond fragments of that slightly baked, wheel-made, heavy grey pottery which Dr. Schliemann has called Lydian. Here, again, there were no vestiges of either bone or charcoal.

We must not, however, consider all these mounds to be mere cenotaphs, though no doubt these were known in pre-Homeric Greece. In the *Odyssey* Menelaos tells how he erected a memorial mound to Agamemnon in Egypt.[2] But a multitude of proofs shows that the mound was destined to cover the burnt bones. Patroklos appears to Achilles in a dream and asks him not to keep their bones apart, but to lay them together in one mound.[3]

---

[1] Philostratus, Her. p. 137 (ed. Kayser). [2] *Odys.* iv. 584.
[3] *Il.* xxiii. 83-91.

In the *Odyssey*[1] it is also told that the bones of Achilles and Patroklos lay together in a "two-handled golden urn," in a tomb "high on a jutting headland over wide Hellespont," and at the close of the *Iliad* the bones of Hector, after being laid in a golden urn, were placed in a grave and covered with a tumulus of stones.[2] Moreover, later generations looked upon these mounds as real graves; occasionally, indeed, they still buried in the same way. Among the tumuli lying about Pergamos, the one which has been opened discloses walls and arches built certainly in Hellenistic if not Roman times. The habit is still more general among barbarous nations, especially among the Scythians, of whom Herodotos[3] says that they burnt their dead king with his cook, his horse, and everything that belonged to him, covered the pile of ashes with a tent, and then buried them under a great hill. This Scythian custom, or its later Greek and Roman imitations, explains the countless tumuli which travellers see to this day in Bulgaria, in the Dobrudscha, in Wallachia, Moldavia, and Southern Russia, as far as the Crimea; these often form long rows of conspicuous monuments on high ridges. Besides, the Egyptian pyramids were nothing but giant burial-mounds. However, since this method of burial rarely occurs on Greek soil, we shall have to seek for its origin elsewhere, perhaps in the far East. As yet no sure result, and no ethnological explanation of the custom, has been arrived at. Only one thing seems certain, and that is, that since the Homeric conception and the later practice of Greeks and barbarians both point to actual burial in these mounds, we should not be justified in considering all the Trojan tumuli to be cenotaphs, in spite of the negative results of Dr. Schliemann's excavations. This opinion receives a welcome confirmation from a discovery made a short while ago. In the spring of 1887 some Turkish peasants discovered several golden objects in the Tschoban-tepeh, near Bunárbashi, amongst them a golden crown of oak leaves and acorns, weighing about $\frac{1}{4}$ lb. They had struck at a depth of 15 feet on a grave built of regular slabs without lime. Everything that the authorities were able to rescue from the people has been brought to Constantinople. These objects seem to belong to a later period than the pottery found in most of the other mounds. Dr. Schliemann and Mr. Calvert assign them to about the fifth century.

[1] *Od.* xxiv. 76-84.   [2] *Il.* xxiv. 664, 665.   [3] Herod. iv. 71.

The mound of Hanaï-tepeh in the garden of Mr. Calvert's estate, about one hour east of Hissarlik, is not a burial-tumulus. In Syria, Assyria, Babylon, and all countries where brick construction was in use, many stately hills are often nothing but the ruins of ancient palaces or settlements. So too, in the thorough excavations undertaken by Mr. Calvert in 1879 with the assistance of Dr. Schliemann, this mound turned out to be the result of a settlement which spread over a considerable time, and in which several periods could be distinguished. In the lowest layer are walls of houses built with quarry-stones or with small clay bricks; among these remains traces of domestic animals are frequently found; the bones of the goat and of the ox have been discovered, and a dog has left its footprints on several clay bricks. Two graves of children have also been discovered here. In the second layer a circuit wall, 8 to 10 feet thick, was built of large unwrought stones bedded in clay; within the walls were several round altars, 15 to 20 feet in diameter, some built of clay and two of stones. Above this houses reappear, and in them were found fragments of fine fifth-century Greek pottery. A short distance off, close to the modern house, large stone slabs had already been excavated, together with the fragment of an inscription giving the inventory of a temple. According to Mr. Calvert's plausible conjecture, this is the site called Thymbra as early as Homer, which in later times continued to be famous because of its temple of Apollo Thymbraios.[1] At the present time this lovely spot is the only oasis in the deserted plain of the Skamander, and every visitor to Troy who gains admission here will in his later reminiscences forget the sandy ride and the melancholy clay huts of the villages in the recollection of the "Villa Thymbra" and its friendly host.

9. Troy and its Inhabitants

The excavations show the wonderful city in all its varying fortunes, during a period of some 1500 years. We learn that the hill of Hissarlik was continuously inhabited. In the time of its oldest settlements, in a period so remote that it can scarcely be reckoned even approximately, it had imposing palaces

[1] Strabo, xiii. p. 598.

and massive fortifications. After this it was inhabited for a
long time by a petty population. Finally, in the days of the
Diadochoi and under the Roman rule, a new era of prosperity
dawned for Ilion and strove to give it back some of its old
splendour. The tradition, general among the Greeks, that Troy
had never been completely destroyed, but had continued on the
old site, is thus shown to be well grounded and correct. This
belief alone could suffice to refute the extraordinary theory which
still insists that the site of the Greek and Roman Ilion was
originally a burial-ground.

Captain E. Bötticher has issued numerous articles since the
year 1883, as well as a separate monograph[1] explaining that
the "so-called citadel" of Hissarlik is not the ancient Ilion, but
only a huge fire-necropolis. The successive strata of the hill
are not, he says, the results of habitation, but of continuous
cremation. The palace and all the houses of Dr. Schliemann's
citadel would therefore merely be buildings in which the bodies
were burnt and the bones preserved. The numerous vases with
human faces were simply funeral urns like their prototypes
the Egyptian *canopi*. The great fortification walls and gates are,
according to Bötticher's view, merely terrace walls with passages
cut through them. The city to which this necropolis belonged, he
says in conclusion, must have been situated in the plain, and have
stretched on either side of the Skamander, perhaps as far as the sea;
its citadel was probably on one of the hills of the Hellespont.

Even granting that one or two of Captain Bötticher's points
might at first sight appear plausible, it will be seen immediately
that his theory as a whole is absolutely untenable. In Babylon
there are real fire-necropoleis, which have, it is true, gradually
formed a whole hill by their accumulated layers. But they
correspond to the citadel of Troy only in their gradual growth;
they have neither colossal "terrace walls" and gates, nor a
monumental building within. The palace is of course the chief
stumbling-block, and the grounds on which Bötticher denies its
existence are typical of his whole method. He asserts that the
plan which Dr. Schliemann's architects published after the last
excavations is not drawn from the actual remains, but made up
from memory; for during the excavations—so Dr. Schliemann is

---

[1] *La Troie de Schliemann une Nécropole à incinération à la manière Assyro-babylonienne* (Louvain 1889).

said to have stated publicly in August 1882—all measuring and
drawing was strictly forbidden.   This was true at the time, but
permission was at last obtained from the Turkish Government
in November of that year, and Dr. Dörpfeld returned to Troy,
where he drew the plans undisturbed.   This, however, was only
a minor offence according to Bötticher.   He proceeds to accuse
Dr. Schliemann and Dr. Dörpfeld of having manufactured the
palace instead of discovering it.   In proof of this he appeals to
the various travellers who in the seventies saw nothing on the
hill but small houses and miserable walls.   He further quotes
the plans made at the time by M. Burnouf, which show a labyrinth of petty walls on the site where the palace afterwards
appeared.   These walls divided the "palace" into numberless
small mortuary chambers, says Bötticher.   Dr. Dörpfeld has had
them all swept away, to obtain the large building which was to
give a new character to his citadel.   When it was urged that
the palace of Tiryns, which was found two years later, had
exactly the same ground-plan, the consistent sceptic explained
that the citadel of Tiryns also was a home of the dead, that it
had been completely closed all round, and had received doors
and gates at the arbitrary will of its discoverers.   And yet
wherever Dr. Schliemann and Dr. Dörpfeld have assumed a
passage, the old door-sills still lie *in situ*, or else the stone bases
of the posts are preserved at the sides.

Such an attack would have best been met by silence.
Unfortunately, however, Dr. Schliemann and Dr. Dörpfeld noticed
all Captain Bötticher's wild theories, and thus bred in him
increasing self-confidence.   As letter followed upon letter during
1889, Dr. Schliemann invited Captain Bötticher to accompany
him to Troy in the autumn of 1889, in hopes that the contention would soon be laid to rest in presence of the actual, indis-
putable facts.   The invitation was accepted, and an arbitration
took place with Captain Steffen and Professor Niemann as witnesses.[1]   Although these gentlemen testified to the absolute
accuracy of the plans, Captain Bötticher merely retracted his
accusation of *mala fides*, and in a recent pamphlet[2] published

---

[1] For an account of the arbitration, which took place December 1-6, and of the
conference, which followed in the spring, see Appendix I.

[2] *Hissarlik wie es ist*, fünftes Sendschreiben über Schliemann's Troja (Berlin
1890).

since the arbitration, he reverts to his former position, and makes a fresh and vigorous attack on Dr. Schliemann and Dr. Dörpfeld on the old grounds.

Captain Bötticher can hardly expect to be treated seriously any longer. He might as well try to prove that the "so-called Acropolis" of Athens was itself but a fire-necropolis, the Propylæa the entrance to the cemetery, the Parthenon and Erechtheion its huge *columbaria*. It is time to dismiss all such theories as mere vagaries, and to pass to a consideration of what the splendid ruins can teach those who study them with an unbiassed mind.

A universal interest has naturally attached to Dr. Schliemann's Trojan excavations, which promised to prove at last whether the groundwork of the Homeric poems was real or purely imaginary. What do they tell us about the citadel of Hissarlik, the nation that held sway there, and the war which is said to have taken place before its walls ? They show us a citadel of very small extent, like the Acropolis of Mycenæ, Tiryns, and Athens; it did not contain the whole city, but only the palace of the rulers. In all these cases the city lay at the foot of the hill, and at Troy it has almost completely disappeared. But the citadel, where we may trace the varying fortunes of the city, had been surrounded with strong walls by the first settlers, and received in its second period a stately circuit of fortifications protected by gates and towers, such as are found on no other site in the Troad or on the Asia Minor coast, at so early a date. Troy must therefore have held a prominent position not only in the Troad but on the whole of that Asia Minor coast, *i.e.* in the maritime intercourse of the Archipelago. It was certainly the capital of the country, and on account of its important position on the straits between two seas it would be called upon to enter actively into wider relations.

When considered individually, the buildings and the objects discovered at Troy are found to occupy a middle position between the three great civilisations of the ancient world, the Assyro-Babylonian, the Egyptian, and the Greek. The use of brick corresponds to a custom that arose out of natural necessities in countries which, like the land of the Euphrates, had no stones but only alluvial deposit. In the same way the scarping of walls, which had its origin in Egypt, was necessitated by the poverty of the material. The later inhabitants of Asia Minor and of

Greece were sufficiently familiar with the rocky formations of this region to build excellently with stone. On the other hand, the form of the Trojan gates and palaces links this Asiatic brickwork with the western shore of the Ægean Sea; for the plan of these gates is not only found again at Tiryns and at Mycenæ, but it became the model for all subsequent Greek gate construction, and the Doric temple was developed from the analogous ground-plans of the royal habitations at Troy, Tiryns, and Mycenæ.

The presence of ivory and of jade proves intercourse with Central Asia; the shapes of several of the vessels betray the influence of Egypt. But the "Mycenæan style" of decoration in a series of gold ornaments shows again the contemporaneous link with Europe.

Thus the inhabitants of Troy are in a state of transition from the Asiatic and Egyptian manner to the Greek. They build according to Oriental methods, which afterwards become the models for Greek architecture; they procure their most precious objects from the East, from the South, and from the West. The common everyday utensils, however, such as cooking-pots, water-jugs, cups, and spools, are made on the spot. They are quite individual, without relation either to the one side or to the other, and so afford another proof of the transitional stage of a people, who have been too long separated from the pure Asiatic races to work in the Asiatic style, but have not yet adopted the Greek manner. And so in their home productions they create a style of their own. This explains why the diadems and ear-pendants of the great treasure and so many vase-shapes are without analogy elsewhere.

We therefore must think of the people, whose king dwelt on the citadel of Troy, as long established in the country. Their architecture shows a period of marked development. It is all the more surprising that many stone implements should still be found in the second city. Tiryns and Mycenæ, however, will show us that stone implements continued in use even in times of high artistic achievement.

Decorative art in Troy is only in its first stages. With the exception of the primitive faces on vases and on stones, no representations of the human form have been discovered. Thus the objects found only scantily satisfy our curiosity as to what the Trojans looked like, how they dressed, or what their occupations were. The finds in Hanaï-tepeh point clearly to an agricultural and pastoral life, such as a long occupation of the soil, and the fertility of the fruitful plain of the Skamander, were bound to bring to high perfection.

The weapons found are lances, arrows, daggers, and axes, but strangely enough no swords. Yet it seems difficult to believe that swords were not in use. Mycenæ has probably only yielded them in such quantities because untouched graves were found there; for in Tiryns, where the excavations have not hit upon any graves, no swords have been found, though this city was so closely connected with Mycenæ both in date and situation. The same circumstance explains the absence of these weapons at Troy.

It remains to discuss the character of the race that inhabited Troy, and the probable historical basis of the war described in Homer. As a necessary preliminary to the even partial solution of these questions, we must obtain some knowledge of the people who dwelt on the other side of the Ægean Sea, and whom legend calls the enemies of the Trojans. Their manner of life is so clearly reflected in the stately ruins of their civilisation both at Tiryns and Mycenæ that a new light is shed at the same time on Troy. Yet even before we enter on this study we can accept one fact as incontestable: there existed on the site of Hissarlik, at a period far anterior to any we know of on Greek soil, a proud and royal city, mistress of sea and land; and the singers of the Trojan War, just as they were familiar with Ida and Skamander, with the Hellespont and the Isle of Tenedos, knew also of this city, knew of its golden age and of its mighty downfall.

CHAPTER III

1. Its Situation and History.   Relation to Mycenæ

MYCENÆ and Tiryns both lie on the borders of the great Argolic plain, which has given its name to the whole region ; for, according to Strabo, *Argos* is the Pelasgic for " plain."   In a rocky and dry land like Greece a stretch of rich low-lying country would in itself appear a fortunate region, but when, like the Argolic plain, it also terminates in a deep sheltered bay, which affords unmolested access to the islands of the Ægean and to the treasures of the Anatolian coast, it is not surprising to find that the most ancient civilisation on Greek soil reached here its highest development.

   The chief stream of the plain is the Inachos ; the Kephissos, now called Dervenaki, flows into it from the north.   Near to their confluence, at the extremity of a ridge of hills that juts out far into the plains, lies Argos ; " it is the natural capital of the plain of the Inachos, and round it the life of the country must always have centred."   So writes Captain Steffen,[1] who in 1881 drew two excellent maps, one of the citadel and one of the neighbourhood of Mycenæ, for the German Archæological Institute.   Tiryns and Mycenæ lie opposite Argos, on the eastern border of the plain. The first is situated on a low, flat, solitary rock, 85 feet high, rising from the marshy plain, at a distance of $1\frac{1}{4}$ mile from the sea ; Mycenæ is $9\frac{1}{4}$ miles inland, on a spur rising from the N.E. extremity of the plain, in the valley of the Kephissos, and not far from the passes which facilitate intercourse between the Argolic and the Corinthian Gulfs.   The hill of the citadel, which is protected by a few spurs, rises to the height of

---

[1] Hauptmann Steffen and Dr. H. Lolling.   *Karten von Mycenæ* (Berlin 1884).

911 feet, and is flanked by two still higher summits—the Prophet Elias (2646 feet) on the north, and the Zara (2160 feet) on the south.

Their relative situations explain at once the hostile attitude in which legend places the foreign founders of these citadels towards the autochthonous lords of Argos. At the dismemberment of the old kingdom of Danaus, Acrisios receives Argos, while Proitos receives the Heraion, Mideia, and Tiryns. These sites accordingly passed for the most ancient. Mycenæ was associated with them later on. During the reign of Megapenthes, son of Proitos, Perseus founds Mycenæ, and makes the older neighbouring city of Tiryns its vassal.[1] This relation between the two cities continued ever after. It comes out very clearly in the myth of the labours which Herakles, the Tirynthian, must accomplish for Eurystheus, King of Mycenæ.

The cities play no part in historic times. Only during the Persian wars eighty Mycenæans are mentioned among those who fell at Thermopylæ,[2] and 400 Mycenæans and Tirynthians took part together in the battle of Platæa.[3] In 468 B.C. Tiryns and Mycenæ were destroyed by the Argives, who asserted over the country a dominion which the position of their citadel gave them. After this the former royal capitals of the Achæans are only known as ruins. But Mycenæ, at least, does not seem to have been left as utterly desolate as ancient writers affirm. Dr. Schliemann had concluded from various indications that there was a new occupation of the citadel in the Macedonian age; and the inscriptions found during the most recent Greek excavations have proved that from the third century B.C. a village (κώμη) existed at Mycenæ for a considerable length of time.

In other respects the excavations thoroughly confirm legendary evidence as to the relative ages of Tiryns and Mycenæ. The walls of Tiryns give a greater impression of antiquity than even the most ancient portions of the Mycenæan fortifications. They consist of colossal roughly hewn blocks, and show no vestiges of later restoration. The Mycenæan wall, on the other hand, was built from the first with somewhat smaller stones, and was afterwards strengthened and restored at different times by a careful masonry either of square or polygonal blocks.

[1] Apollod. ii. 2, 1. Paus. ii. 25, 6; 16, 2, 3.
[2] Herod. vii. 202. [3] Herod. ix. 28.

· It is difficult at first to understand how the hill city of
Mycenæ came to overshadow a city like Tiryns, favourably
situated on the sea. This fact is not explained by the following
remark of Aristotle, who says : " At the time of the Trojan War
the land of the Argives, on account of its marshy soil, could only
support few inhabitants, but the land of Mycenæ, on the other
hand, was good, and highly esteemed accordingly." [1]   The finds of
Tiryns and Mycenæ point too clearly to a maritime civilisation,
and to wealth obtained through commerce, for us to venture to
explain the greater or lesser power of these cities by the condition of their soil. The real answer must be sought in the situation of Mycenæ on a height between the Corinthian and the
Argolic Gulfs.   Especially since Captain Steffen has shown in his
maps a perfect labyrinth of Cyclopean road-tracks, all intended
to keep Mycenæ in communication with Corinth by the most
varied routes, there can be no doubt that this mountain site was
chosen in order to ensure the new city a twofold outlet for its
activity, and that the amazing prosperity and power to which the
city attained were the practical result of that endeavour. It now
only remains to inquire what the starting-point of the founders
of Mycenæ was ; did they come from the Argolic Gulf, wishing to
secure the Corinthian as well, or, coming from Corinth, did they
aim at Argos ?   It is difficult to accept Captain Steffen's view of
the matter.   He considered Mycenæ to be an outpost of Corinth
in its effort to reach Argos.   He believes that another offshoot
of the same people, who coming by sea had settled in Tiryns,
now came into Argolis by land, through Corinth.   On the
contrary, it is more probable that the founders of Mycenæ came
from the Argolic Gulf, and established the city in order to facilitate the road to the Corinthian Gulf.   In the first place, Mycenæ
and Tiryns are too evidently allied by their situation, and too
intimately connected in legend, for the close similarity of their
finds to be explained by the accidental reunion of two peoples
who, though originally belonging to the same stock, had become
completely separated.   Secondly, it is more difficult to see why
Corinth, who by her unrivalled situation already commanded two
seas, should have aimed at the Argolic Gulf by an overland route,
than to suppose that a people who had a firm footing in the plain
of the Inachos, pressed farther to the north in order to win the

[1] *Meteor.* i. 14.

western sea. A rich field for trade was open in the west, towards the Ionian Islands, the land of the Phæacians. We must remember that legend names the king of Ithaca as one of the most faithful paladins of Agamemnon.

We may therefore presume that the civilisation which began at Tiryns spread thence to Mycenæ, where it reached its full development. Power and civilisation travelled here in an opposite direction to what they did in the Troad. The ancestors of Priam had a small fortress in the hills; they became a mighty State only when they came down into the plain. In Argolis Tiryns first holds sway, then Mycenæ grows in the mountains and over-shadows everything. This is why the finds of Troy always bear the stamp of inland fabrics, while those of Mycenæ, with their ornamentation borrowed from marine plants and animals, find their analogy in the islands of the Ægean.

The greater age of Tiryns makes it desirable to depart from the order of time of Dr. Schliemann's excavations, and to describe its ruins before those of Mycenæ. This is the more necessary, as the most important excavations at Tiryns—those of the city walls and of the palace—often form the basis for our explanation of the similar buildings at Mycenæ, which are much less well preserved.

2. Walls and Gates

In the spring of 1884 Dr. Schliemann, who had already sunk several shafts at Tiryns in 1876, undertook its complete excavation, and discovered in a good state of preservation the whole ground-plan of the palace with its gates and courts, its men's and women's apartments, and its walls still standing in some places 3 feet high. The arrival of the summer heat stopped the work for that year. In the following year Dr. Schliemann entrusted the excavations to Dr. Dörpfeld. The work of this second season proved most interesting, and resulted in laying bare a great portion of the colossal enclosure wall, with its towers, galleries, and chambers.

Tiryns is built on a limestone rock, only 328 yards long and 109 yards broad, which rises, isolated on every side, 59 feet from the surface of the surrounding plain and 72 feet above the level of the sea. It falls several feet from south to north, and forms three terraces, which were utilised for different purposes in the scheme of building, and which we shall respectively call the *Upper*, *Middle*, and *Lower* citadels.

On the upper citadel, in the south, was situated the palace; it occupied the whole space between the fortification walls; on the middle citadel are some petty habitations much dilapidated, probably destined to the servants; the lower citadel is not yet excavated. Its circuit is much smaller than that of the upper and middle citadels, and cannot possibly have enclosed the city belonging to the royal palace. It is much more likely that this city lay, as at Troy, at the foot of the hill. We cannot tell

94.—PORTION OF THE WESTERN CITADEL-WALL.

whether it was surrounded by a wall, or how far it stretched, as no excavations have been undertaken here, and they would probably be of little use in a region which has been uninterruptedly cultivated for centuries.

The circuit wall of the citadel is built throughout of very large stones. It is not scarped, and does not support a wall of clay bricks like the Trojan wall. It is well known that the ancients believed that King Proitos invited the Cyclopes to come from Lycia and build his citadel walls. Such was the wonder they excited, that their erection could not be attributed to ordinary men. In reality several stones are 6 to 10 feet long by

H

more than a yard both in height and in thickness. The stones are not, however, as was long commonly supposed, quite *unhewn*: several of them have received a lower bed, others a smooth facing roughly worked with the pick-hammer. Moreover, they are not irregularly piled up on one another, but have been arranged as much as possible in layers running right through (see Fig. 94); and finally, they were not joined without binding material, as was universally believed up to the time of the last excavations, but they were bonded with clay mortar: in places which have lately been laid bare the yellowish dust of the clay is being continually brought out by the lizards and rats which live in countless numbers in these walls. The walls are built of blocks of limestone, which was also employed as a rule for the buildings inside the citadel. "This limestone has been quarried in the neighbourhood of Tiryns from the rocks lying south and east, where one

95.—STONE WITH A BORE-HOLE.

may still recognise the vestiges of ancient stone-quarries." A few stones give a clear indication of the manner in which they were obtained. They show on their edge (sometimes right in the centre of the face, as in Fig. 95, sometimes in the corner) a deep round bored hole, into which a thick wooden stave was introduced; this was wetted, and as it swelled loosened the block.

The strength and the structure of the walls vary in the different parts of the citadel. Around the lower citadel the thickness is uniformly from 23 to 26 feet, and the elevation has been preserved to a height of 24 feet 6 inches. The continuity is only interrupted by a few niches, built on the inner side; their exact purpose is uncertain. Around the upper citadel, on the other hand, the thickness varies from 16 feet up to the astonishing figure of 57 feet; moreover, the line of wall is here divided up by numerous projecting or re-entering angles, it is fortified by towers, and pierced by galleries and chambers. The latter are best preserved in the southern portion of the wall (see Fig. 96). Here in the great tower at the angle of the wall (A A on the plan of Tiryns) are two chambers closely adjoining; they have no entrance on any side, and may have served as

provision cellars, or more probably as cisterns. From the
quantity of brick rubbish found inside these chambers, their
upper structure must have been built of clay bricks. The
adjoining south line of wall, the most massive of the whole
circuit, was, before the complete clearance, thought to consist
of two different portions; on a substructure 36 feet thick a re-
treating superstructure 14 feet 7 inches in thickness was assumed.
This would leave a free space 21 feet 5 inches broad along the top
of the lower wall in front of the upper wall. The long corridor

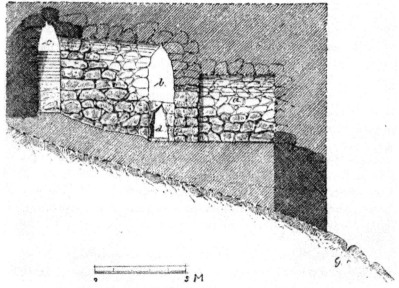

96.—TRANSVERSE SECTION THROUGH THE SOUTH WALL.
a, Vaulted chamber; *b*, gallery with window *d*; *c*, gallery with staircase.

or "gallery" of the upper structure, with the five doors leading
from it, had long been known, but the object of these unique
features was much disputed till an explanation offered by Captain
Steffen gained universal acceptance. He suggested that these
arches served as sallyports, by which the soldiers issued from
the corridor on to the platform on the lower wall, in order to
defend the citadel. But the thorough clearance of this portion
of the wall undertaken in 1885 has meanwhile led to quite new
results. It appears that there never was a platform along the
top of the lower wall. In its place five separate chambers were

found, which, as is still clear in some portions, had a pointed vaulted ceiling formed by the gradual converging of the stones of the side walls. Above these chambers the walls must certainly have been built up to the same height which they had inside above the corridor and the staircase.

The whole disposition of this new system can be understood from the ground-plan of the citadel (iv), with the additional help of the annexed transverse section (Fig. 96). From the great court F in the interior of the citadel a connecting passage which has not been preserved, though several indications point to a small portico with columns (E), gave access to a staircase D (c), leading with two bends down into the long corridor C (b), 24 feet 6 inches lower. This corridor is from 5 feet to 5 feet 7 inches broad; its western end is completely closed, the eastern end is lighted by a window (d), which, starting with the same breadth as the corridor, contracts towards the outside down to 4 inches in the shape of a loophole. The ceiling of the corridor is formed by the converging stones of the side walls, so that it had the shape of a pointed vaulting. From the corridor five distinct doors whose sills are preserved led into five separate chambers. The two on the west are somewhat larger than the three on the east; they have a depth of 17 feet 4 inches as against 14 feet 2 inches. These chambers, like the corridor, have a pointed vault produced by the convergence of the side walls, and perhaps had a window similar to the corridor.

This whole system is exceedingly interesting through its re-semblance to that of the city walls of several Phœnician colonies on the north coast of Africa. The following illustrations (Figs. 97 and 98) show a portion of the ground-plan of the east wall at Tiryns and a portion of that of the Acropolis wall of Carthage. Although at Carthage the corridor lies to the outside and the chambers to the inside of the citadel, the similarity, even in the dimensions, is so remarkable that it cannot be attributed to mere coincidence. We naturally are led to think of the various Phœ-nician settlements on the Greek coast of which legend and the new methods of comparative philology tell us. However, we need not suppose that the workmen employed by Proitos to build his walls were Phœnician; the art of the Tirynthians goes back for its pattern to the same old Asiatic type which was adopted, consciously or unconsciously, not only by the Phœnicians, but also by several other nations of that time.[1] With reference to the remarkable system of galleries and chambers in the Tiryns walls, Dr. Dörpfeld writes: "They can no longer be assumed to have served a purpose of fortification, for even supposing that each room had a window which could serve as a loophole, yet within the whole southern wall only six combatants could have found standing room for defence. And for six combatants so elaborate a construction would certainly never have been made. The chambers and corridors cannot have been anything but storage

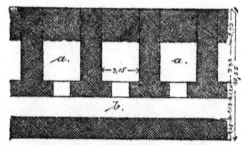

97.—GROUND-PLAN OF THE EASTERN WALL OF TIRYNS.

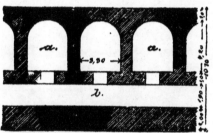

98.—GROUND-PLAN OF THE WALL OF CARTHAGE.
a, Vaulted chambers ; b, gallery.

cellars, in which all kinds of provisions and other objects could be conveniently and safely stored."

A similar arrangement of chambers with a gallery behind may be seen in the south part of the east wall. The view of this gallery in Fig. 99 also explains the distribution of the different parts of the south wall just described. The staircase in this east wall is completely destroyed ; but it can only have ascended from the corridor at the spot marked Σ in the plan, and doubtless opened out into the small colonnade J, which leads

[1] See W. Dörpfeld in Tiryns, p. 325.

19.—VIEW INTO THE GALLERY OF THE EASTERN WALL.   *d*, Doors to the chambers; *b*, partition walls of the chambers.

into the great fore-court F, so that both sets of chambers in the southern and in the eastern wall would directly communicate with this court. While the southern wall offers no hint of how its huge upper superficies (57 feet broad) was utilised, whether dwellings or magazines were erected there, or whether only a broad rampart ran along it, four stone bases of columns preserved on the western or inner side of the eastern walls prove that a colonnade (probably a broad hall) was situated on this wall and opened on to the interior of the citadel.

The same elaborate care has been bestowed on the various entrances which pierce these massive walls as upon the walls themselves. The chief ascent is a road on the east side. It rises to the citadel at an easy gradient by a ramp (Δ), which begins some way back to the north, and debouches exactly at the point of junction of the middle and the upper citadel. The ramp is 19 feet 4 inches broad, and this breadth is preserved for the upper part of the entrance passage between the walls; but the lower part of this passage is reduced to 8 feet by blocks built up on either side. It is remarkable that no gate-portal seems to have existed here, for neither threshold nor posts have been found. This chief ascent is planned on the ancient strategical principle, in accordance with which the assailing enemy would have their unprotected right side exposed to the defenders.

The last excavations brought to light a second smaller ascent (T on plan) on the west side of the citadel. For this ascent a separate semicircular structure was built in front of the angular trace of the wall which follows the shape of the palace. A great staircase winds up it inside. The massive structure is entered from outside by a gate 6 feet 6 inches broad (T) rising into the usual pointed arch. At a distance of 18 feet the stairs are reached; the first steps are cut in the rock, and up to the twentieth step they wind up through the natural rock (see Fig. 100). After the sixty-fifth step the stairs are completely destroyed; farther on a portion of the substructure about 21 feet long has been preserved. Most likely they opened out at V into the court Y at the back of the palace. From this point the little staircase X would give quick and easy access to the chief apartments. This side ascent by means of stairs, which afforded the inhabitants of the citadel a very convenient mode of communication with the Lower City, and occasionally a very favourable sallyport, was absolutely impregnable by the enemy, who would have found themselves shut in within a long narrow passage with certain death threatening them on all sides.

100.—STAIRCASE OF THE SIDE ENTRANCE.
a, External fortress wall ; *b,* rock ; *c,* lateral walls of the staircase ; *d,* enclosure wall of the palace.

Besides this last ascent and the chief entrance, the citadel wall had two small gates or posterns, one on the west side of the middle citadel, and one at the northern corner of the lower citadel.

3. The Palace

Of all the excavations at Tiryns the palace has yielded the most important results. It seems best, in examining all the various buildings in their order, only to mention at first what is peculiar to each, and to reserve to the end all general observations on the technique of the masonry or of the wooden posts and columns, and on the construction of the roof.

If we pass through the chief entrance, which, as remarked above, had no portals, and turn to the left, we find ourselves in an approach shut in on one side by the citadel wall, and on the other by the palace wall, which is here extraordinarily massive. At 49 feet from the chief entrance we reach the folding gate θ. If we can imagine these two walls occupied as they were manifestly intended to be by defenders, we shall see that on this side also the assailants would have found it practically impossible to reach the gate.

This gate (θ) corresponds closely in material, construction, and even in dimension with the Lions' Gate at Mycenæ. It is built of huge slabs of breccia.[1] The large threshold, 4 feet 9 inches broad, lies there intact; the right door-post (10 feet 6 inches high) is also preserved; but the door-post on the left has had its upper portion broken off, and along with it the lintel, and all the upper structures have disappeared. The entrance on the outside has a clear width of 8 feet 4 inches, on the inside of 10 feet $4\frac{1}{4}$ inches, as each door-post is rebated at a right angle. The folding gates were fixed into the recess thus formed; they opened inwards, and when closed rested against the projecting part of the uprights, which thus formed a door-rebate or door-case. The closed portals were finally made secure by means of a huge round wooden bolt; the holes meant to receive it can still be seen half-way up each post; on the side of the palace the hole is only 1 foot $4\frac{1}{8}$ inches deep, but on the opposite side it passes right through the post into the outer wall of the citadel; so that when the gate was open, the bolt could be pushed right back into the wall.

If we pass through the gate, and continue our way in the same direction between the high walls, we find ourselves next in a fore-court, bounded on the east by the citadel wall with the covered colonnade; on the west we find a new large gate-way H. Its ground-plan is one with which we are already familiar at Troy, and which was adopted for all Greek gate-building down to the Propylæa at Athens. It has an outer and an inner vestibule, and the wall which divided the two held the actual folding-doors. In Troy the vestibules have no columns in front, because, owing to the smaller dimensions, the architrave

---

[1] *Breccia*, a conglomerate of pebbles, used at Tiryns as freestone for door-sills and antæ blocks.

beams could be laid across from anta to anta. But in Tiryns
the great width of the gate (45 feet 9 inches) is quite sufficient to
explain the additional support of two columns between the antæ.
The ground-plan of the building is absolutely certain ; the walls
are still standing 18 inches above ground, and the four bases
of the columns, as well as the great stone threshold, are all *in
situ* : moreover, in the vestibules portions of a concrete pavement
of pebbles and lime are preserved. The inner vestibule is somewhat deeper than the outer one. A door in its northern side-
wall gives access on the right to some inferior chambers, and to
a corridor leading right up to the women's apartments.

After leaving the great gate H, we find ourselves in the large
court F, which reaches on the east and south to the citadel walls
with their little colonnaded vestibules (E and I). The west side
has been utterly destroyed ; the citadel wall must at some time
have given way here, and caused a sort of landslip of all the
western portion. Moreover, the ancient disposition of the interior
of the court was almost entirely effaced by the building of the
Byzantine church. On the north side of the court, close to the
great gate H, a small side-door leads by the shortest way into
the colonnade of the men's court. Westward, on the left, are
two chambers, which must have been entered from the large court
F, as there are no doors on their other sides ; but their front
walls are completely destroyed. These may have been the guard-
rooms. Next to these rooms comes the gate K, which in spite of
its ruined condition shows the same plan as the great gate, but
its dimensions are smaller. The inner vestibule can be approximately measured, and gives us 36 feet as the breadth of the gate.

This second gate closes the entrance into the court of the
men's apartments (*a*). This court brings us close in front of the
chief rooms of the palace. Hitherto the way has been one continuous ascent ; while the threshold of the gate (θ) of the upper
citadel is 70 feet above the level of the sea, that of the great
gate H of the palace is 80 feet 6 inches and that of the
following gate (K) 84 feet above the sea-level. And from there
to the steps of the entrance to the men's apartments the ground
rises further to 85 feet 10 inches. The court forms a rectangle,
measuring 51 feet 7 inches by 66 feet 4 inches. It has a very
solid concrete floor, the composition of which can be clearly seen
at the spot where Dr. Schliemann sunk a deep shaft in 1876.

Dr. Dörpfeld says of it: "Lowermost on the *remblai* there is a stratum of stones and lime, $1\frac{1}{2}$ inch to $2\frac{1}{2}$ inches thick, a sort of *Beton*, intended as a secure basis for the actual concrete ; above it follows a second layer about 1 inch thick, consisting of pebbles and a very solid reddish lime ; uppermost lies a layer of about $\frac{3}{4}$ inch thick, made of lime and small pebbles, and affording a most durable concrete." [1] This concrete floor is skilfully laid so as to form a fall for carrying off the rain-water towards a point on the south side, whence it escaped by a drain. The court, according to its Homeric epithet of "the fair porticoed," is surrounded on all sides by porticoes. On the south side next to the inner vestibule of the gate was a two-columned portico only half the depth of the vestibule. Both on the west and on the east side was a portico with three columns, on the north side was the vestibule of the men's chamber. Exactly in the middle of the south side of the court lies a quadrangular block of masonry,

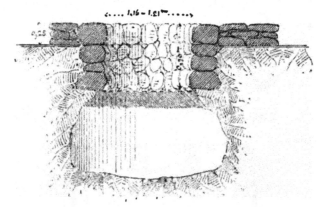

101.—TRANSVERSE SECTION OF THE SACRIFICIAL PIT.

in which a round hole was discovered at the time of the last excavations ; when this was excavated "it was found that the circular masonry only reached to a depth of 3 feet. Further down, there were neither side walls of masonry nor any artificial floor. As the hole, consequently, could not have been either a cistern or a well, it must have been a *sacrificial pit*." [2] Probably it is an altar in the shape of a sacrificial pit (Fig. 101). In Homer an altar of Zeus is mentioned in the court of the palace

[1] *Tiryns*, p. 203.   [2] *Ibid.* p. 339.

of Odysseus,[1] and the existence of one can be proved in the old palace on the Acropolis at Athens. Up to now pits have only been found in the Asklepieion at Athens,[2] and in the temple of

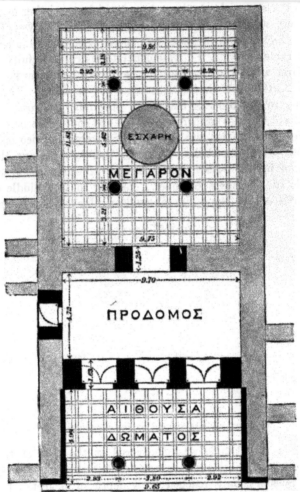

102.—THE MEN'S APARTMENT, WITH ANTE-CHAMBER AND VESTIBULE.

the Kabeiroi in Samothrake.[3] They may have been more general in very ancient ritual than was the case later on.

On the north side of the court, and on exactly the same

---

[1] *Od.* xxii. 332-336.   [2] Köhler, *Athen. Mittheil.* ii. p. 223 to end.
[3] *Untersuchungen auf Samothrake,* i. p. 20 and ii. p. 21.

axis, are situated the men's apartments (M on the plan; see also
Fig. 102). Two stone steps, an enrichment which is only found
here, bring one up into the vestibule; the bases of its two
columns and of its two antæ are still well preserved (Fig. 103).
The vestibule is connected with the ante-chamber by three doors,
whose three thresholds still lie *in situ*. Between each, and to
the right and left in each of the walls, stood massive wooden
uprights; the doors were not as usual placed behind the threshold, but were set forward in the threshold itself, so that when opened

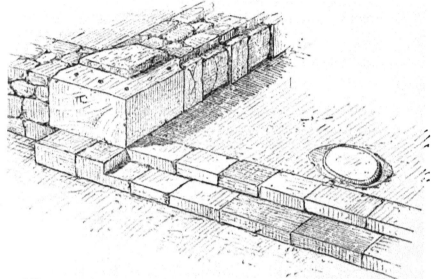

103.—ENTRANCE TO THE VESTIBULE OF THE MEN'S APARTMENT, SHOWING THE BASIS
OF THE WESTERN ANTA AND THE BASIS OF A COLUMN.

the wings of each of the doors rested against the uprights. In
this way they did not stand out awkwardly behind and get into
the way of the inmates. In order to match this wooden cross-wall
both the side walls of the vestibule were wainscoted with wood.
Traces of grooves on the stone wall suggest that it was cased
with wooden boards fastened by dowel-holes; besides, the side-
walls, on one of which is a splendid alabaster frieze to be
described later on (p. 117), became 1 foot $3\frac{3}{4}$ inches thinner immediately behind the antæ, thus clearly pointing to a casing in some
other material.

It is very remarkable that the bases of the columns stand

back the whole depth of the upper step from the line of the antæ. Consequently the beams which the columns supported did not lie on the front of the antæ but receded somewhat. We know from the finds at Mycenæ that the columns of this style of architecture thickened towards the top. But, given the above relative position of the bases, this swelling is by no means considerable enough to bring the front of the capitals of the columns in a line with the front of the antæ. We are therefore led to assume that the antæ advanced considerably beyond the architrave, and passed upwards beyond the architrave and the superimposed frieze, a system which we shall meet with again at Mycenæ in the façade of the bee-hive tomb excavated by Mrs. Schliemann.

The following ante-chamber is of about the same depth as the vestibule. The door in its left side-wall opens into a corridor leading to the bath-room. Exactly opposite the entrance a doorway in the north wall gives access to the megaron. As this doorway had no contrivances for fixing door-wings, it was probably only closed by a curtain. In the middle of the megaron, just as

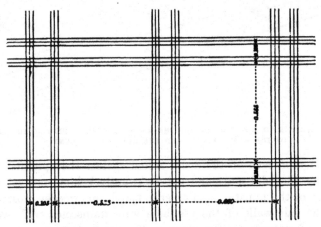

104.—PATTERN ON THE FLOOR OF THE MEGARON.

at Troy, is the big round hearth, here surrounded by four pillars which helped to support the roof. The concrete floor of the vestibule and of the megaron has a design composed of scratched lines; its pattern is shown in Fig. 104. "In the northern part of the hall there are still distinct traces of red colour on the

larger central squares of the concrete. On the small strips
separating these are faint traces of blue. Hence the floor was
originally of a bright simple carpet pattern." [1]

In later times a building was erected on the site of the men's
apartments. Its foundations show a rectangle stretching from
the north-west central pillar of the megaron to its east wall in
one direction, and in the other to the entrance of the vestibule. [2]
In all probability this building was the temple of which some
architectural fragments, among others a Doric capital (Fig. 133),
have been discovered. [3]

It has already been mentioned that in the west wall of the

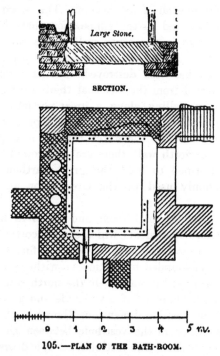

105.—PLAN OF THE BATH-ROOM.

ante-chamber a door opened into a corridor which gave access, a
little farther on, to the bath-room, one of the most interesting
portions of the palace (Fig. 105). The floor is formed by one

[1] W. Dörpfeld, *Tiryns*, p. 225.

[2] For the other sides the old walls were utilised.

[3] This later building is not shown on the accompanying plan ; it may be seen in
plan ii. of " *Tiryns*."

gigantic block of limestone. 13 feet 1 inch long, over 10 feet broad, and averaging 2 feet $3\frac{1}{2}$ inches in thickness. This gives a weight of about 20 tons. Its projecting rough edges ran under the masonry of the wall. Its exposed surface is worked so as to form close to the walls a border about $4\frac{3}{4}$ inches to $5\frac{1}{4}$ inches broad, raised $\frac{1}{5}$ inch above the well-polished rectangle in the centre. At fixed intervals along this border are found two holes close together; their object was doubtless to receive wooden dowels serving to fasten panels of wainscot lining the whole of the walls. The two holes on each side of every wider interval must have belonged to the same panel, which they would secure at each of its corners. This wooden lining on the inside might have led to the supposition that this room was a reservoir, but a door in the south wall shows that this cannot have been the case. This door is not actually preserved, as the whole of that wall has been destroyed; but its former existence may be safely inferred from the fact that there are no dowel-holes and therefore no panelling along a great portion of this wall. The central portion of the great block of the floor is well polished, and forms a fall which let the water run off at a point in the east side. In the north wall there are two round holes, which were probably destined to hold the great earthen jars full of the oil so commonly used by the Greeks for anointing after the bath.

A corridor skirts the bath-room, and winds in many zigzags round to the women's apartments, which exactly correspond in their arrangements to those of the men. We again find ourselves in a great court partly surrounded by porticoes: within these are traces of benches fixed against the wall. On the north side of the court is the chief building, composed of a vestibule and a large hall (O). On account of the smaller dimensions (breadth 18 feet), there are no columns either in the vestibule between the antæ or in the hall round the hearth. The vestibule has side doors both on the left and on the right. In the centre of the hall O was situated a square hearth, and on the walls there are traces of painting, all the more interesting because in the other rooms the fragments of painted plaster are no longer on the walls, but were found fallen on the floor.

The women's megaron also is surrounded by a corridor—it leads to some apartments lying parallel to the megaron on the east.

Among these a large chamber with an ante-room is the most remarkable; it may have been the bedchamber of the royal couple. South of this chamber, in the two long and narrow rooms adjoining one another, were probably the stairs leading up to the upper floor; presumably they began at the east end of the southern room, and ascending in a westerly direction, passed into the next room, where they would continue to rise from west to east till they reached the next story.

Quite in the north-east corner of the enclosure wall of the palace were several rooms of varying sizes which probably served as treasuries, armouries, etc. South-east of the women's court is another court; and again south of this a labyrinth of walls has been discovered; but it is impossible to reconstruct their original ground-plan with any certainty. It is interesting, however, to note that amongst them are several traces of other very ancient walls, which, in opposition to the whole of the rest of the palace, have the same orientation as the great Propylæum (H). It would appear accordingly that the plan of the latter was a survival from an earlier stage in the building of the citadel. Traces of an older epoch have been found in various parts during the excavations, and especially in the north-west corner, where about 10 feet below the later floor, and even under parts of the circuit wall, a floor of clay concrete exactly similar to the one at Troy was discovered, along with walls built of rubble, and fragments of a rough monochrome pottery. There can be no doubt that the palace lately excavated does not represent the first settlement on the citadel, but is only the last stage in a development of incalculable antiquity. It is well, however, to emphasise the fact that the circuit wall has nothing to do with the earlier settlement, but belongs to the later palace.

We will now examine some of the peculiarities of the buildings described, in order to gain a clearer insight into the method of construction of their most important portions.

Lime is used at Tiryns and at Mycenæ in every wall and every floor; never, however, as binding material, but only as plaster. As such it was indispensable, for walls bonded with clay, or built completely of unbaked bricks, could not long have resisted the destructive effects of the weather.

It has often been stated that the antæ and the columns were

of wood, but the proof of this has not yet been given. Practically it is based on three observations. First, the antæ bases of the vestibule of the megaron (see Fig. 103) cannot have carried other blocks, nor yet stone or brick masonry; they have a smoothed surface deeply sunk and pierced with dowel-holes; this surface could only have carried wooden boards. Secondly, the other antæ bases whose surface is not worked in this characteristic manner, but only smoothed, cannot have received a stone super-structure, because it is inconceivable that when twenty-six of these bases have been preserved not a single block of the antæ itself should be preserved. Thirdly, the traces of fire are most strong exactly at the portions under consideration; the surface of the bases, both of antæ and of columns, is reduced to the condition of lime just round the shaft; and when there are portions of wall near the antæ, the stone-rubble has likewise been reduced to lime, while the binding clay has become a shapeless red mass, and the bricks have been vitrified.

At Troy and at Mycenæ the wooden posts of the antæ rested on a base-stone scarcely raised above the level of the floor, and so differed from the antæ at Tiryns, where the base is usually 2 feet high. The manner in which these bases were prepared and the dowel-holes bored can be distinctly traced. The vertical outer surfaces are sawed. The saw was not, however, carried straight through from side to side; but, as may be seen in the drawing of the anta base (Fig. 103), the stone was sawed from three sides, each time almost to the middle, when the piece that remained unsawed was broken off. The curved marks made by the saw, and the shape of the portion broken off, which is that of a spherical triangle, prove, as Dr. Dörpfeld remarks, that the instrument was not held by two people, one at each end, and drawn backwards and forwards, but that "it had the shape of a knife, which a single workman held by the handle, and with the point of which he made the incision." The thickness of the saw may be ascertained in some places from the width of incision it made; it was about $\frac{3}{32}$ inch. The instrument must consequently have been of metal, and since iron has not yet been discovered in any of these sites, it must have been of bronze. "The saw," says Dr. Dörpfeld further on, "certainly had no teeth, for only the very softest stone can be cut with the toothed-saw; the hard limestone, and particularly the *breccia* of Tiryns, belong, however,

to the class of hard stones which can only be cut through with a
smooth saw and extremely sharp sand (emery). . . . When the
stone was sawn some inches deep, the piece to be removed was
struck off as far as the incision reached, and the sawing was
begun anew. It is of these separate incisions that the still visible
curves remain on the stone. This primitive method of sawing
had the effect of leaving the surface not quite even, but often
very warped. On this account, too, the antæ seem to have been
all covered with lime-plastering, although traces of this coating
remain only on some of them." [1]

Besides the antæ bases of the vestibule of the men's megaron,
this method of sawing may also be recognised on the antæ bases
of the great Propylæum, and those of the vestibule of the
women's apartments. The saw was also probably employed for
the harder sorts of stone, such as the compact limestone and
breccia of which almost all the antæ and door-sills are formed.
The surface of the softer sandstone blocks employed for the bases
of columns and the walls inside the megaron and other rooms is
too much weathered to allow any definite conclusion as to the
instruments with which they were dressed.

It is, however, clear that the softer stone was dressed in a
different manner from the hard stone, from the different shape of
the dowel-holes in the different materials. Thus, while the soft
sandstone had square holes cut with a sharp instrument, the dowel-
stones of the hard limestone and the breccia were made with the
auger; indeed, the drill-auger would be needed, and we have
many proofs that this instrument was known to the ancients.
The lower end of the drill-auger used at Tiryns must have been
a hollow cylinder, and was in fact like a strong reed. Emery
was employed as with the saw, and the rapid twirling of the
drill bored a cylindrical hole in the midst of which a stone
core remained standing. This was afterwards broken off; but
as it naturally did not always break exactly at the bottom, a
stump was often left, which now affords us this interesting explanation of their method of boring.

We now pass to the description of some isolated fragments
of the interior decorations of the palace; in the first place
the frieze of alabaster, and then the remains of the wall-
paintings.

[1] *Tiryns*, p. 264.

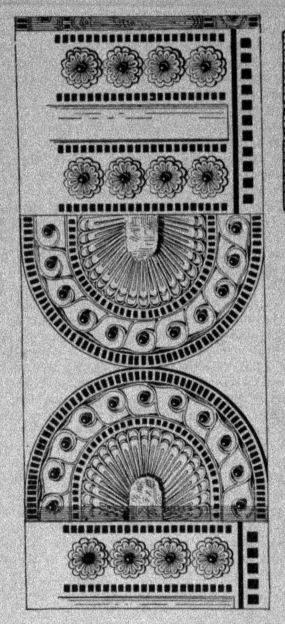

166.—ALABASTER FRIEZE INLAID WITH BLUE GLASS, RESTORED.

167.—GLASS PASTE FROM MENIDI.

This frieze was found, as already stated, in the vestibule of the men's megaron, occupying with its seven slabs the whole length of the lower portion of the left wall. It was at first thought from several signs that the frieze could not originally have been intended for this place. A narrow slab alternates with a wider one, and the narrower projects beyond the broader, just as in the frieze of a Doric temple the triglyph slab projects beyond the metope. Now if the frieze originally belonged here, then the concrete floor should have been cut out to fit into the broken line of the frieze. This is not, however, the case. The concrete floor is cut off in a straight line in front of the frieze, and its edge skirts the projecting slabs, and leaves in front of the receding ones a gap which has just been filled in with sand. Quite as primitive was the filling of the gap behind the slabs. Since these were only 6 inches to 8 inches thick, they could not fill in the foot of wall space, which was probably reserved, as we saw, for a wood panelling, and the space thus left was filled in with *débris*. However, though all this goes to prove that the wall and the concrete were not actually prepared to receive the frieze, and that consequently this portion of the building was not originally decorated with it, yet (and such is Dr. Dörpfeld's latest opinion) the frieze may have been made for the vestibule at the time of some thorough restoration of the old building, and it need not be assumed that it had been placed elsewhere first.

The pattern in its main lines is one which is frequently found in the Mycenæan style of ornamentation (Fig. 107), an elliptical, palmetto divided into two halves by a vertical band. Only in this case the pattern is much richer; on the centre field are rows of rosettes, and round the palmettes is a band of spirals resembling plaited work. The middle of the rosettes and of the spirals, and the dentils which form the frames of both, are inlaid with another material, and there can be little doubt what this material really was. In Homer a splendid frieze of *kyanos* is mentioned in the Palace of Alkinoos: "Brazen were the walls which ran this way and that from the threshold to the inmost chamber, and round them was a frieze of blue" [1] (κύανος). By cyanus, however, as the researches of R. Lepsius and of Professor Helbig prove, we must understand not blue steel, but *smalt, i.e.* a

[1] *Od.* vii. 86, 7.

glass paste coloured blue with copper ore.   Quantities of objects
made of it have been found in Egypt, and it also appears in the
layers of the Mycenæan period for every kind of ornaments, such as
pearls, necklaces, etc.   These blue pastes must have had a splendid

108.—WALL-PAINTING IN THE PALACE.

effect on the white alabaster.   A similar frieze seems to have
formed the main decoration of apartments in the Mycenæan period.
Quite lately the excavations at Mycenæ have shown us that there
also, wherever a frieze had not been actually let into the wall, a
painted band in imitation of one ran round the room.

The wall-paintings which have been found in fragments in several of the rooms of the palace, especially in the megaron of the men, were executed *al fresco* on the wall-plaster. Dr. Dörpfeld has recognised this from observing that .the brush had sometimes entered into the lime, leaving the painted surface rough to this day, while the surrounding part is smooth. Only four colours are employed—white, yellow, red, and blue; green and all half tones are wanting. Their wealth of forms exhibits all the varied systems of Mycenæan ornamentation, and accordingly finds its analogies now in Mycenæ, now in Orchomenos, at times also in Menidi or in the islands. For example, Fig. 108, giving a portion of a border carried out in the four colours mentioned, shows the pattern on the ceiling of the tomb at Orchomenos combined with rosettes and the familiar frame of dentils. In Fig. 109 we see the characteristic heart-shaped ornament, which appears also on the ivory slabs from Menidi. Fig. 110 shows the net-like pattern which is so often found on the vases. Finally, in Fig. 111 we have the *chef d'œuvre* of the wall-paintings,

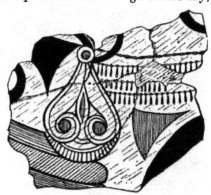

109.—WALL-PAINTING IN THE PALACE.

110.—WALL-PAINTING IN THE PALACE.

the great bull with the so-called acrobat on its back. A mighty bull is galloping at full speed to the left. Its body is painted a yellowish colour with many red spots. The short head with big round eyes carries a pair of strong horns, curved to the front. A man balances himself on its back, just touching the animal with his right knee and the tip of his toe, while he throws his other leg high up into the air, and holds on to the bull's horn with his right hand. His other hand is laid in front of his body. The dress of the man cannot be clearly made out; on his knees and above his ankles are several bands, which at first are not easy of explana-

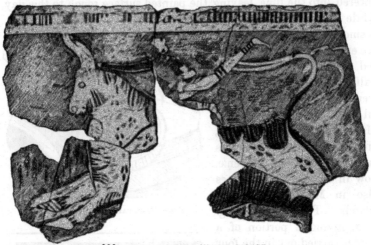

111.—WALL-PAINTING IN THE PALACE.

tion. The whole background is painted blue. The bull was apparently spared out on the original ground, and its contour brought out by a thick blue line, while the man was painted over the blue ground. The painter originally sketched in the tail and the forelegs differently, and then painted his mistaken attempt over. We now pass to the meaning of the picture. Up to now the man has been explained as an acrobat, such as Homer describes leaping on to the back of horses in full career,[1] and here performing the same feat on a bull. On the other hand, Dr. Friedrich Marx lately tried to make another interpretation probable, by pointing out a very interesting analogy.[2] On Greek coins from Catana in Sicily (Fig. 112) we find a man-headed bull with a figure surprisingly like the acrobat of Tiryns on its back. Here the bull must be a river-god, as is so frequently the case in the most widely distant parts of the Greek world; and the man on his back would then probably be one of the Sileni, who as personifica-

112.—COIN OF CATANA.

[1] *Il.* xv. 679.   [2] *Jahrbuch*, 1889.

tions of streams and springs often appear in the train of river-deities. The remarkable similarity in the representation suggested that the bull and the man of Tiryns might also be river-divinities. This interpretation might have led to most important results with regard to the nationality of the inhabitants of Tiryns. However, the remarkable finds of the summer of 1889 have led us back again to the original conception, and afford us at the same time the desired information about some of the peculiarities of the picture, especially about the curious rings on the man's legs. The Greek Archæological Society have, through their representative M. Tsountas, excavated a domed grave at Amyclæ near Sparta, and there, amongst other very important objects, two gold cups have been found. At the time of their discovery Dr. Paul Wolters sent the following short account of the subjects they represent. "They unquestionably give us scenes from everyday life, and represent the capture of mighty bulls, which we must imagine to be in a half-wild condition. On the one cup we see a palm-tree under one of the handles, which partially covers it, then farther on to the right a bull rushing furiously to the left. He has caught a man on his powerful horns, and throws him headlong to the earth. By the side of the bull another man is falling to the ground : apparently he has not been knocked down, but thrown off the bull's back. Not only in Mycenæan, but in any art, the treatment of these scenes would deserve the highest praise. Their value is specially enhanced by the fact that they offer us what was previously unknown in this style, careful representations of men in comparatively large size, and in good preservation. The peculiar costume, which could only be guessed at in the smaller representations, now becomes clear. The men have long hair, and are naked except for a thick projecting girdle, from which hangs a little apron both before and behind. Further, they wear shoes with slightly turned-up points, which are tied half-way up the calf by horizontal thongs.

"The whole scene reminds us vividly of the wall-painting at Tiryns (the bull). Not only the general character of the scene, but the strong build of the bull and the costume of the men, find here their closest parallel. For it seems certain that we must restore the figure of the 'acrobat' from the men on the cups; these only differ from the former in having no bands round the knee. After the new find every one will admit that the traces of yellow colour on the thighs are the remnants of the little apron.

"It is important to emphasise these points, as they refute Dr. Marx's interpretation of the Tirynthian painting, an interpretation which, could it be proved, would be of the greatest importance to the whole question of Mycenæan civilisation. The shoes and the apron worn by the man would alone suffice to weaken a mythological explanation, and this falls to the ground completely in presence of the scenes on the gold cups.

"Further, we must note two cut gems from Mycenæ found during the recent excavations, and to be shortly published in the *Ephemeris*.[1] Of these, one repeats the scene of the fresco, except that the animal is standing still, and is apparently not a bull. The other shows a man in the act of swinging himself on to the back of a bull. We shall not need to attribute any mythological meaning to these scenes when we remember the evident tendency of Mycenæan art towards representing the objects and events of daily life."

Dr. Wolters is surely right. The bull is no river-god, and the man on his back is only an ordinary mortal trying to capture the animal. Still, it remains a striking fact that the motive which the Sicilian Dorians of the seventh or sixth century represented on their coins is the same as the one which had been employed by the Tirynthians many centuries before. Even if this analogy does not prove the two races to have had the same origin, it yet shows that there was close intercourse between them and a continuous tradition.[2]

4. *The Separate Finds*

The excavations at Tiryns have not been very productive in single finds, and what little has been brought to light consists almost entirely of fragments of vases and of terra-cotta figures. A study of these objects is chiefly valuable as establishing the marked difference between the pottery found in the oldest settlement and that which comes from the later palace. It has already been stated that in the north-west corner of the upper

[1] Published *Eph. Arch.* 1888. *Pin.* 10, 34 and 35.
[2] These cups have since been published in the *Ephemeris Archaiologike*. A drawing from the plate is given in Appendix II, with a few remarks supplementary to Dr. Wolters' account.—(Tr.)

citadel, where the big stairs open, traces of an older settlement, consisting of rough walls and a concrete floor of clay, have been found 10 feet below the level of the adjoining portions of the palace. On this spot vases and jugs were dug up which have their nearest analogy in the earthenware vessels of Troy, especially in those of the first and second settlements. A few of the

113.—TERRA-COTTA VASE (size 1 : 2).

114.—TERRA-COTTA VASE (size 1 : 2).

principal objects will suffice to support this assertion. The hand-made vessel of Fig. 113 has, in common with many of the Trojan vases, perforated projections through which a string was passed to serve as a handle. The clay, which is of a reddish-yellow, is fairly well baked. A terra-cotta cup without a foot is given in Fig. 114. Round its upper edge is laid a stripe decorated with rough round impressions. This laying on of a clay stripe, on which impressions have been made obviously with the finger, is a Trojan practice. Similar stripes are seen on the fragment in Fig. 115; here they are decorated with concentric circles, and the so-called "herring-bone" pattern, both of which are also found at Troy. The dish in Fig. 116 marks an advance; it has been made on the potter's wheel; like the preceding vessels, it reminds one of the Trojan finds. A thread

115.—FRAGMENT OF A LARGE JAR (size 1 : 3).

116.—DEEP PLATE OF TERRA-COTTA (size 1 : 2).

117.—BLACK STONE SPOOL (actual size).

spool (Fig. 117), which, like the earliest ones found at Troy, shows as yet no attempt at imitating the human form, affords once more a striking analogy to those from the oldest Trojan strata. A few terra-cotta whorls, some rough knives and arrow-heads of obsidian, as well as a bead of cobalt-glass, were found in the oldest layer.

It is quite needless to conclude from the agreement between the oldest Tirynthian and Trojan finds that the same people

originally lived in these two places, or even that a common
market supplied both with closely analogous objects. Not only
are these rough primitive vessels found in Troy, Cyprus, and
Tiryns, but similar shapes have come to light in Hungary, in
Mecklenburg, in Lower Sax-
ony, in Upper Italy, in France,
and generally in every spot
where the excavator's spade
reaches the oldest strata. They
are the forms which occur
naturally to all nations, however far apart, when they have
to fashion the utensils necessary
for the simplest needs of life.
We may accordingly consider
the oldest layer at Tiryns to
represent a period in which men
ate and drank out of home-
made pottery, and only pur-
chased the objects made of
uncommon materials, such as
knives or arrow-heads of obsidian, from some itinerant vendor.

118.—VASE WITH "STIRRUP HANDLE"
(size 1 : 3).

On the other hand, the finds from the palace, like the wall-
paintings, bear everywhere the impress of the Mycenæan civilisation. The vases, indeed, do not belong
to that older Mycenæan pottery which
the "shaft-graves" have preserved for
us, but correspond to the types found
"outside the graves." One shape characteristic of this class is the so-called
"Bügelkanne," a jug with a stirrup
handle, of which Fig. 118 gives an
intact instance. The stripes around
the body of the vase keep recurring

119.—VASE (size 1 : 2).

with different variations, or enlivened by connecting members.
Thus in Fig. 119 we see a vase adorned with broad and narrow
stripes, receiving additional zigzag lines on the shoulder. The
following wood-cuts show the various forms of the other connecting patterns. In Figs. 121-123 the vertical members connecting
the horizontal bands are disposed so as to form a frame which is

filled in now by wave-lines (Fig. 121), now by squares (Fig.122), or by plain thick dots (Fig. 123). In Figs. 121 and 122 these broad vertical members support on each side a semi circular or semi-elliptical ornament, and thus form a pattern similar to the leading motive

120. —CUP (size 1 : 2).

121, 122.—FRAGMENTS OF VASES (sizes 1 : 2 and 1 : 3).

of the alabaster frieze (Fig. 106). This conception of two symmetrical figures to the right and left of a vertical centre field is seen more and more to have been a leading motive throughout the whole range of Mycenæan art. It may be that it underlies the relief of the celebrated gate with its column guarded on either side by a lion rampant. The fragment in Fig. 125, however tiny, is sufficient proof that the pattern of the wall-painting of Fig. 110 reappears on the vases; and the long-necked birds so common in this class of vases are, as we should expect, found here also (Fig. 124).

123.—FRAGMENT OF VASE (size about 2 : 3).

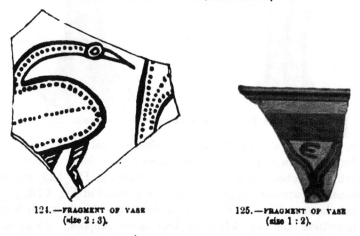

124.—FRAGMENT OF VASE
(size 2 : 3).

125.—FRAGMENT OF VASE
(size 1 : 2).

Next to the ordinary low cup without a foot, the most usual shape for drinking-vessels is that of Fig. 120; moreover, it predominates in all other finds of the Mycenæan period.

Numerous terra-cottas have been found, similar to those so common at Mycenæ and kindred sites; they represent a female figure with arms raised in the shape of a sickle, or else clasped together in a circle (Figs. 126, 127). Dr. Schliemann saw here an allusion to the shape of the half moon and the full moon, which he brought into relation with the Argive Hera, tracing her back to the old Pelasgic moon-goddess Io. Without accepting

126, 127.—TERRA-COTTA "IDOLS" (actual size).

the premises on which this conclusion rests, we must yet admit the possibility of these figures being idols. The figure with long robes and a rich breast ornament in Fig. 129, and the woman apparently engaged in kneading bread of Fig. 128, prove that the modelling of the human form was already much better understood than the idols could lead us to suppose. As in spite of this the more primitive forms kept on being steadily reproduced, this fact can be best accounted for by assuming some old traditional custom necessitating the reproduction of ancient *cultus* images; consequently it is highly probable that these figures do represent the image of a goddess.

FOR PAGE 129 - TURN
TO PAGE 172.

fragment ; but the remnants of another figure on the right, where
the breakage occurs, shows that several were represented, and we
probably have the picture of a round dance or *choros*. Fig. 131
gives as a contrast to this feminine pastime the more earnest
occupation of the men. A man is walking in front of a horse,
which he is probably leading by the bridle. His waist is even
more tightened in than that of the women, and his chest forms
a complete triangle. A sword is sticking out horizontally from
his girdle. Under the horse, simply to fill up the space, a fish
is painted, and by the side of the man, as well as above and

131.—FRAGMENT OF VASE (size 1 : 2).

below him, all kinds of ornaments have been introduced for the
same purpose, a mæander, a swastika or hooked cross 卍, and
several lozenges with a dot in the middle.

Besides the vases of the Mycenæan group and the Dipylon
vases, some fragments have been discovered at Tiryns of a style
not hitherto found elsewhere. They represent a transition —
between the Mycenæan and the Dipylon vases. The most noteworthy instance is given in Fig. 132. On the left we see a
horse with very stiff legs, with large round eyes and a fluttering
mane. The reins are visible in his mouth, but the horizontal
lines above his back do not seem to be their continuation; along
with the four arches which support them, they probably merely

help to fill up the space, just like the two spirals farther up. Under the horse is a dog, no less wooden in appearance ; his tail curls up into a spiral.   In front of the horse are two men, both in the same attitude ; their left hand is raised and holds a small round shield, and their right holds the spear ready for hurling. Their legs are as thin as sticks, their waist is very much drawn in, but not shaped as on the Dipylon vases.   The men are drawing themselves back to gather strength for the throw.

132.—FRAGMENT OF VASE.

From their hips hangs down a long strip, which has been explained, probably correctly, as the tail of an animal's skin thrown over their back.   The drawing of neck and head is particularly primitive ; the neck is very long and stiff, and the head consists almost entirely of one huge round eye.

The whole scene is painted in brown lustrous paint on a light yellow ground, but above the varnish white body colour has been copiously used for inner markings and dottings.   The drawing of the figures with their thin legs and wooden attitude comes very near to the Dipylon vases.   A glance at the " acrobat " in the fresco of the bull, with his well-developed muscles and easy gliding attitude, will suffice to show how completely this later drawing differed from the Mycenæan. In other respects, however, the design of the vase belongs to the Mycenæan period—white, for instance, is not employed in the Dipylon vases. Genuine Dipylon painting also had the *horror vacui*, but where in our vase the empty space happens to be artificially filled up, as above the back of the horse, it has been done with Mycenæan ornaments. We may therefore consider this style of painting as transitional between the art of Mycenæ and that of the Dipylon.

After the cessation of the Dipylon period Tiryns must have remained empty and deserted for centuries, for after the Doric temple, built in the middle of the megaron, which may belong to the seventh century B.C., the traces of habitation first reappear in Byzantine times ; numerous Byzantine graves have been found on the southern portion of the citadel, and a Byzantine church in the great courtyard of the palace F. These Byzantine ruins were the reason why Dr. Schliemann's excavation of the real Tirynthian palace was distrusted for a time, just as his discovery of the real site of Troy had been distrusted before. Mr. Penrose, who has since the publication of his famous work on the Athenian Acropolis held a leading position among archæologists, had visited Tiryns with a correspondent of the *Times*, and thought that the excavators had mistaken rude mediæval masonry for masonry of the heroic age. In the spring of 1886 several articles to this effect appeared in the *Times*. The matter was discussed at a special meeting of the Hellenic Society ; Dr. Schliemann and Dr. Dörpfeld came from Athens expressly to attend it. It appeared that the mistake was due entirely to the church and other Byzantine ruins, on which it was supposed that the excavators relied to support their theory. Explanation was easy, and the objections made were withdrawn.

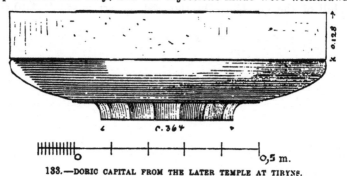

133.—DORIC CAPITAL FROM THE LATER TEMPLE AT TIRYNS.

CHAPTER IV

1. Situation and Fortifications of the Citadel

ALL that is known about the origin and history of Mycenæ has been told at the beginning of the preceding chapter, where it was shown that this city was a daughter or younger sister of Tiryns, and owed to her favourable situation between the Eastern and the Western seas a wealth that became proverbial and a power that won her the foremost position in the oldest age of Greece.

Our present knowledge of the former importance of Mycenæ rests in the first place on the excavations of Dr. Schliemann. In the year 1876 the pit graves filled with gold were opened, and afforded the fullest illustration of the life and habits of the lords of the citadel. Captain Steffen's map of Mycenæ in 1881 marked a further and welcome advance; and a most important supplement to the work was added by the excavations of the Greek Archæological Society in 1886 to 1888, when the palace was discovered on the summit of the citadel, as well as a number of graves situated either within or close to the area of the city. These last results are reserved for the end of this chapter.

The two high peaks, the Prophet Elias and the Zara, between which Mycenæ lies, are separated by the ravine of the Chavos. This brook closely skirts Mount Zara in a westerly direction, and then bends sharply round to the south. About 150 yards north of the bend begins another ravine, that of the Kokoretza, which bends in a westerly direction towards the Kephissos. In the angle thus formed by the two ravines the soil rises to an isolated height of 912 feet; it was this spot which was selected for the hill of the citadel. On the east a narrow saddle 100 feet lower joins the citadel hill to the Prophet Elias; on the west an insignificant depression connects it with the long stretch of hill extending from north to south, upon which the chief portion of the ancient lower city, including the famous bee-hive tombs, was built.

Behind the above-mentioned saddle, 400 yards east of the citadel wall, and at a height of 1282 feet, rises a copious spring, evidently the celebrated fountain of Perseia mentioned by Pausanias, which furnished the citadel with water. The aqueduct, which between spring and citadel had to pass over a saddle 836 feet high, would notwithstanding reach the interior of the fortress with a moderate fall, as the corner of the north-west wall has an altitude of 817 feet at the outlet. A water-supply under pressure, which would have been possible under the circumstances, could hardly be expected in those early times.

Exactly north of the citadel, and on the same side of the Kokoretza, are to be seen several traces of the ancient road-tracks which went from Mycenæ to Corinth in three branches. They are either cut in the rock or are supported by Cyclopean masonry. When the road had to be carried across a stream, bridges which may still be seen were constructed in the same masonry, with small passages for the water—so small that several are generally found close together. These passages have pointed arches, constructed with side blocks converging towards the top, while a great block covers the top. The roads are only about 11 or 12 feet broad, and, unlike our modern roads, are not taken up a hill or down a valley gradually and by the most regular incline, but are kept horizontal as long as possible, and then carried across the obstructing feature with a sudden rise or descent. The narrowness of the roads, as well as their peculiar engineering, shows that they were not intended for the traffic of carriages, but only for beasts of burden. Moreover, no wheel-marks have been discovered, except close to the city, on a line which in all probability joined on to the great high road to Corinth. This road probably followed at that time the same direction as ever since, along the Kephissos and past Cleonæ; for this very reason, however, there is absolutely no trace of it left.

The roads are often protected by forts, which sometimes completely cover the road, and thus could easily bar its passage; sometimes they are situated a little distance off the road, in which

case they are usually built on a commanding spot. Apparently
several towers protected the great high road in the neighbourhood
of the modern railway station at Phichtia. But the most imposing remains of a watch-tower are to be seen on the summit of
Mount Elias; they consist of a circuit wall, a well-preserved gate,
and the ruins of a number of dwellings.

The fortifications of the citadel of Mycenæ form an almost
equilateral triangle; one of the angles is turned to the east, while
the side subtending it forms the front which dominates the lower
city, and is pierced by the chief entrance, the celebrated Gate of
the Lions. Opposite the Lions' Gate in the north-east corner is a
second smaller gate.

The wall of the citadel has been preserved, almost along its
whole circuit, with the exception of the southern line over the
steep incline to the Chavos stream, where a short piece has been
swept away by a landslip. With its many salient and re-entering
angles and its numerous projecting towers, the wall follows the
edge of the hill. Three kinds of masonry may be distinguished
in its structure. That which is apparently the oldest, and in
which the greater part of the circuit has been built, closely
resembles the masonry of the walls of Tiryns. Limestone blocks
only slightly hewn or even quite unhewn are heaped one on another;
only the slighter dimensions of the blocks throughout the structure,
and here and there the occasional introduction of a well-hewn
block, betray a later period (Fig. 134). Another style of masonry

134.—CYCLOPEAN MASONRY.

is employed for the entrances and the towers of both the gates,
as well as for the tower (C) on the middle of the south-east
line. Here carefully hewn rectangular blocks are laid on one
another in regular courses (Fig. 135). The third style, which
is found south of the Lions' Gate near to the circle of graves,
farther on in the same line, in the great tower (B), and finally
at the north-east point of the circuit, is composed of polygonal

blocks fitting together with the most accurate joints (Fig. 136). It
remains to find out the relation of the second and third kind of
masonry to the first.

The coursing with rectangular blocks occurs again in the
Tholos buildings of the lower city; these belong without a
doubt to the Mycenæan period. This kind of masonry therefore

135.—RECTANGULAR MASONRY.

need not signify a later restoration of the walls; seeing, moreover, that it has only been employed in much-exposed places, it
may very well have formed part of the original plan, and have
had the object of giving additional strength to the most
important points. In that case it would be unnecessary to
suppose that the Gate of the Lions was erected, as has been

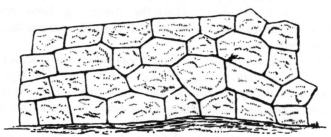

136.—POLYGONAL MASONRY.

suggested, at the time of a later restoration of the fortifications.
It would, on the contrary, be of the same age as the walls.
This view, however, is not yet placed beyond all doubt.

It has always been held certain that polygonal work marked
later restorations. Although this assertion can nowhere be
proved true of the Mycenæan period, it yet holds good in the
case of all other Greek wall masonry from the seventh to the
third century B.C. Now close to the circle of graves the line of
the circuit wall forms a bend; this curious projection, which in

itself is sufficiently remarkable, is constructed in polygonal masonry. It was therefore natural to suppose that we had here an alteration in the natural line of wall, caused by the circle of graves. It was thought that the burial-place had originally been outside the walls, and was enclosed within them at a later period. This view has now turned out to be erroneous. The wall running east of the circle of graves cannot, as was thought, have been the original citadel wall, but was intended from the first merely as a support to the terrace above it; while the citadel wall on the other side must, from the shape of the rock-surface, have always run along the edge of the ravine, *outside* the burial-place. Originally, however, the wall may have formed a less marked bend; at the time of a later alteration, its course may have had to be accommodated to the ring of slabs newly erected round the ancient graves.

The thickness of the wall varies from 10 to 23 feet in the places where both the inner and outer line can be still discerned. Two portions, however, in spite of the complete destruction of the inner line, show, from the lie of the ruins, an original thickness of as much as 46 feet. This great variation of breadth is clearly explained by the walls of Tiryns, which are so much better preserved. There the broadest portions contain galleries, similar to our casemates, and probably constructed for the same purposes ·

The experience gained at Tiryns has led to the discovery of traces of a similar gallery in the north wall of Mycenæ. Another presumably existed in the south line. The nature of these inner passages and chambers was probably much the same as that of the similar contrivances at Tiryns.

Both the gates of the citadel are planned in such a manner that a narrow approach between wall and tower must be traversed before the actual entrance is reached. The assaulting enemy would here have been exposed to missiles from both sides. The approach to the Lions' Gate is 27 feet 10 inches broad; the gate itself, which is somewhat narrower at the top than at the bottom, has a clear breadth of 9 feet 10 inches to 9 feet, and a clear height of 10 feet 4 inches. In the colossal lintel are still to be seen the deep round holes for the hinges; in the threshold the hinges fitted into quadrant-shaped holes, and at the place where the wings of the gate met when closed there is a great rectangular depression (12

by 15 inches).   On the exterior of the threshold there is a curious hole, almost triangular in shape; according to Dr. Schliemann, one like it is also to be seen in the great gate at Troy; its object is not yet explained.   The uprights likewise have several holes whose purpose is not very obvious; a large square hole on the right received the bolting beam.

While in Tiryns, after passing through the gate, a long passage specially favourable for defence had to be traversed, in Mycenæ there is only a court 13 feet square, formed by two side walls, whose extremities turn inwards at right angles for the distance of 3 feet, and, with the help of further small projections, form two small sentry-boxes—one turned towards the gate, the other towards the interior of the citadel.   Behind the most northern of these side walls, close to the gate, and accessible by a small doorway, is a recess 26 feet square.   These small corners were probably reserved not so much with a strategical purpose, as for the daily guard in times of peace.

Far the most interesting and important part of the gate is the celebrated relief of the lions which adorns it.   In order to lighten the pressure over the lintel, a triangular space was reserved in the wall; this space was closed by a slab worked in relief.   The slab is of a hard greyish limestone—anhydrite, according to a chemical analysis.   The place whence this stone is obtained is not yet known.   The relief represents two lions rampant, heraldically opposed, with their fore-paws resting on two bases or altars placed side by side (Fig. 137).   The traces of dowel-holes show that the heads were fastened on separately; probably they faced the spectator.   Between the animals is a column of remarkable shape.[1]   It stands on a stone plinth over the point of contact of the two bases; it increases in thickness towards the top, and is crowned by a curious capital, composed of a fillet, cyma moulding, roll, and abacus.   Over the latter are four round discs, and these again are covered by a slab shaped like an abacus.   The discs are obviously meant to imitate the ends of beams, and we actually have here the different members of wood construction translated into stone.   Thus the slab or abacus above the bigger roll of the capital represents the beam of the architrave, which reached from one column to the other.

[1] The best publication is in *Arch. Zeitung*, 1865, Taf. 193, p. 1.   An instructive section of the profile of the column is given here.

Upon it rested a roof of beams in rough-hewn timber, and these again were covered by planks, laid parallel to the architrave and forming the floor of the upper story.

The meaning of the column between the lions is not yet satisfactorily explained. The introduction of animals as supports reminds us of the Assyrian custom of sculpturing lions or griffins as guardians on each side of a gate. In Phrygia, moreover, Professor Ramsay has found two lions, exactly similar to those of Mycenæ, on either side of a column above the door of a rock tomb;[1] and on a carved ivory handle from Menidi we seem to behold a faithful copy of the great relief of the gate. All this forbids our looking upon these lions as the special heraldic device of Mycenæ; still less ought we to indulge in interpretations resting on a deep symbolism. For the rest, Egyptian monuments show us Anubis as guardian of the tomb, symmetrically repeated on each side of the central post of the entrance.

When compared with Assyrian sculpture, the technique of the Mycenæan relief produces a much more natural effect. Both exaggerate the inner bone structure, so that the joints are visible through the flesh, but in the Mycenæan lions the gradations of the muscles are more softly modelled, and the varying projection of the relief gives a more plastic expression to the forms.

The gate was first cleared down to the threshold by Dr. Schliemann. The relief, on the other hand, had been visible from time immemorial, and has always been quoted as marking the first stage in the history of Greek art.[2] It has long been well known through casts.[3]

The other gate of the citadel in the north wall is smaller than the Lions' Gate, and has a simpler ground-plan. The outer

[1] Professor Ramsay has found as many as eight of these heraldic groups of lions in Phrygia (see *J. H. S.* iii. pl. 17, 18, pp. 18, 256). Generally they guard a column, once also they place their paws against the image of the goddess (Cybele) herself (*J. H. S.* v. p. 242). In a *Study of Phrygian Art* (*J. H. S.* ix.), p. 371, Professor Ramsay maintains "that the idea of the lions as guardians of the gate arose in a country where Cybele was worshipped, and where the dead chief was believed to be gathered to his mother the goddess. . . . The Phrygians adapted an old oriental heraldic type to represent this idea. . . . In the interchange of artistic forms and improvements in civilisation which obtained between Phrygia and the Greeks, the lion-type passed into Mycenæ during the ninth, or more probably the eighth, century B.C."

[2] Mrs. Mitchell, *A History of Ancient Sculpture*, p. 154 ; Friedrichs-Wolter, *Gipsabgüsse*, pp. 1-3 ; also Baedeker's *Greece*, p. lxxv. (R. Kékulé).

[3] There is a fine cast at the South Kensington Museum.

approach, formed in this case also by the city wall on the left and a strongly projecting tower on the right, is barely 10 feet broad. This is also the width of the gate itself. Above its lintel a triangular slab, this time left unsculptured, closes the relieving space.

2. Lower City. The Bee-hive Tombs

Both at Troy and at Tiryns the existence of a lower city was inferred chiefly from the fact that the citadel was completely occupied by the king's palace; at Mycenæ, on the other hand, there are actual traces of a settlement adjacent to, and dependent on, the royal fortress.

The wall of the lower city branches off from the two extremities of the south-western side of the citadel triangle. Like the oldest portions of the citadel walls, it is of Cyclopean construction, but it is only some 6 feet thick, and large portions of it are completely destroyed. Apparently the wall ran along the ridge of the adjoining hill in a southerly direction, was pierced by a gateway at its southern end (at Makry Lithari), and then passed along the eastern slope of the hill back to the citadel. The area thus enclosed was 1000 yards long, with a breadth of only 275 yards. This space, however, by no means represents the whole lower city, but rather its original limits, which were soon too small to contain the increasing population. The same house or terrace walls, almost always of Cyclopean masonry, which crowd the walled portion of the city, are also found in great numbers far beyond its limits, both on the other side of the Chavos, on Mount Zara, and more especially on the other side of the Kokoretza on Mount Elias. Moreover, far beyond the walls to the south and south-west were the only two ancient fountains which have yet been found.

The most important features in this extensive lower city are the large, vaulted, "bee-hive" tombs, commonly called treasuries; two of these are within the old city enclosure, the other four outside it to the west and south-west.

The biggest and best preserved of these is the so-called Treasury of Atreus,[1] situated about half-way down the eastern slope of the hill. The building consists of a long entrance

---

[1] Known popularly as the "Tomb of Agamemnon" (*Mycenæ*, p. 49; and Baedeker's *Greece*, p. 255).

passage (*dromos*), a large vaulted chamber (*tholos*), and a small square chamber adjoining it. Its peculiar construction is shown in the following woodcut (Fig 138). The passage AB leads horizontally into the hill from an artificially constructed terrace. BC is the deep doorway to the bee-hive vault, from which a little door D gives access to the small side-chamber. The approach is 20 feet broad and 115 feet long. Its sides, as they run

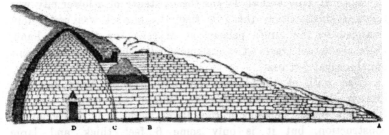

138.—SECTIONAL PLAN OF THE SO-CALLED GRAVE OF ATREUS.

inwards, rise with the slope of the hill. They are revetted with the same massive ashlar masonry which is employed for the angles and gates of the citadel fortifications. At the end of the dromos we find ourselves in front of the vertical façade wall, about 46 feet high. Its architectural structure can still for the greater part be made out. Some notion of its appearance may be obtained from the illustration, showing the second biggest of the bee-hive tombs (see below, Fig. 140). The door itself is 17 feet 9 inches high, 8 feet 9 inches broad at its base, and 8 feet 1 inch at the top. It is framed by a moulding of three *fasciæ* or bands, which, as is so often the case in the Mycenæan and Tirynthian buildings, have been made not by carving but by sawing the stone. Close to the door on low square plinths stood dark grey alabaster half columns of curious shape. The fragments found show a shaft thickening towards the top, round which ran a spiral band, with triangles and lozenges carved on it in relief. A fragment of the capital has been known for many years, but has only lately been recognised as such; it was formerly considered to be a base (Fig. 139).[1] Its resemblance to the capital of the Lions' Gate makes this new view practically certain. This capital is composed of a curving *cymatium* or

---

[1] These fragments of shaft and capital are now in the British Museum. A restoration is given at the end of this chapter (p. 298).

concave moulding adorned with lancet-shaped leaves, then follows a broad roll or *echinos*, on which spirals alternate with lozenges, then a second smaller con-cave moulding with a slab, and finally the *abacus*. The lower moulding with its leaf pattern closely resembles the capitals of the Temple at Pæstum. The capital found at Tiryns also has marked analogy to them. Dr. Puchstein is therefore

139.—HALF-CAPITAL FROM THE FAÇADE OF THE SO-CALLED GRAVE OF ATREUS.

of opinion that probably we have in the Mycenæan capital the first stage in the development of the Doric capital.[1]

The columns doubtless carried a cornice which lay along the upper edge of the door-lintel. Not a fragment of the cornice remains, but we are able to conjecture its shape from the fragments of cornice of the second bee-hive grave, and shall discuss it in this connection. In order to relieve the door-lintel of pressure, a triangular space, the sides of which are 10 feet long, was reserved in the massive wall, and closed by horizontal courses of slabs of red porphyry, decorated with spirals. The slab which filled the apex and a few fragments from the middle courses have been found and are in the Polytechnic Institute at Athens.[2]

This rich framing of the door was not enough. All round it the façade, as the many dowel-holes show, was coated right up to the top with another material, perhaps with variegated marbles or with bronze ornaments. If we try to picture to ourselves this façade with its polished square masonry, its many-coloured marble coating, and its elegant bronze decorations, we feel that the age was one not only of advanced technique, but capable

---

[1] *Das dorische Capitell*—Otto Puchstein ; Programm z. Winckelmannfeste, 1887, p. 51.

[2] The angle slab from the right corner is in the British Museum (Cat. No. 1). Professor Middleton (*J. H. S.* 1886, p. 168—"A suggested restoration of the great hall in the Palace of Tiryns ") notes that this marble fragment affords an illustration of the alabaster frieze studded with blue paste found at Tiryns. In this fragment "each spiral in the central bend was once set with a small boss, probably of glass, which in every case is now lost, though the marks of the cement used to fix the false jewel are still visible."

of appreciating refined splendour in decoration. And the conception grows when we consider what the façade covers. The door-lintel, answering to the unusual depth of the entrance passage, consists of two huge blocks, the innermost of which projects far beyond the door on both sides; it is 29 feet 6 inches long, 16 feet 6 inches deep, and 3 feet high; these measurements represent the colossal weight of about 120 tons. Great mechanical ability in quarrying and conveying stone must have been necessary to hew out such a block and bring it to the spot, and then to work it so accurately and lay it so carefully.

In the middle of the entrance the holes for the hinges of the folding-doors have been preserved, and on the sides are many dowel-holes, partly connected with the actual doors, partly no doubt meant to receive bronze decorations.

Passing to the interior, we find ourselves within a large and impressive circular vault. Its lowest diameter and its height are each about 50 feet. The construction is not that of the later dome, where the stones are wedge-shaped, and the joints run towards a common centre, but the vaulting is formed by thirty-three horizontal courses, gradually becoming narrower as they ascend, and closed at the top by a single slab. With the building there went on an accumulation outside of excavated earth and stone, and with this the vault was finally covered over. Within, the stones are cut to follow the spring of the vault, and most carefully polished, so that the upward flow of the lines from floor to apex is nowhere interrupted. This simplicity, this fusion of wall and roof, makes a powerful impression. "The artificial space produces the effect of a natural vault, simply from its proportions, adjustment, and texture," says Professor Adler.[1]

The stone layers become thinner towards the top, and from the third layer upwards are to be seen small and large holes regularly distributed, some of them with bronze nails still fixed into them. Large holes, produced by two borings close together, are to be seen, according to Dr. Dörpfeld's latest examination, over the third, fourth, and fifth layers, close on the joint, at intervals of 3 feet 5 inches to 4 feet, while small holes occur in the middle of the fifth course, between the sixth and seventh courses, and so on with the other courses, up to the seventeenth, at horizontal intervals of about 32 inches. Higher up nothing can now

[1] Preface to *Tiryns*, p. xxxix.

be clearly distinguished. A fixed scheme cannot as yet be made out ; but it seems certain, at any rate, that the holes did not serve to fasten metal plates, with which it was at one time thought the whole room had been cased. Had this supposition been correct, then a row of holes running one above the other, and serving to fasten the extremities of the plates, would have been found near the door-frame, where the plates terminated. But this is not the case, and Dr. Dörpfeld is doubtless correct in his conjecture that just as in the so-called "Treasury of Minyas" at Orchomenos bronze rosettes in groups of five $\overset{.\;.}{.\;\cdot\;.}$ were distributed in the vault, so also at Mycenæ the dome was decorated by larger and smaller ornaments, arranged according to a fixed pattern.

A side door, with a similar framing to that of the chief entrance, and relieved like it by a triangular space, led from the large domelike structure into a chamber cut in the rock. Many vestiges remain to show that this chamber was not originally left as rough as it is now. Lord Elgin's engineer saw on the walls remains of a rubble masonry, which, as at Orchomenos, would be revetted with sculptured slabs. An important indication of this is afforded by small pieces of alabaster slabs said to have been found in the Treasury of Atreus, and now scattered about in the Museums of Athens, London, Munich, and Berlin.

In Orchomenos, the exquisite slate ceiling of which an illustration is given further on (Fig. 290) was found in a chamber corresponding to the one under consideration. In the centre of the Mycenæan chamber there is an almost circular depression, 3 feet in diameter and 2 feet in depth, cut into the rocky ground. In spite of its unusual shape, we must recognise in it the actual site of the grave. The interpretation of these buildings as "treasuries" and not tombs was never quite satisfactory, and has been completely disproved since the excavations at Menidi, near Athens, in 1879 yielded a similar structure, within which were found six corpses lying undisturbed with all their ornaments about them.[1] Besides, no prince would ever have kept his treasures outside the walls of his citadel. However, the rich mode of burial of that period might well induce in the fortunate discoverers the belief that some powerful king had here deposited in safety his most valued possessions.

While the smaller chamber thus enclosed the actual grave,

---

[1] Köhler, *Das Kuppelgrab von Menidi.*

and was probably never opened except to admit a new corpse, the great vault in front of it was doubtless devoted to the cult of the dead. It was and remained easily accessible; the rich façade and the expensively built approach conclusively show that the entrance to the vault was not blocked up after the reception of the bodies. This entrance was only closed up, after the desertion of the citadel, by a deposit of earth brought down by the rain of centuries.

On the same slope of the hill there lies, farther to the north, facing obliquely towards the Lions' Gate, a second bee-hive tomb, not much inferior in size; it was excavated by Mrs. Schliemann, and is generally named after her (Fig. 140). Unfortunately, only the central part of the building has been cleared down to the ground; but even so it enables us in many points to supplement our previous observations on the structure of these tombs. The best and completest description of this building, and of the other tholoi, is due to Professor Adler.[1] On the supporting side walls of the approach several covering-stones have been preserved, which project somewhat beyond the walls; they give us a further proof that this approach was never meant to be blocked up. The façade was richly constructed with various kinds of stone. The half-columns are of dark green alabaster, and have Doric flutings; as the impressions left in the walls show, they thickened towards the top. Unfortunately none of their capitals have been found. They carried a projecting slab of bluish-grey marble, on which little circular discs are carved in relief. They can only represent, as already remarked in connection with the relief of the lions, the ends of the round wooden beams which formed the roof. Thus, what in wood architecture were structural elements are transformed here into features which are merely ornamental. The outer door-lintel is of leek-green marble. The relieving triangle above it was closed on the outside by thick slabs of red marble; inside it is still completely walled up by rows of flat square slabs, a strong proof that the triangular space was never used as a window. The upper breadth of the door is about 7 feet 11 inches; it is thus only 2 inches narrower than in the Treasury of Atreus. The whole lintel consists of three slabs, in the centre one of which the pivot-holes of the folding-doors are visible. The innermost block runs far into the wall

[1] Preface to *Tiryns*, pp. xxix.-xliv.

140.—BEE-HIVE TOMB EXCAVATED BY MRS. SCHLIEMANN.

on both sides, and joins a stone course of the same height, running right through; while in the remaining courses the blocks are very much lower, and are cut almost like slabs. The upper courses have fallen in. On the walls no nail-holes for bronze decorations have been found. Moreover, this tomb has no side chamber.

Four other bee-hive tombs lie, still unexcavated, on the western and north-western slope of the city hill. In all of them the vault has fallen in, and only the upper portion of the façade shows above the ground. During the Greek excavations of the year 1888 another of these tombs, bringing up their number at Mycenæ to seven, was found among a quantity of small, miserable graves, which, in contrast to the royal mausoleums, undoubtedly represent the graves of the people. These tombs will be described further on.

Besides those at Mycenæ we know of only five other tholos structures on Greek soil. Three have already been mentioned in this and the preceding chapter; they are those of Menidi in Attica, of Orchomenos in Bœotia, and of Pharis near Amyclæ in Laconia. The fourth is at the Heraion near Argos, $2\frac{1}{2}$ miles south of Mycenæ, and the fifth and last is at Volo in Thessaly. All five have now been excavated; and we see in all of them the architecture of the Mycenæan tombs, although somewhat less elaborated. Moreover, the objects found all bear the impress of that stage of civilisation which we are accustomed to call Mycenæan. Thus we have, in the shape of these remarkable burial structures, a characteristic belonging exclusively to that highly developed period. Professor Adler traces the shape back to Phrygia, where, according to Vitruvius, the inhabitants of the valleys lived in similar underground chambers. They erected these, it appears, by " excavating a pit on a hill, and setting up posts over it in a conical form. These posts they bound together at the top, then covered them with reeds and brushwood, and finally piled over them the greatest heap of earth they could bear; the entrance was made by cutting a passage from outside. Such dwellings are very warm in winter and very cool in summer."

The analogy is certainly significant. Men in all ages have fashioned the dwellings of the dead in accordance with those of the living; but the dead are conservative, and long after a new

generation has sought° a new home and a new pattern for its
houses, the habitations of the dead are still constructed in
ancestral fashion.

3. The Shaft-Graves

Only a few steps from the Gate of the Lions, on the right of
the way leading to the upper citadel, is a circular space enclosed
by upright slabs; within it, in the year 1876, Dr. Schliemann
discovered the celebrated graves with their astounding wealth of
gold. He himself opened five of them within a few months,
and a sixth one was found immediately after his departure. His
excavations at that time were almost entirely confined to this
spot. The trial shafts which he sank in all parts of the citadel
showed that here the greatest depth of *débris* had accumulated, so
it seemed probable that the undermost layers would be in a good
state of preservation.

Fortune favoured Dr. Schliemann from the beginning. At a
distance of 40 feet from the Lions' Gate he dug a trench 113
feet square, which thus almost exactly covered the circle of the
graves. The first *stelai* were discovered after only a few days,
and in the following weeks treasure after treasure was revealed
in the depths.

The diameter of the circle is about 87 feet; and the ground
enclosed by the circle had been levelled. The precinct wall
is formed by two rows of vertical slabs about 3 feet distant
from one another, and connected at the top by horizontal slabs.
The intervening space was not originally left hollow, as it is
now, but there are signs that it was filled up with small stones
and earth, and the slabs, which are now the only remaining
portion of the structure, were originally the mere outward revetment of a massive wall (Fig. 141). At the point nearest to the
Lions' Gate there is an entrance of rather more than 6 feet
clear width; its sides stand out like broad door-posts on each
side of the precinct wall, and are constructed in the same way.
The eastern portion of the ring rests directly on the rock; its
west side, on the other hand, where the hill falls away abruptly,
stands on a scarped Cyclopean wall as much as 13 feet high.
The slabs on the east side are about 3 feet high; those on the
west side, on the supporting wall, about 5 feet. The portion
resting on the higher ground is the best preserved, though it

141.—GENERAL VIEW OF THE CIRCLE OF GRAVES.

is by no means perfect. The pressure of the *débris* washed down from above has caused the upright slabs to slope inwards, and the horizontal covering slabs to fall down. Dr. Schliemann considered the upright slabs to have had this inclination from the first, and thought the ring formed a continuous bench; accordingly he interpreted the whole enclosure to be the agora of Mycenæ, the place where its citizens assembled for council or for judgment. This view, however, is contradicted in the first place by the fact that the slabs are much too high for seats; they are 3 to 5 feet instead of the average height of 18 inches. Moreover, they once certainly stood upright, for the edges both of the vertical and of the horizontal slabs are cut at right angles. And finally, as we shall see later on, the citadel of Mycenæ had not, like later Greek cities, a separate agora, but it merely contained the dwelling of the kings, with all that belonged to it, just like the fortress of King Alkinoos in the *Odyssey*,[1] who, when he wished to gather his folk together, goes down " to the assembly place of the Phæacians, which they had established hard by the ships."

Consequently, since no vestige of any single ancient building has been discovered on the level of the ring of slabs, a fact all the more remarkable as all the other parts of the citadel are strewn with ruins of buildings, the ring can only have been erected in some relation to the graves lying below it. It has already been stated that its level on the west is very considerably above that of the natural rock, while on the east the two levels coincide. The graves, however, do not lie in the layer of earth, helping to form the level of the ring, but they are all *under* it, hewn in the rock. In what relation of time, then, do the graves and the circle of slabs stand to one another? Were they planned at the same time, so that the graves were arranged with reference to the ring, or did the ring only come into existence later?

It is self-evident that the great filling up and levelling of the ring must have been simultaneous with the erection of the ring of slabs. It is impossible to understand why the enclosure was raised on the west by a great foundation wall, unless the surface within the ring was levelled up in proportion. The rough masonry of that wall is a proof that it was never intended to be seen. On the other hand, had this filling up of earth existed

---

[1] *Od.* viii. 5.

from the first, then, at each new burial, some 13 feet of earth would have had to be turned up, a thing altogether improbable. Furthermore, the enclosing ring, as is shown in the plan, cuts a corner off each of the graves V and VI, which would not have been the case had it with its foundation wall been older than the graves.

The point at issue has been finally decided by the finds yielded by the layer of earth under discussion. Dr. Schliemann found in it an altar and a number of most interesting *stelai*. The depth of these remains below the ring is exactly fixed by his observations. At the beginning of the excavations there still lay above the layer forming the level of the ring of slabs a further layer of the *débris* washed down from the terrace above: this last layer was as much as 3·50 metres deep. "The altar," says Dr. Schliemann, "was precisely over the centre of the fourth tomb "— it consisted of "an almost circular mass of Cyclopean masonry, with a large round opening in the form of a well" (see Fig. 142); it was 4 feet high, and measured 7 feet from north to south, and $5\frac{1}{4}$ feet from east to west.[1]

The size of this structure, the fact that it is built of masonry and not formed by a single stone, and the round hole in the centre, vividly remind us of the small stone structure in the court of the palace at Tiryns. Dr. Schliemann is no doubt right in recognising it as an altar. It was found "20 feet below the former surface of the mount." This surface, as already stated, rose in its highest portions to 3·50 metres, or about 12 feet above the level of the ring of slabs. Deducting these 12 feet the altar was still at least 8 feet below the ring of slabs. In the same

---

[1] Dr. Schliemann and M. Stamatakis, who superintended the excavations for the Greek Government, and who arranged the Mycenæan collection at Athens, differ from one another in the numbering of the graves. Dr. Schliemann calls the grave which was first recognised as such by its upper edge, the first, while M. Stamatakis calls it the fifth, because its excavation was interrupted, and its contents were only obtained after the other four graves had been emptied. Although one numbering is just as good as the other, it seems more convenient to follow that of M. Stamatakis, which is adopted in the Athenian Museum and in most archæological works (for instance, by Furtwängler and Löschcke, *Myk. Thongef.*) The correspondence of the numbers is as follows :—

Our grave I is Dr. Schliemann's grave II.
    ,,   II   ,,   ,,   ,, V.
    ,,   V   ,,   ,,   ,, I.

Nos. III, IV, and VI are the same as Dr. Schliemann's.

way we can reckon the height of the altar above the grave. According to Dr. Schliemann the bottom of the grave was "33 feet below the former surface of the mount"; so that the altar found at a depth of 20 feet lay 13 feet above the grave. As the sides of the grave were about 10 feet high, there would thus be left between them and the altar an interval of 3 feet.

These numbers show that close above the graves a cultus of the dead had already been established; and that this cultus was not merely temporary is proved by the *stelai*, which were set up as lasting memorials of the dead. Dr. Schliemann gives 4 feet as the uniform depth at which they were found. The apparent discrepancy between this measurement and the depth at which

142.—ALTAR FOUND OVER THE FOURTH GRAVE.

the altar lay, disappears when we remember that the *stelai* were almost all found farther to the north, where the hill rises and the layer of *débris* was thinner. It seems certain, therefore, that the slope of the original rock itself had been for a long period of time the seat of a cultus of the dead. Later on all traces of it were concealed by a great layer of earth, and the upper surface was thoroughly levelled.

The graves are cut vertically into the rock; the upper portion of the sides has generally crumbled away, but graves I and V show that the sides were from 10 to 16 feet high. The bottoms of the graves are all horizontal, but they lie at different levels, according to the position of the grave on the slope. The plan of each grave is rectangular, but varies considerably in size. In II, the smallest, it measures 9 feet by 10; in the biggest, IV, it measures 16 feet by 22; accordingly, we find that the former contained only one corpse, the latter five.

The interior arrangement of the graves, Dr. Schliemann tells us, was as follows. / The sides were lined with a wall of small quarry-stones and clay, which has been preserved up to different heights; in the fifth grave it still reaches 7 feet 8 inches. Several slate slabs were leaning against this wall; others were lying cross-ways or slanting over the bodies. / Dr. Schliemann saw in them the revetment of the clay walls.

The bodies themselves were embedded in a layer of small river-pebbles, surrounded with a wealth of ornaments, utensils, and arms, and covered over with a layer of fine clay. On the side walls Dr. Schliemann noticed places blackened by smoke, and concluded from this, and from the presence of some ashes and much unconsumed wood, that the dead had been cremated within the tomb. Immediately over the small pebbles, which he thought served as a sort of ventilator, he maintained that a funeral pyre was erected, and that the bodies were burnt upon it.

As, however, in the excavations, portions of the bodies were discovered in a mummified condition, and as the utensils had not suffered at all, and even many fragments of wood were quite untouched by fire, he assumed that only a small fire was lit, so to speak, *pro forma*, which was not strong enough to consume the bodies or their equipment.[1] The space above the bodies was in all the graves filled with *débris*; and as there were no vestiges of a former artificial closing of the tomb, Dr. Schliemann thought it had been blocked up immediately after burial. He naturally shrank from the notion that the graves could be reopened to admit fresh corpses. When he considered that it would be necessary to close the grave after the first burial, and impossible to reopen it because of the method by which it was blocked up, he gradually became convinced that the corpses in each grave must have been buried simultaneously. From "the identity of the mode of burial in all the tombs, the similar style and decoration of the ornaments," he further concluded that there was no interval between the burials, but that the whole group of graves were the result of a burial *en masse*. The rich offerings proved the high estate of the dead; and certain unmistakable signs of disorder, the position of one body whose head was squeezed down

[1] See *Mycenæ*, p. 155 *seq.*

on to the breast, and similar observations, were all proofs of a hurried and careless burial. Dr. Schliemann accordingly thought he might safely conclude he had discovered the graves of Agamemnon and his companions. The well-known tradition of the tragic fate of the leader of the Greek host, who at his return from the Trojan War finds wife and throne in possession of another, and is treacherously murdered by his enemy, seemed to explain exactly the mingled signs of wealth and haste in these graves. Further, there was the remarkable coincidence of the testimony of Pausanias, who saw in Mycenæ the five graves of Agamemnon and his companions, and says expressly that they were within the walls.

Dr. Schliemann, in the little work[1] which gives an account of his first researches, had as early as 1869 expressed his opinion that those "walls" of Pausanias did not refer, as had hitherto been supposed, to the enclosure of the lower city, but to the fortification wall of the citadel. He undertook his excavations at Mycenæ solely with the object of discovering the five graves mentioned by Pausanias. When during the first months of the work five graves, apparently belonging to a simultaneous burial, came to light, revealing a wealth and splendour such as could only have been displayed by a kingly race, Dr. Schliemann's interpretation of the ancient passage seemed indeed to receive a dazzling confirmation. Critical German philologists might smile at the notion that Agamemnon had been found bodily with sword and sceptre, but the world at large accepted the discovery with an enthusiasm which found a lasting monument in Mr. Gladstone's preface to Dr. Schliemann's *Mycenæ*.

In order to be able to form an independent opinion on this point, we must subject the arguments on which Dr. Schliemann builds his hypothesis to a close investigation. They fall under two heads—the manner of the burial, and the passage in Pausanias.

No one has ever actually admitted with Dr. Schliemann the simultaneous interment of the bodies. Yet every one believed that the graves had been blocked up after the burial, and also admitted that a frequent reopening was improbable, especially as Dr. Schliemann thought the later disturbance and partial plundering of one corpse had left its traces. Only a short while ago Dr.

---

[1] *Archäol. Forschungen. Ithaka, der Peloponnes u. Troja*, 1869.

Dörpfeld, whose loyal collaboration with Dr. Schliemann has
enriched science with such great results, succeeded in throwing a
new light on this point also.   He made special oral inquiries
concerning the position, at the time of excavation, of the irregular
slate slabs with which Dr. Schliemann thought the walls of the
graves had been revetted, and when he heard that one of them was
actually found on a body, it became plain to him that the
disorder in the graves was not the result of a hasty burial, but of
the falling in of a roof or lid formed by those slabs.   The presence
of the many well-preserved pieces of wood was now explained;

143.—COPPER CASING OF THE BEAM-END (size about 3 : 10).

across the grave lay one or two strong beams which carried the
slabs ; when the beams rotted the lid fell in, and the greater part
of the slabs just slipped down against the wall, and remained there
in an erect position ; but some of them also fell on the bodies.
Then the whole space got filled up with the earth which had
covered the lid of the grave, and which probably already rose to
the level of the ring of slabs.   Next, on closer inspection the
bronze casings with which the ends of the beams had been shod
were discovered in the museum among the finds from the third
grave.   These are what Dr. Schliemann calls "four little boxes
of stout sheet copper"; one of them is shown in Fig. 143.   Each is

10 inches long, 5 inches high, and $4\frac{1}{3}$ inches broad, and is filled
with wood in fair preservation, which was fastened all round by
a number of strong copper nails.

The side plates are not soldered, but hammered together.
Dr. Schliemann found no other explanation for these boxes,
than that they "served as head pillows for the dead, and
perhaps also for the living," just as pillows of marble or alabaster
have been found in Egyptian tombs.   However, he expressly adds
that not one of the would-be pillows was found under a head.
It is scarcely necessary to argue in support of the new explanation
of these objects.   The fragments of wood fastened by such a
number of nails can only be explained on the supposition that
a beam end filled the hollow space.

The fact that these casings have only been found in the third
grave accords with the whole stately furnishing of this grave.
Here were found the richest offerings to the dead; here too the
style of ornamentation was most developed; consequently more
care was also bestowed on the closing of this grave.   As four
beam casings have been preserved, there must have been two
beams lying across the grave.   The walls built against the sides

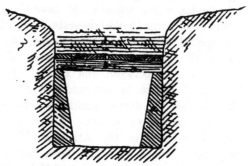

144.—CROSS SECTION OF A GRAVE.   a, Side walls ; b, beams ; c, stone slabs.

were in all probability destined to carry the beams.   All these
facts tend to show that the main point in the conception hitherto
formed of the Mycenæan mode of burial is erroneous.   The
graves were not filled up immediately after the interment of
all the bodies or of each single body, but were carefully closed
with slabs in such a manner that a high cavity remained within.
The layer of clay which Dr. Schliemann found over the bodies
was washed down, as Dr. Dörpfeld has already remarked, by the

moisture trickling down through the earth. The beam-ends lying deep below show that there was as yet no deposit of débris when the lid gave way. Everything that lay above the layer of clay must have fallen when the roof collapsed. The débris consisted of a mass of thick clay interspersed with bone implements and potsherds; partly also, as Dr. Schliemann repeatedly states, it was "mixed with natural earth, brought there from some other place": indeed, the first grave seems to have been completely filled with the unmixed earth. This confirms the conjecture hazarded above, that at the time when the graves fell in, the ring of slabs with its great filling of earth already existed. Accordingly, the final closing of the graves and the levelling of the ring form the limits within which the objects found in the accumulated débris must be dated. Dr. Schliemann's conjecture of a hurried and irreverent burial, one of the main supports of his Agamemnon theory, also proves unfounded, since the disorder in the grave, the displacement and compression of the corpses, were all caused by the fall of the lids. His further assumption of a simultaneous interment of all these bodies is equally baseless; for, as the graves were simply closed with slabs just like our modern family vaults, a new burial could take place without any difficulty. When we come to the separate finds of each grave, we shall give special attention to the question whether, from a consideration of the furniture of the graves, a difference in date can be made out between the several graves, or even between the several bodies in one and the same grave. Unfortunately we cannot yet decide positively whether the bodies were burnt within the grave or not. A few heaps of a grey pulverised substance now in the Athenian Museum certainly appear to be ashes. Ashes have also been found in analogous graves at the Heraion, as well as at Spata and Volo. But in all these cases the bodies do not seem to have been burnt. In his description of the graves on the slope of the Palamidi near Nauplia, Dr. Lolling expressly remarks "that the dead have been buried there intact, and cremation of the bodies is not to be thought of."[1] However, in these very graves unmistakable traces of fire have been found on two vases, and "between these two vases, on the narrow empty spaces near the heads of the dead, lay a few thinly

---

[1] *Athen. Mitth.* v. pp. 154, 155. See also Köhler, *Das Kuppelgrab von Menidi,* p. 55.

scattered bones of sheep or of goats, and similar bones were also scattered singly over the place where the bodies had lain. These bones of animals and the two vases evidently came from sacrifices offered to the dead, and had been placed in the grave with the corpses."

In the same way, at Mycenæ also, offerings may have been burnt at the tomb and their remains afterwards scattered in the grave. But since here, as at Nauplia, the skeletons have been found intact, in some cases even with mummified flesh and portions of skin still adhering to them, we must assume that in this case also the bodies were merely buried and not burnt. We need not wonder at meeting with a mode of burial differing from the custom, universal in Homer, of burning the dead; for among the later Greeks there still lived on the tradition of an original burial by interment. Herodotos, Pausanias, and Plutarch all imagine the mortal remains of Pelops,[1] of Theseus,[2] and of Protesilaos[3] and Orestes[4] not as mere ashes, but as whole skeletons.

We now come to the last and most important argument in Dr. Schliemann's theory—to the question whether the graves which he has discovered are really the same which Pausanias saw and described as those of Agamemnon and his followers, *i.e.* which the popular tradition of his time ascribed to those heroes.

This question can now be clearly answered by the help of the researches mentioned above. The passage in Pausanias's description of Mycenæ runs as follows (ii. 16, 5-7): "Some remains of the circuit wall are still to be seen, and the gate which has lions over it. These were built, they say, by the Cyclopes, who made the wall at Tiryns for Proitos. Among the ruins at Mycenæ is the fountain called Perseia, and some subterranean buildings belonging to Atreus and his children, where their treasures were kept.' There is the tomb of Atreus, and of those whom Aigisthos slew at the banquet, on their return from Ilion with Agamemnon. Kassandra's tomb is there, but its authenticity is denied by the Lacedæmonians of Amyklæ.[5] There is also the tomb of Agamemnon, and that of Eurymedon

---

[1] Paus. v. 13, 5, 6.   [2] Plut. *Thes.* 36.   [3] Herod. ix. 120.   [4] Herod. i. 67, 68.

[5] τοῦ μὲν δὴ Κασσάνδρας μνήματος ἀμφισβητοῦσι Λακεδαιμονίων οἱ περὶ 'Αμύκλας οἰκοῦντες.

the charioteer, and the joint tomb of Teledamos and Pelops, the twin children of Kassandra, whom Aigisthos slew with their parents while still mere babes . . . for Orestes gave her (Elektra) in marriage to Pylades. Hellanikos adds that Medon and Strophios were the children of Pylades and Elektra. Klytemnestra and Aigisthos were buried a little way outside the wall, for they were not thought worthy to be within, where Agamemnon lay and those who fell with him."

We must first consider how many graves Pausanias really saw. "The people of Amyklæ deny the authenticity of the grave of Kassandra," but this only means that Amyklæ itself claimed to possess the genuine grave of Kassandra, and therefore would not accept the one shown at Mycenæ. In any case, however, the grave of Kassandra *was* shown at Mycenæ, and Professor Adler is incorrect in leaving it out of his enumeration of the graves. Dr. Schliemann, on the other hand, is not any more justified in disposing of the grave of Atreus as though it never existed. Both make Pausanias mention five graves, whereas he undoubtedly names six, those of (1) Atreus, (2) Kassandra, (3) Agamemnon, (4) Eurymedon, (5) Teledamos and Pelops, (6) Elektra. However, as a sixth grave in addition to the former five has been discovered since the close of Dr. Schliemann's excavations, the number of the graves seen by Pausanias, and that of the graves preserved to this day, agree just as well as before. It is well known that Dr. Schliemann understood from the passage in Pausanias that the graves were *within* the citadel walls. The walls within which Agamemnon and his followers were buried, but which might not contain the graves of the adulterous Klytemnestra and her paramour, are, Dr. Schliemann maintains, the same walls whose ruins and gates have been described at the beginning of the chapter.

This interpretation, though quite possible in itself, was not accepted by scholars simply because burial within the citadel wall seemed quite incredible. But there are other objections. For instance, it is scarcely conceivable that, after the citadel had lain deserted and in ruins since the year 468 B.C., there should in the age of the Antonines be any external traces of the exact situation and number of the shaft-graves or even any knowledge of their existence. No *stelai* or former memorials of a burial or of a *cultus* of the dead have been found in the upper level of the

ring of slabs, which, failing a more definite date, must at any rate
have been erected in the " Mycenæan " period.

Moreover, the ring has been so exposed to constant accumula-
tions washed down from the overhanging terraces above it, that
certainly not one stone of it can have been visible in the time of
Pausanias. Dr. Schliemann has rightly concluded from a few finds
on the summit of the citadel that the city was again inhabited
for a short while in Hellenistic times; he found specimens of
good Greek work, separated by a thick layer of *débris* from the
remains of the great epoch long gone by. He himself argues
from this fact with respect to the " Agora," *i.e.* the ring of slabs,
that Euripides, who he believes had personal knowledge of the
site, must have visited it in his youth soon after the capture of
the city by the Argives, for later, towards the year 400 B.C., the
accumulation of *débris* would already have been too considerable.
If Euripides was only just in time to get a glimpse of the
renowned site, the unfortunate Pausanias must have arrived
considerably too late.

The notion that Pausanias could see with his own eyes either
the pit-graves or their circular precinct is therefore absolutely out
of the question. It has, however, been hinted that he here
employed a method suspected in many of his descriptions, and
spoke of things which he did not personally see, but the accounts
of which he borrowed from older literary sources. Dr. Belger
attempts to explain the mention of the Agamemnon graves in
this manner.[1] He considers the informant of Pausanias to have
been Hellanikos, who was a predecessor of Herodotos and who
might well have visited Mycenæ before its destruction and seen the
graves. But the description of Mycenæ by Pausanias bears the
impress of personal knowledge. The few points he mentions, the
fortification walls, the gate, fountain, and treasuries must have
been as visible then as they were up to the time of Dr.
Schliemann's excavations. Dr. Belger himself cannot rid himself
of the supposition that Pausanias visited Mycenæ and described
all these things from his own experience. He can only support
his theory of the literary sources for the mention of the grave by
the somewhat curious notion that Pausanias, owing to some
accident, did not penetrate to the interior of the citadel, and so
when he got home filled up the gap in his book of travels from

[1] Belger, *Beitrage zur Kenntniss d. Griech. Kuppelgräber.*

the contents of his library. This explanation is so artificial and incredible that the whole theory may well fall to the ground along with it.

But where did Pausanias see his graves, if not in the citadel within the precinct of slabs ? Many maintain that he saw them in the lower city, and meant by them the bee-hive buildings, which were at all times the most prominent monuments on the soil of the ancient city, and to which popular tradition would be most likely to attach the names of its ancient heroes. This interpretation is, however, also open to doubt. Besides the Lions' Gate and the spring, Pausanias saw at Mycenæ firstly treasuries and secondly graves. From his description of Orchomenos it is clear that by a treasury he means a bee-hive building. He mentions there the treasure-house of Minyas, and describes as such the "tholos" which Dr. Schliemann excavated in the year 1881. "Minyas," says Pausanias, "had such great revenues that he surpassed in wealth all that were before him ; he was the first we know of who built a treasury for his riches." And further,[1] "the treasury of Minyas is a marvel surpassed by none, either in Greece or in any other country, and is built as follows. It is of stone, and rises from a circular base to a blunt conical point, of which the topmost stone is said to act as a keystone to the whole structure."

There can be no doubt that when Pausanias says he saw in Mycenæ "underground treasuries," he means tholos buildings. But where were his graves? Professor Adler and Dr. Dörpfeld are both of opinion that he also saw these in the tholoi of which he considered the big vaulted room to be the treasury, and the small side-chamber the grave. It is also conceivable that the two bee-hive tombs on the slope of the city hill, which were probably then as now the only accessible ones (namely, the one excavated by Mrs. Schliemann, and the so-called treasury of Atreus), were pointed out to him as the "treasuries of Atreus and his sons," but that the remaining buildings, which were filled up and probably only marked by the tumulus which they formed, passed as mere graves. Which exactly of the many graves still extant there were pointed out as the six of Agamemnon and his companions, and which as those of Klytemnestra and Aigisthos, which were reputed to lie beyond the circuit walls, cannot be proved.

[1] Paus. ix. 38, 2.

The exact line of the walls is also uncertain. The fortifications of the lower city are so badly preserved, that their course in the west cannot be made out. Perhaps they took a great bend towards the Kokoretza, perhaps also the wall had disappeared long before the days of Pausanias, and he only assumed its former existence on the outermost limit of the ruins of the settlement.

At any rate, one important result has been arrived at—the pit-graves on the citadel are *not* those which were shown to Pausanias as the graves of Agamemnon and his companions. This, however, does not dispose of the further question whether these graves are in any way connected with Agamemnon. As the pit-graves got blocked up and gradually sank into oblivion, the popular belief found no other monuments to which to attach the names of the great heroes, except the tholos buildings which have outlasted all their surroundings in the lower city. Thus this later attribution may very possibly be erroneous, and perhaps one ought to connect the name of the great leader rather with the older and simpler burial-ground than with those later and more splendid structures.

These are points, however, which can only be discussed in relation to other questions.

4. The Stelai

The *stelai* found above the graves are of a porous grey-brown limestone; their average dimension is a height of 5 feet to a breadth of 3 feet 3 inches. Some of them are adorned with representations in low relief. The others are simply polished stone slabs. Hitherto, owing to the presence both of sculptured and unsculptured *stelai*, it has been supposed that these grave memorials belonged to different periods—that the ruder unsculptured ones were the earliest, and were afterwards replaced by sculptured slabs. This view, however, does not hold good on a closer inspection of the *stelai*. Dr. Schliemann says that he found, close to almost every grave, at a depth of from 1 to 3 feet below the slabs still standing, unsculptured slabs in various positions, lying sometimes horizontally, sometimes obliquely. Near to graves II and V the standing slabs were carved in relief: in this case the slabs lying beneath might well have been the predecessors of the sculptured ones. But the circumstances are different in the case of graves

I and III. The *stelai* that stood over them were *unsculptured*, and yet the same plain slabs were found beneath them as in graves II and V. Dr. Schliemann describes the find of slabs above the third grave as follows: "The two unsculptured tombstones were extremely well fastened with horizontal square slabs, so that they could not be got out without great effort. Two feet below them I found two large slabs in the form of *stelai* lying horizontally. At a depth of 5 feet lower I brought to light three more slabs, the one lying, the other two standing." [1]

After Dr. Dörpfeld's new theory as to the method by which the graves were closed, we can no longer look upon all these stones as former grave *stelai*, but may consider those which lay deep down as portions of the lid. We shall then find that a different explanation of the relation between sculptured and unsculptured *stelai* easily suggests itself from a closer inspection of the manner in which the *stelai* lay when excavated.

Dr. Schliemann found the first three sculptured *stelai* over the grave V. All three were standing upright in one line, about 1 or $1\frac{1}{2}$ foot apart, with their sculptured side turned to the west. In the same line, and 10 feet farther south, a fourth sculptured *stele* was found over the second grave. Again, in the same line, and at a distance of only $1\frac{1}{2}$ foot from the last *stele*, was found the first unsculptured slab. As grave II only contained one body, it would only have one *stele*, i.e. the fourth sculptured one, so that the following unsculptured slab must belong to grave IV close by, otherwise no *stele* is mentioned as belonging to grave IV.

We now pass to the remaining unsculptured slabs. Two of these Dr. Schliemann discovered 23 feet to the east of the three first sculptured *stelai*, that is, over grave I. And 40 feet farther south he found two more unsculptured slabs over grave III. All these were standing upright like the sculptured *stelai*, and had their face to the west.

To sum up:—sculptured *stelai* were found over graves II and V, unsculptured over graves I, III, and IV. As we shall see later on, the contents of the graves show that men alone were buried in II and V, women alone in I. and III, and in grave IV both men and women. Accordingly everything seems to show that only the graves of the men were marked by sculptured slabs, with reliefs representing occupations which belong exclusively to

[1] *Mycenæ*, p. 161.

men, whilst the graves of the women only received modest polished stones.

We now turn to the reliefs of the sculptured *stelai*. The three that were found first and are also the best preserved (Figs. 145, 146, 147) show a figure-subject, typical of the active life of the dead man, with the addition of artistic combinations of spirals. In 145 and 146 the framed rectangular upper portion of the *stele* is divided into two fields by a horizontal fillet. In one relief the upper space, in the other the lower, is utilised for the figure-subject, and the remaining space is filled up with decorations in spirals.

In all three examples the centre of the composition is a war or hunting chariot mounted by one man and drawn by a horse at full gallop. The chariot-box is apparently quite low, like that of the chariots on Egyptian monuments, and seems to rest on a four-spoked wheel. We must naturally suppose a second wheel on the other side, and probably two horses are intended, though only one can be seen, since a one-horsed chariot was unknown to the ancients; besides in the hunting-scene on the gold ring given below (see Fig. 220), the chariot is unmistakably drawn by two horses.

Neither pole nor traces are represented in the relief, though in each instance the reins passing through the mouth of the horse and held by the charioteer are clearly shown. The charioteer (Fig. 146) is fully armed. On his right side hangs a big sword; the blade is very broad at the hilt and ends in a sharp point. In Fig. 145 we must identify the object fastened at the back of the charioteer's seat as a sword with round hilt. The blade is much curtailed owing to the lack of space. According to information due to Dr. Puchstein's kindness, shields are fastened in the same way behind chariots in some Hittite reliefs, not yet published, from Boghaskoï in Asia Minor and Sendjirli in Syria. When the chariot stood still the sword would hang down between the two wheels, but when the chariot is going at full speed, as here, then the sword flies out behind. This observation might lead us to suppose that in Fig. 146 the sword is not buckled on to the man's waist, but hangs by the side of the chariot-box. But in that case the box would have to be much higher than we should suppose from the analogous examples in 145 and 221. It is more probable that the chariot-box only reaches as far as the

division seen about in a line with the back of the horse, and that
the curved line farther up, ending under the reins close to the
man's chin, is either his left shoulder, or, and this seems more
likely, a great round shield with which he is armed.

145.—GRAVE STELE FROM GRAVE V (size about 1 : 10).

The only relief clearly indicating the object of the expedition
is the one given in Fig. 145. We see here, close in front of the
horses, the figure of a man; the position of his feet shows us that
he is facing the charioteer, and is apparently threatening him with
a long spear. This, then, is a battle-scene.

146.—GRAVE STELE FROM GRAVE V (size about 1 : 12).

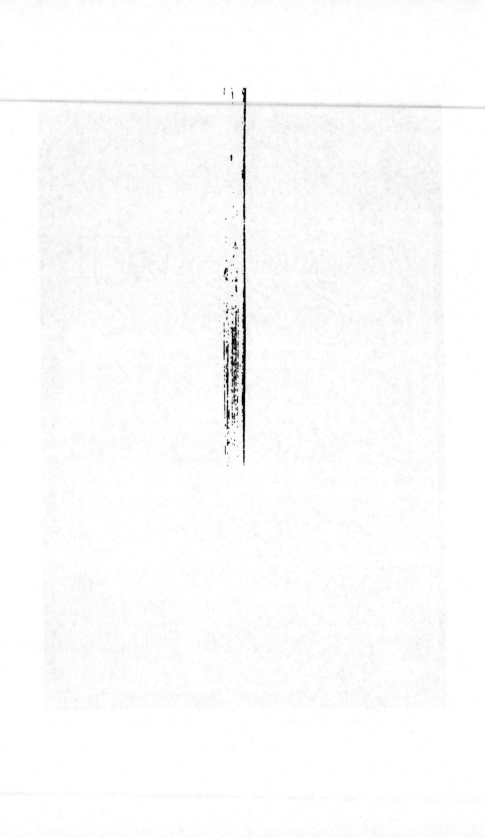

The group of finds first mentioned showed us that the oldest settlement on the hill of Tiryns reaches back to a time when almost all objects of daily use were of a rough home-made manufacture. The second group proves that the palace discovered at Tiryns belongs to that great period of prosperity which active commercial intercourse between the various coast-towns fostered at one time in all the lands of the Greek sea.

128, 129.—FEMALE FIGURES OF CLAY (size 2 : 3).

It is this period which has received its character and its name from the finds of Mycenæ. At Tiryns we not only get a glimpse into this great epoch, but also into the one that followed it. It has long been observed that although the vases of the Mycenæan style are followed by those of the so-called "Dipylon" style, the two coexisted side by side for a time, till the culture of Mycenæ gradually left the field clear for that of the Dipylon. Just as the Mycenæan vases are called after the place where they have been

K

chiefly found, so the Dipylon vases are named after the great double gate at Athens, which leads to the street of tombs.

The chief difference between them and the Mycenæan vases is that a system based on angles takes the place of one based on curves; instead of spirals we have the mæander, instead of wave-lines we find zigzags. As in the later Mycenæan vases so here seaweed and polyps have completely disappeared. On the other hand, figures are more frequently attempted than was hitherto the case, but they have a rude and clumsy appearance

130.—FRAGMENT OF VASE (size 1 : 2).

which leaves them very far behind what the Mycenæans had achieved in this line.

The clay of these vases is much rougher than that of the Mycenæan pottery; the paint used is always lustrous.

Many fragments of Dipylon vases have been found in Tiryns, a sign that the citadel continued to be inhabited for a considerable length of time after the decline of the Mycenæan period. In this case, again, we shall only give quite a few examples. Fig. 130 shows, in the midst of a maze of horizontal and vertical zigzag lines, women carrying bunches of flowers, and holding one another by the hand. Only two women have been preserved on the

In Fig. 146 there is also the figure of a man in front of the
horse, only here he is turned to the right; in his left hand he holds
up a sword, slightly different in shape from the two kinds of swords
known to us up to now.   It is broadest in the middle, and
decreases in thickness both above and below.   The right arm,
like the left arm, is bent at the elbow and then raised up to the
height of the shoulder.   It is a mere accident that the hand
seems to touch the head of the horse; it does not mean that the
man is holding the horse, for the swift movement of the animal
contradicts any such notion.

There is nothing to show whether the second man wishes to
attack the charioteer or is merely running along as an escort;
but the analogy of the preceding relief, as well as the raised
sword, leads us to look upon him as a foe rather than as a friend.

The empty space above and under the horse, as well as
behind the warrior in the chariot, is filled with spirals.   The
most ancient art, like nature, is wont to feel a *horror vacui*.

On the third relief (Fig. 147) the charioteer seems to be out
hunting.   At any rate, *under* the horses (a position which is
perhaps intended to imply "in front of" or "beside" them) there
runs an ibex or some such creature, followed by an animal of
about the same size.   The pursuer, from the strength of its build,
especially about the head and neck, bears a strong resemblance
to a lion, but seems hitherto to have been taken for a dog.
This view is hardly tenable.   A glance at the various representations of a stag pursued by a lion on the gold plates in Figs.
260, 261, immediately suggests that this is also the subject of
our *stele*.   On the gold plates the hunted animal has the same
horns curving backwards.   With regard to the second animal,
there is absolutely no proof that dogs were employed in the chase
at that period, while running lions are a subject dear to the
artists of the Mycenæan period.   These two facts tend to confirm
us in our suspicion that the pursuer cannot be a dog.

If we can safely identify the animal as a lion, then the gold
plates (Figs. 260, 261), which it should be noted came from the
grave over which our *stele* stood, leave no doubt whatsoever that
we have in the group of two animals a motive common in the
art of the time, and utilised in the most various cases for mere
decorative purposes.   This, then, is an isolated scene, and has no
connection with the driving-scene.   If the artist wished to

picture a hunt, he ought not to have represented at the same time the chase of the lion and the ibex, who are already sufficiently occupied with one another. It is much more probable that the group of animals on the *stele* is as complete in itself as are the compartments filled with spiral decorations in Figs. 145 and 146. Certainly the latter are separated from the main subject by a horizontal fillet, while in the third slab main and subordinate subjects are juxtaposed in the same compartment. On the other hand, what remains of the framed compartment of Fig. 147, even without the piece which has been broken off, is higher than the compartments in Figs. 145 and 146. Moreover, the addition of a second figure-subject, instead of mere linear decoration, corresponds to the greater artistic skill which has been expended on this relief. This is shown in its rich and elegant frame, as compared with the simple polished borders of the other slabs.

After the solution of the lower scene, we shall naturally have to consider the upper one by itself, and must recognise in the charioteer a warrior starting for the battle. But where is the adversary represented on both the other reliefs, whose presence seems a necessary complement to the scene? A figure can scarcely have been broken away in front of the horses, even had it been placed as high as it is in Fig. 145. For on the ground of the relief between the horses and the edge, on a piece that has not been sunk, there is a pattern which, like the one behind the chariot, must have run upwards in waved lines. Likewise, a portion of the surface below the horses has not been sunk and has been left rough; however shapeless it appears at first sight, a few lines betray the object with which it was left standing. The lower edge, shaped like two semicircles connected by a short horizontal line, corresponds exactly to the outline of the great double shield, so often represented on Mycenæan monuments. It may be clearly seen on the idols in Figs. 281 and 288, and on the dagger-blade in Fig. 227. The last-named example shows that a man could almost completely disappear behind such a shield. We next find that the shapeless mass has two projections on its left edge, which are probably legs; on the right side we see the head, which is thrust between the horns of the ibex. Only the upper edge is left quite straight and unfinished. All this proves, it seems, without a doubt that the artist intended to

represent a warrior fallen on his shield. If we have a front
view instead of a side view of the shield, it is only what we
should expect from this primitive art.

We thus have on all the *stelai* a scene of battle. The
struggle is between a mighty and distinguished warrior and a
humbler foe, whose overthrow is foreshadowed by the fact of his

147.—GRAVE STELE FROM GRAVE V (size about 1 : 12).

being on foot, a suggestion of ultimate defeat repeatedly employed
on Egyptian monuments representing the warlike exploits of the
Pharaoh.

The fourth and last of the well-preserved *stelai* has no figure-
subject. Its surface is framed by a narrow fillet, and divided
into two vertical compartments by a broad inner band. Each of
these compartments is filled with a band running in regular

loops; it might be called a rounded mæander or wave-pattern. Of the other fragments found, only two are worthy of mention. One of these shows a man, and in front of him there is probably a horse's tail, so that here again we have a charioteer; on the other are two galloping horses; the space on the right is filled up, as in Fig. 146, with spirals. On all the other fragments only spiral ornaments have been preserved.

The technique of the *stelai* and of all the fragments is peculiar. The figures and ornaments are not modelled, but always lie in the same plane with the edge of the slab. They resemble work cut out with the fret-saw and stuck on to a background. A simple incised line gives here and there indispensable inner markings. In technique, therefore, the *stelai* are greatly behind the relief of the lions with its plastic modelling, and also much inferior to it in material, so that they must belong to a considerably earlier date. Their technique seems to be developed from the inlaid work seen on the dagger-blades from graves IV and V.

5. *The First and Third Graves*

The objects from the first and third graves are so closely analogous that they must be described together. The following is Dr. Schliemann's account of the discovery of the first grave: "At a depth of 15 feet below the level of the rock, or at 25 feet below the former surface of the ground as I found it when I began the excavations, I reached a layer of pebbles, below which I found at a distance of 3 feet from each other three human bodies, all with the head turned to the east and the feet to the west. They were only separated from the surface of the levelled rock by another layer of small stones, on which they were lying." [1] The most important objects found in the grave were three large diadems (Fig. 148) belonging to these three bodies. All these are similar in shape and design, and consist of an oval gold plate 20 inches long, decorated with a system of concentric bands and bosses in *repoussé* work. The centre line of the design is formed by bosses each surrounded by two concentric circles, and gradually diminishing in size on either side of the largest central boss; the intervening spaces both on the upper and lower edge are in each case filled up with a smaller circle and boss.

[1] *Mycenæ*, p. 155.

In addition to these large ornaments there were found in the
same grave a number of similar ornaments of semi-oval shape, with designs
matching those of the diadems. It
was Dr. Schliemann's opinion that
two of them went together to form
one diadem (Fig. 150). Not only is
this in itself unlikely, as the join
would then be exactly in the middle
of the forehead, but the great number
of the pieces renders the theory altogether inadmissible. Twenty-four
perfect pieces are known, without
counting a few fragments, so that
more than eight would fall to the
share of each body. The similar
finds from grave III teach us how
these objects were really worn.

This grave is only a little smaller
than the first. Dr. Schliemann's
account of its discovery is: " I found
in this sepulchre the mortal remains
of three persons, who, to judge from
the smallness of the bones and
particularly of the teeth, and by the
masses of female ornaments found
here, must have been women. As
the teeth of one of these bodies,
though all preserved, were evidently
much worn away and very irregular,
they appear to belong to a very old
woman. All had the head turned
to the east, and the feet to the west.
As in the former tomb, the bodies
lay at a distance of 3 feet from each
other. They were literally laden
with golden jewellery." [1]

148.—GOLD DIADEM FROM GRAVE I
(size about 1 : 3).

The chief ornaments here were two large diadems. A third,

[1] *Mycenæ*, p. 164.

149.—GOLD DIADEM FROM GRAVE III
(size about 1 : 3).

which Dr. Schliemann reckons with these and has published with them, is placed in the Museum among the finds from grave IV, where, according to M. Stamatakis's notes, it presumably belongs. We can therefore come to no conclusion about this diadem, and must leave it an open question whether one body may not have been buried without ornamental headgear. The other two diadems differ in design, not only from those of the first grave, but also from one another. One (Fig. 149) shows a mere elaboration of the system of design found in the first grave—large bosses decreasing towards the ends and surrounded by concentric circles; the circles, however, no longer consist of simple raised rings, but are composed partly of dots, partly also of leaves. The intervening spaces towards the edges are filled up by bosses encircled by dots, and the diadem has a border of plain and dotted lines, outside which, along the edge, runs a pattern of interlaced spirals formed like an S. The diadem is pierced with a hole at each end.

The other diadem (Fig. 153) supports on its upper edge a crest of small plates. The solid portion is decorated with a treble row of circles alternately filled with a rosette or with seven smaller circles. The intervening spaces on the lower edge are filled by circles with a boss in the centre, and on the upper edge by Ψ and Υ shaped ornaments—motives probably borrowed from the palm. On the small plates which form the crest, rosettes and bosses alternate with circles and spirals.

Here, as in grave I, the diadems are matched by semi-oval ornaments. Apparently a fixed number of these belonged

150.—PENDANT FROM GRAVE I (size about 2 : 9).

151.—PENDANT FROM GRAVE III (size about 2 : 9).

152.—PENDANT FROM GRAVE III (size about 2 : 9).

to each diadem. Six repeat the system of decoration of the first diadem, bosses surrounded by circles of points or leaves (Fig. 151). Seven others show the decoration of the second, circles alternately filled with rosettes or with seven little bosses (Fig. 152). These gold plates are far better preserved than those of the first grave. Even in the latter it could be seen that a thread had run along the edge, which was folded back; but in those of the third grave the actual fold on the broader end is preserved,

and shows, without a doubt, that the ornament was
pendant (Fig. 154). Moreover, these plates are, pier

hole in the middle of each of their lo
the thin wire still preserved in some of
was evidently intended to carry little
pendants, which can be found without n

154.—BACK VIEW
OF A PENDANT   culty among the objects in the grave,
FROM GRAVE III.   small triangular plates of gold, also
some with the circle and boss, others
with rosettes (Fig. 155).

The pendants, then, hung point downwards, and with their tassels must have
produced a gay and rich effect. It now
remains to settle how they were worn. Dr.
Studniczka has proved that large pendants   155.—ACCESSORY
were sometimes worn on the girdle.[1]

Pendants similar to these may be seen on the side of
breast-plate from Olympia, possibly of the seventh cen
In Homer[2] Hera wears a girdle with a hundred θύσαι
are most probably to be understood as pendants, and
identical with our gold plates. An image, however, m
closely related to Mycenæan art than either Homer or
gives us a different suggestion. A small female terra-co
found in Tiryns (see above, Fig. 129) wears over the
ornament composed of large pendants, decorated like this
large bosses. Nine can be counted between shou
shoulder. From the illustration the pendants seem to
shape of long rectangles; however, as the figure itse
intact, it is possible that the points have been broke
that the pendants originally resembled ours more cle
presence of this figure it seems as if there could be no d
the Mycenæan pendants were worn, not hanging from
but on the breast, perhaps in imitation of the we
Egyptian breast-pendants.

In the Tiryns figurine the pendants seem to be fast
broad band, likewise adorned with bosses, and reach

---

[1] F. Studniczka, *Beiträge z. Geschichte d. Altgriechischen Tracht* (
pp. 121-123 ; see also Helbig, *Epos*, p. 207.

[2] This breast-plate is given in Helbig, *Epos*, p. 175, Fig. 48, wl
references will be found.   [3] *Il.* xiv. 181.

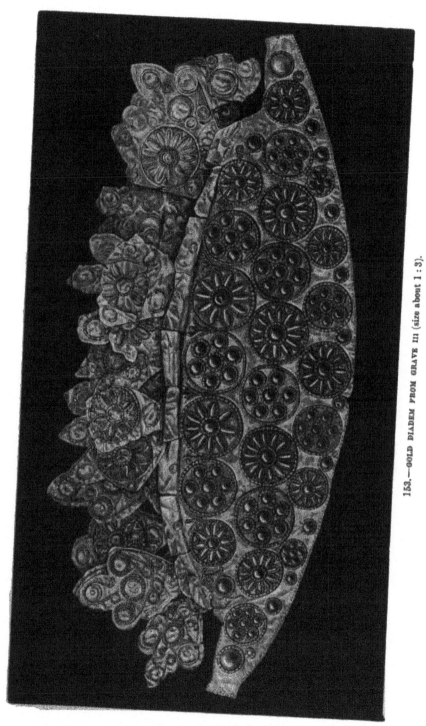

153.—GOLD DIADEM FROM GRAVE III (size about 1 : 3).

· shoulder to shoulder. The further question now arises whether
the so-called diadems may not also have been worn on the
breast. Their shape, however, seems scarcely adapted to this.
Had our gold plates been worn like the band supporting the
pendants on the figurine, they would have been shaped like
crescents, instead of ovals. Besides, head-frontlets accord with
Mycenæan custom; almost all the terra-cotta figurines wear
them; and finally, Dr. Schliemann's account of the find decides
the point. He says: " On the head of one of the three bodies was
found the splendid crown of gold " (Fig. 153), and again:
" Around the head of another of the three bodies was found the
magnificent and artistically worked diadem (Fig. 149), *to which
was still attached part of the skull.*" These objects must therefore still be looked upon as diadems. As to the breast-pendants,
it is possible that they were fastened on to a band made of
leather or some other perishable material.

The contents hitherto described, *i.e.* the great diadems and
pendants, give the finds from graves I and III a unique importance. Plates resembling these diadems have also been found in
the other graves, but they are always much smaller and more
insignificant, and some of them at all events were destined to a
different purpose; pendants like those of these two graves are
not found again. As a number of the objects in grave III, such
as earrings, hair-pins, bead necklaces, are only worn by women,
and as Dr. Schliemann has concluded from the shape of the bones
that the bodies are those of women, it already seems highly
probable, without further proof, that women were buried in these
two graves. The point is confirmed by the observation that
while the remaining graves were all packed with weapons, in
graves I and III no single sword or dagger, not one spear or
arrow-head, was found. We must therefore further conclude that
only women were buried in these graves; accordingly, among the
Mycenæans the large diadems and breast-pendants we have
described were exclusively part of women's apparel.

The diadems and pendants help us to a further conclusion.
As all the gold plates in the first grave are identical in workmanship, the three bodies to which they belong must have been
buried at about the same epoch. Between the first and third
graves a considerable interval of time can be noticed. The
diadems of the third grave show a far more developed scheme of

decoration, and must therefore belong to another and more luxurious period. Moreover, the two last diadems with their corresponding pendants differ from one another. While one group is merely adorned with richer and more advanced combinations of the circle, which was already found on the diadems of the first grave, the second diadem is enriched by a crest of gold leaves, and the pendants by additional tassels. Thus the whole of the third grave with its contents belongs to a later period than the first; and further, within the grave the body adorned with the richer ornaments must have been buried later than the others. This second proposition cannot receive further confirmation from the other finds, as it is impossible to ascertain how

156.—GOLD CROSS FROM GRAVE I (size about 4 : 5).

these were apportioned among the bodies; on the other hand, the first proposition, that grave I was much more simply furnished than grave III, is confirmed by a whole series of facts.

We shall now proceed to examine the contents of each grave separately.

The only other gold ornaments in grave I were a number of great crosses. One of these is given in Fig. 156; as many as fourteen perfect instances and a few fragments have been collected, so that five would belong to each body. The pattern of the crosses is that of four laurel leaves meeting at right angles; these are cut out in two plates, fastened together in the middle by a small bronze nail with broad head. Each leaf is decorated with three bosses along its spine, and all round the edges runs a leaf pattern like the one surrounding the bosses on one of the diadems from grave III (Fig. 149). The edges of the leaves had not, as was supposed, been strengthened by a piping of wire.

The pin in the centre of these crosses suggests that they were fastened to some solid object, like a wooden jewel-casket, or else that they studded a leather girdle. Still, we may adhere to the original explanation that they were stitched on to garments. In real life they were doubtless more securely fastened; for the apparel of the dead the simple pin bent round at the back would suffice.

The objects of other metals from this grave are a narrow bronze knife-blade, about 8 inches long; the gilt rim of a bronze vase, adorned with a leaf pattern; and a much-corroded copper ring, about the size of a bracelet.

A number of partly cylindrical, partly egg-shaped objects of blue paste, with a hole pierced through them, were also found. They had evidently been strung together for necklaces. Two-and-twenty are of the shape shown in Fig. 157, four others are composed of four cylinders juxtaposed (Fig. 158), and one or two had a more oval shape.

157, 158.—GLASS BEADS FROM GRAVE I (size 4 : 5).

Beyond the small fragment of a box of bone with an incised design apparently representing a flower-stem, the other objects yielded by this grave were all of terra-cotta; for example, first two small female figures, exactly similar to those found in such numbers elsewhere on the citadel (Figs. 159, 160). The heads of both are broken off, the arms are raised in a very clumsy " sickle shape " attitude. The colouring is red on the natural yellow of the clay; under the breast, in Fig. 159 round the neck as well, a horizontal line has been drawn, and the space between waist and neck has been covered with slanting hatchings. In Fig. 159 two lines descend from the waist.

This same method of decoration is found in almost all

statuettes of this kind, except that sometimes more lines run
downwards from the waist than in our example.   As these lines
and the closer lines on the breast and arms are never found on
the head, they must indicate the folds of the garments; they

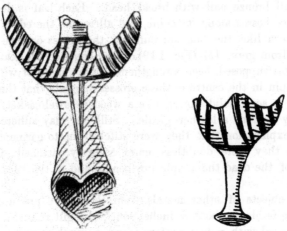

159, 160.—TERRA-COTTA IDOLS FROM GRAVE I (size 4 : 5 and 3 : 4).

suggest a fuller scheme of drapery over the breast, and closer-
fitting folds over the lower part of the figure.   The horizontal
line round the neck shows the upper finish of the garment, and
the line round the waist the girdle.

The rest of the find consists of terra-cotta vases, and the
number found in this grave almost equals that of all the other
graves put together.   They are of that fine yellowish-brown clay
which distinguishes all the vases of Mycenæan fabric; they are
all made on the potter's wheel, and have very thin sides, so that
they are characterised by that lightness for which later Greek
vases are justly celebrated.   They may be divided into two
classes according to their ornamentation.   In the class which
preponderates in this grave, the design is carried out in a dark
brown lustrous varnish on the natural clay.   Where this varnish
has been injured, or been thinly laid on, it has various paler
shades down to a dull yellowish brown.   As a rule, the foot and
neck of the vase are uniformly covered with this varnish: the
body, on the other hand, is covered all round with designs, which
are consistently borrowed from marine plants or animals.   Thus,
on the finest instance (Fig. 161), the stalk of a seaweed winds

upwards; from either side of it spring smaller twigs and beautiful triangular leaves, here and there in the intervening spaces are
small five-rayed polyps. In Fig. 162 an umbelliferous plant
appears to be growing between two lettuce-like leaves. On four
others (see Fig. 163) creepers alternate with a curious double

161-163.—TERRA-COTTA VASES FROM GRAVE I (sizes 1 : 4, 1 : 3, and 1 : 4).

object, which has been doubtless correctly explained as an open
shell. The small low bowl (Figs. 164 and 165) is decorated
outside with stars and points, inside with small polyps. These
are apparently the "argonauts," so common in the Mediterranean.

All these vases are painted with the lustrous varnish
mentioned above, and, with the single exception of the bowl, are

all of the same shape. They have full bodies, with broad round spouts, and three or four small handles on the shoulder. The two remaining vases from the same grave are clearly distinguishable from these. Both are painted in a dull brown and red colour, and they stand completely alone both in their

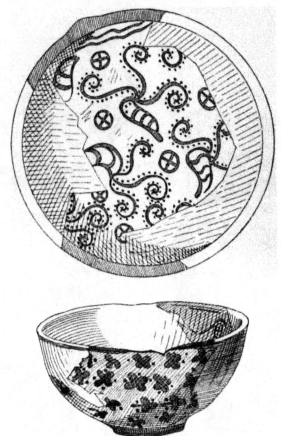

164, 165.—TERRA-COTTA VASES FROM GRAVE 1.

decoration and in their shape. The big vase (Fig. 166) is almost spherical. It has a narrow neck, which, to judge from the small portion left, ended in the long beak - like spout which is characteristic of the vases of grave VI. Around the body runs a broad band of narrow brown lines, alternating with wide red ones. On the neck are two broad red circles, and between them, in front, opposite the only handle, are two plastic imitations of the human breast. The shoulder is decorated with elaborate spirals. The other vase, also painted with a dull colour, has the shape of a bowl with two large handles on the shoulders. Its decoration also consists of simple horizontal lines and a band of spirals.

The relation of the vases with varnish to those with dull paint within this grave, holds good for the whole class of Mycenæan vases. All the more important examples of this class

166.—TERRA-COTTA VASE FROM GRAVE I (size 1 : 4).

of vases, which spreads over the islands of the Archipelago as far as Rhodes and Crete, and on the west as far as Sicily and Sardinia, have been collected and published by Drs. Furtwängler and Löschcke for the German Archæological Institute.[1] They divide the whole of these vases into two classes, the one painted in lustrous varnish, the other in a dull colour; and they have proved that the vases with varnish employ as ornaments natural objects, especially those connected with the sea, such as

[1] *Mykenische Vasen. Vorhellenische Thongefässe aus dem Gebiete des Mittelmeeres.* (Berlin 1886).

seaweed, shells, polyps, and sea-nettles; those with dull brown
paint employ linear ornaments, and above all the spiral.
Further, they connect this linear ornamentation with that of the
oldest seats of civilisation in Cyprus, Thera, Sicily, Assyria,
Phœnicia, and with the systems still followed nowadays among
barbarous nations. The lustre paint, on the other hand, they
consider to be a genuine and exclusively Greek method. "Only
Greeks, and those who can be proved to have learnt it from
Greeks, like the Etruscans, the Iapygians, and certain Cypriote
fabrics, have painted with lustrous varnish; the Mycenæan vases
show us the beginnings of this important innovation."

Although the result of these observations seems to be that
the painting of vases in a dull colour came into use earlier than
the lustre-painting, yet every dull-coloured vase need not be older
than the lustre vases. In the first grave the technique of the
gold diadems, as we saw, proved that the bodies were buried
almost simultaneously; therefore the vases which were deposited
with them cannot be far removed from one another in date.

At that time vases with lustre paint and vases with dull
paint must have been manufactured side by side, and the question
whether a greater number of the one or of the other class was
found in a grave cannot have any weight in fixing the date of
that grave. It is more likely that the two kinds were not
manufactured in the same place. If we take into account the
wide distribution of the so-called Mycenæan vases, we are
astonished at the conformity in the clay, the shape, and the
systems of decoration. This homogeneous character has long ago
led to the conviction that the vases were not always manufactured
where they were found, but that they formed the staple of an
extensive trade carried on between the islands and the coasts of
the Greek Sea. Hitherto, however, no fixed place of manufacture has been ascertained. It would be a mistake to imagine
there was only one central fabric. If, on the other hand, there
were several, it would then be easy to understand why in one
place the traditional oriental manner was preserved, with its dull
washes and its designs clearly imitated from the flat, hammered
hoops and the wire spirals of metal work, while in another place
the painter was already using a new lustrous paint, and had
realised that he was not working in a stubborn material, but with
a brush that gave him the power of imitating every living form.

We now turn to the finds from the third grave, whose chief
objects, the diadems and pendants, have been described and
figured above. Beside the three full-grown women, there lay in
this grave two bodies of children, to which various objects can
easily be attributed. Not only were the little faces covered with
tiny masks of gold leaf, in one of which the eyes were cut out,
while in both the forms were moulded by the hand over the

167.—GOLD CROSS FROM GRAVE III (size 2 : 3).

face itself; but the hands and feet were likewise enveloped in
gold leaf, which still shows clearly the shape of the fingers and
toes.

The gold ornaments next in order of importance are six
crosses similar to the fourteen crosses from grave I, though of more
elaborate shape and design. The simplest is given in Fig. 167,
the most elaborate in Fig. 168. In each instance a cross of
narrow lancet-shaped leaves is laid on a cross of broad leaves,
the four arms of which are imitations in the one case of the
laurel leaf, in the other most likely of the fig leaf. The narrow
cross is quite smooth in Fig. 167, but in Fig. 168 it is decorated

with a branch of symmetrically opposed leaves. Through the
centre of the cross we again have a pin with a broad head;
unfortunately nothing definite can be arrived at with regard to
the use of these crosses any more than in grave I.

The annexed illustrations give three interesting ornaments

168.—GOLD CROSS FROM GRAVE III (size 3 : 7).

(Figs. 169-171). The only explanation offered of them hitherto
has been that they served "to hold together locks of hair."[1] In
spite of their size they are undoubtedly earrings. Each ornament
is one of a pair, and in Fig. 171 the little ring which passed
through the lobe of the ear is still preserved; in the other
instances it is lost, but the point where it should be fixed at the

[1] See *Mycenæ*, p. 195, for this interpretation of these particular ornaments; and
Helbig, *Epos*, p. 242, etc., for the Homeric custom of tying plaits or locks of hair
with gold or silver "holders" (cf. *Iliad*, xvii. 52).

end of the ornament is so much worn on the inside, that
identally obtain a proof that these earrings had been worn
time during life.   The ear-pendant in Fig. 171 consists of
ld plates in *repoussé* open work ; they were joined together

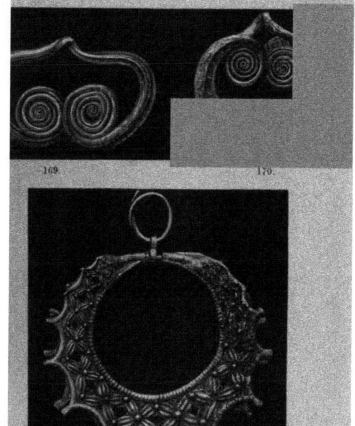

169-171. —GOLD EARRINGS FROM GRAVE III (size 5 : 6).

ling over the edges, and have now got separated from one
r.   This pair was probably not worn in life, but made
ly as an ornament for the dead.   The pattern on Fig. 170
elled.
e ladies of Mycenæ were evidently in the habit of loading

9

themselves with gold.   It would be difficult to match even their hair-pins for size and weight.   One of these, originally thought to be a brooch, is given in Fig. 172 ; the pin, which is much too broad and long for a brooch, is of silver.   The bent upper end supports a semicircular ornament, within which is a female figure with upraised arms.   She wears a necklace round her throat, and a bracelet on her left arm near the shoulder.   Her dress flows

172.—GOLD HAIR-PIN WITH SILVER STEM FROM GRAVE III (natural size).

downwards in long parallel folds.   The encircling frame apparently consists of small leaves, growing on long stalks which end in lotus blossoms.

In Fig. 173 again, we have two views of a hemispherical ball of rock-crystal, which must have been the head of a hair-pin. The ball is hollow, and inside the hollow are traces of a pattern of pointed arches carried out in bright red and white.   Many gold sheaths have also been found in which bronze or wooden pins must have been encased; thus forming a kind of hair-pin, which would of course be of no use except as an ornament for the dead.

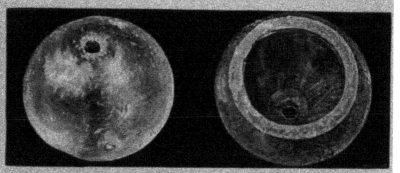

173.—BALL OF ROCK-CRYSTAL FROM GRAVE III (natural size).

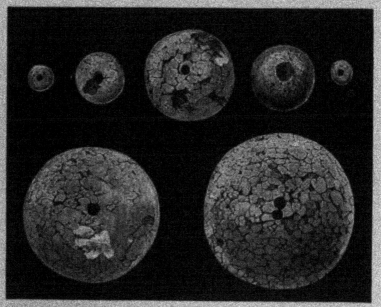

174.—AMBER BEADS FROM GRAVE III (natural size).

The high head-dress of the Mycenæan women is further confirmed by the representation on the gold ring found outside the graves, and given below, Fig. 281.

An extraordinary number of fragments of necklaces were

found.   In the first place, several amber beads of the most various sizes (Fig. 174).   They are now of a dark yellow colour, and are cracked all over.   The chemical analysis made for Dr. Schliemann by Dr. O. Helm, of Danzig, has shown that these beads are most closely allied, not to Sicilian amber, but to that of the Baltic, whence they probably came.   The Sicilian and Upper Italian amber, says Dr. Helm, has absolutely no succinic acid ; only Baltic amber contains it in a proportion of three to seven per cent.   The beads from the Mycenæan graves contain six per cent of succinic acid, and must therefore come from the Baltic, for "there has been no instance hitherto of a product, physically and chemically identical with the Baltic amber, being found in another spot."

With the amber agate beads have also been found, and lenticular gems of sardonyx or amethyst adorned with spirals or

175, 176.—GOLD ORNAMENTS OF NECKLACES (size 5 : 6).

even with figure-subjects, and finally gold ornaments which were probably threaded together to form necklaces, as they always have a tubular perforation lengthways.   Some are given in Figs.

177-179.—GOLD INTAGLIOS FROM GRAVE III (natural size).

175 and 176 ; these are composed of a hollow spine with wire spirals soldered together on each side of it.   Another kind is seen in Figs. 177-179, three rectangular ornaments, also perforated, and adorned with figure-subjects in intaglio.   On the first a man is fighting with a lion, which he has seized round the neck with his left hand, while with his right hand he thrusts his

sword into the beast's throat. The lion has clutched hold of the man's outstretched leg with his front claws. The man wears a sort of bathing-trousers, the regular costume on the so-called "Island-stones," or oldest gems from the Greek Archipelago : its details can now be more accurately determined from the recent finds in the bee-hive tomb near Amyklæ. The drawing, especially of the man's figure, is surprisingly natural and easy.

The skill of the artist is still more admirable in the second example, where we have a scene of two warriors in close combat. The one is pressing forward lustily from the left, and thrusts his sword into the neck of his sinking foe just above the edge of the shield. The conqueror appears to wear no other garment beyond the one mentioned above. The lines behind his back are not clear, they may be the ill-preserved outline of a shield. The conquered man is almost completely covered by his large round shield. He wears a helmet, apparently with a crest and big plume. The bipartite shield is strongly arched ; it is decorated with a double row of points ; these are doubtless the bosses which have been found in such numbers in the men's graves, and to which we shall return later on.

On the third ornament is 'represented a lion looking back, while running swiftly away to the right. The bent forelegs do not mean that the beast has sunk on the ground, but are merely expressive of swift running. Later art, even in the seventh century, rendered rapid motion in the same manner, *e.g.* on the metopes of Selinus, on black-figured vases, etc. Under the animal is a clear indication of rocky ground.

A number of tiny figures in gold plate found here were destined to be stitched on to garments as trimming. Among the most important are a few representations of female divinities. Figs. 180 and 181 each show a naked female figure, standing upright with hands crossed over the breast. Head and feet are turned to the left, but the rest of the body faces full to the front, according to the method usual in archaic art. The head is bound by a diadem made up of large balls ; it bears a close resemblance to the diadems from the first and third graves. Above the figure hovers a dove ; in Fig. 181 two more doves are flying away, one on each side. Fig. 180 is a simple *repoussé* gold plate, hollow at the back, and pierced with six holes to sew it on by. Fig. 181, on the other hand, was meant to be seen on both sides, for it consists of two plates equally wrought, and fastened together by the two rivets visible in the middle of the body and

180, 181.—FIGURES OF ASTARTE IN GOLD LEAF FROM GRAVE III (natural size).

between the knees. The exact way in which this object was worn is not known, but very probably it formed the head of a hair-pin. Both statuettes may be safely assumed to represent Aphrodite, who, as the Phœnician Astarte, had already received the dove as her attribute, and is the only female divinity ever represented quite nude.

One of two duplicate little female images in gold plate is given in Fig. 182. The figure is clothed and is turned full to the

182.—SEATED FEMALE FIGURE IN GOLD LEAF FROM GRAVE III (natural size).

front in a sitting posture; only the feet are here again turned, the one to the right, the other to the left. The hands are joined on the breast. The garment on the upper part of the figure falls in a bulging fold below the breast, and the skirt forms one large fold between the knees. It is adorned with two rows of points and several plain stripes which may represent tucks (see p. 276). The points or discs are probably identical with the round gold plates found in this grave in numbers exceeding 700 (Figs. 189-192). The sitting attitude of the figure, the arms folded on the breast, the full-face position of the head, all correspond so closely to the ancient figure of Cybele on the rocky side of Mount Sipylos near

Magnesia,[1] a figure which goes back to a mythical Greek past, that we may venture to see in our gold trinket an image either of Cybele or of the Great Mother Rhea.

Many might resent the supposition that these sacred images served as ornaments; but in Egypt small effigies of the gods were strung together in numbers and worn round the neck or on the breast, and the modern custom of wearing a cross on a neck-ribbon is scarcely different.

There may also be a religious significance attaching to the little house in Fig. 183. It was found in duplicate in this grave,

183.—TEMPLE IN GOLD LEAF FROM GRAVE III (natural size).

and three more exactly similar instances were found in grave V. It affords a most interesting example of the complete elevation of a building; this is all the more valuable as only the ground-plan of even the best preserved of the actual buildings of that remote period has been found. Our little gold plate shows first a foundation of well-jointed slabs; above this follow three niches, apparently framed by wooden beams; the central niche is the highest. In the midst of each stands a column with a capital composed of

[1] The famous so-called "Niobe." See W. M. Ramsay, *J. H. S.* ii. p. 33, "Sipylos and Cybele."

two square slabs. The line shaped like a calyx, within which the column stands, is at first sight enigmatical.

The central opening is further surmounted by an upper part; first four superimposed beams followed by a framed rectangular space, which is adorned with two semicircular ornaments turned back to back. The whole erection is crowned by an object of peculiar shape. The low side niches also end in ornaments, on each of which perches a dove.

This triple division of the façade reappears on Lycian tombs built in imitation of wooden houses. The ground-plans of the palaces of Troy, Tiryns, and Mycenæ, where the front is invariably formed by two columns standing between two antæ, further show that this is the typical façade for the most ancient Greek buildings. Moreover, the central upper-structure confirms in a most satisfactory manner the conjecture offered on many sides that these ancient buildings were of the basilica type—a raised central nave between two aisles. The windows which let in air and light, and at the same time afforded an escape to the smoke of the hearth, were introduced in the walls that rose above the aisles. Dr. Dörpfeld has already thought of this construction for the roof of the palace of Tiryns, the ground-plan of which is the only one completely preserved. In this case, however, special reasons have led him to conclude that the central raised structure was not continued the whole length of the chief room up to the vestibule, but only covered the four pillars in the centre.[1] The little gold house, on the other hand, seems to represent a building where the central upper structure is continued up to the front. Had it only existed far back on the roof, it would not have been visible to the spectator standing in front of the façade, and would consequently not have been represented, as it is here, crowning the façade.

We may therefore consider the rectangle of the upper structure to represent a window. The semicircles are introduced either to fill up the space or as ornaments on the shutters. The curved lines under the columns of the niches should be interpreted in the same manner: they merely cover the empty space, or else they are patterns decorating the doors. Still the position of the columns themselves in the centre of the openings remains a problem. Perhaps the artist wished to indicate single columns

---

[1] *Tiryns*, ch. v. p. 215, etc.

or rows of columns standing in the interior, and clumsily showed one through each entrance.

It seems impossible to take the crown of the central structure to be an altar, as some are inclined to do. It seems to be a simple akroterion. The doves at the corners are too certainly suggestive of an Aphrodite or Astarte cultus, for the whole building to be considered as merely secular.

184, 185.—GOLD PLATES FROM GRAVE III (natural size).

The other ornaments destined to be sewn on to garments are chiefly in the shape of two animals facing one another heraldically in the scheme which the Gate of the Lions has made familiar. At

186.—FLYING GRIFFIN IN GOLD PLATE FROM GRAVE III (natural size).

one time we have stags, as in Fig. 184 (10 examples), at another cat-like creatures (Fig. 185) supported on a palm tree as on a bracket. Swans are also found and eagles, the oldest prototypes of the double eagle. As instances of one animal alone, we have, in addition to foxes and jackals, the sphinx of Fig. 187, which is repeated as often as six times, and once we find a flying griffin

(Fig. 186). Some of these ornaments were fixed on to pins to serve as hair-pins. However, as most of them are not pierced at all (e.g. the octopus of Fig. 188, of which eighteen replicas have

187, 188.—SPHINX AND OCTOPUS IN GOLD PLATE FROM GRAVE III (natural size).

been found, and another similar octopus, with ten replicas), it is difficult to tell exactly how they were fastened.

189.—GOLD PLATE FROM GRAVE III (natural size).

In addition to these no less than 701 large round gold plates have been found in this grave: we can only imagine that they served as ornaments for dresses. Not one of them shows any trace of how they were fastened. Dr. Schliemann found them

190, 191.—GOLD PLATES FROM GRAVE III (natural size).

" as well below as above and around the bodies."[1]   They may
have been fixed on the garments with some kind of glue,[2] so that
with the garments which they adorned they would enfold the body
on all sides (Figs. 189-192).

The patterns on these beautiful and exquisitely worked plates
show us the Mycenæan technique in all its wealth of design.
We find in them, in equal proportion, the two styles of decoration
which may be distinguished on the vases of the first grave; in
imitation of natural objects, not artistically copied, but con-

192.—GOLD PLATE FROM GRAVE III (natural size).

ventionalised, we find cuttle-fish, butterflies, and palm leaves; as
an echo of the old metal work we have patterns composed of
circles, wave-lines, and spirals.

These same round plates, adorned in one case with a
butterfly, in the other with a pattern of leaf and circle combined,
are utilised as trays for two small pairs of scales, evidently

---

[1] *Mycenæ*, p. 165.

[2] It would seem reasonable to suppose that they were kept in place by a " button-
hole " stitch all around the rim—much as pieces of glass, etc., are fixed to Eastern
stuffs up to this day.—(Tr.)

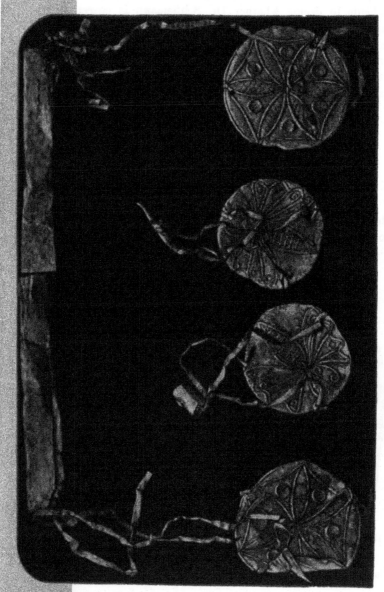

193.—SCALES IN GOLD PLATE FROM GRAVE III (see above 6 : 1).

destined only as furniture for the dead (Fig. 193). Only the thin
gold leaf covering of the beams of the scales has been preserved.
it undoubtedly clothed a wooden or bronze bar: the cords which
support the trays are quite thin strips of gold leaf. It is
difficult to decide whether Dr. Schliemann is correct when he
attributes a symbolic significance to these scales, and asserts that
as on Egyptian grave-paintings, so here also the good and the
evil deeds of the dead were to be weighed with them. May we
not rather have here an illustration of Greek modes of thought,
naïvely realistic and utterly opposed to all mysticism, so that

194.—BRONZE KNIFE-BLADE FROM GRAVE III.

the scales are simply to be looked upon as a gift just as necessary
to the worthy housewife in her grave as sword and drinking-cup

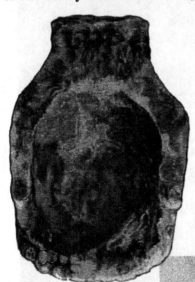

195.—ALABASTER SPOON FROM GRAVE III
(size 7 : 10).

are to the man in his? At
any rate, this would not be the
only article of household furniture discovered in this grave
where only women were buried.
Here also was found a bronze
blade, which owing to its shape
cannot possibly have belonged
to a sword or a dagger, and is
probably a piece of kitchen
furniture (Fig. 194), just like
the alabaster spoon in Fig. 195.
The latter has the shape of
two hands juxtaposed so as to
form a hollow. So too, in the
lower city, M. Tsountas has
noticed that small knives were
only found in the women's
graves.

Among other gold finds we
have a cup (Fig. 196), charmingly decorated with two rows of

fish; the cup proper is beaten out of a single plate, the handle is riveted on. Likewise the gold box (Fig. 197) is not soldered, but the bottom is made fast to the sides merely by folding over the edges. The lid in this box and in the following three vases is fastened on by means of a wire. The same arrangement is

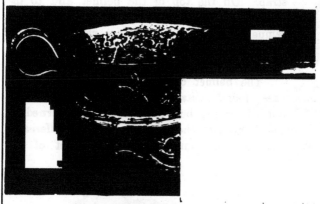

196, 197.—GOLD CUP AND BOX FROM GRAVE III (size 3 : 8).

often found in the Trojan vases, just as in Homer the lids of coffers are fastened down by skilfully tied knots.[1] The gold vessels given in Figs. 199-201 are exceedingly small. One is a shallow round box. The two others are shaped like *amphoræ*; the one, decorated with a leaf pattern, consists of two separate pieces one above the other; the other, of which a somewhat larger duplicate has been found, is quite smooth. It is probable that these miniature water-jugs and caskets were laid by the side of the children's corpses in imitation of the real objects offered to grown-up people.

A few other vases of silver, a cup of the same material, and some copper caldrons need no special description. On the other hand, among the objects made of the so-called Egyptian porcelain—a fine white paste with a sand-like grain—one fragment with the helmeted head of a warrior is of special interest. It is published here for the first time (Fig. 198). The face is shown in profile. The nose is large, the eye, which is big and staring, has its pupil

[1] *Od.* viii. 443-445. "Now when the steadfast goodly Odysseus heard this saying, forthwith he fixed on the lid, and quickly tied the curious knot, which the lady Circe once on a time had taught him."

given in black paint.   The neck is concealed by the upper rim of
a huge shield.   The helmet is low, and fits closely to the head.
It consists of several superimposed bands, each of which is

separately plaited, probably out of leather
thongs.   Over the ear can be seen the chin
strap.   On the top of the helmet and to the
front is an appendage shaped like a horn; the
remnant of a second appendage can be seen to
the centre, but it is unfortunately impossible
to know how it terminated.

198.—FRAGMENT OF
A VESSEL IN EGYP-
TIAN PORCELAIN
(natural size).

The helmet of the warriors on the large
vase found outside the graves has similar
horned crests, but these are both turned to
the front, and the whole helmet is differently
fashioned.   We have a closer analogy in the helmet of the

199-201.—GOLD VESSELS FROM GRAVE III (size 2 : 3).

Schardana (Fig. 202), who are represented as enemies of the
Egyptians in the chronicles of Ramses III.   Here we again meet

with the low semicircular helmet, fitting close to the
head, with a horn to the back and front and a knob
in the middle.   The Schardana are generally understood to be the inhabitants of Sardis, and it is highly
probable that the shape and crowning of the helmet
in question came from Asia Minor to Mycenæ.   The

202.—HELMET
OF   THE
SCHARDANA.

only painted vase found in this grave is given in Fig. 203.   It
shows us a combination of linear and naturalistic decorations

rendered in lustrous paint. The body is surrounded by two
bands; above these, palm leaves are inserted within circles, which
are bound together by an undulating line.

In the Museum of the Polytechnicon a few small vases are
placed along with the contents of this grave, though they do not
belong to them, but have a quite distinct provenience. Dr.
Schliemann gives the following account of their find : " At
about 9 feet above the mouth of the third grave, I discovered
close to it, on the slope of the rock, at a depth of 21 feet below
the former surface, a number of skeletons of men, which had
evidently not been on the funeral pyre, but were so much
destroyed by moisture that none of the skulls could be taken

203.—VASE FROM GRAVE III (size 7 : 10).

out entire. The only objects found with these skeletons were
knives of obsidian, and five very pretty hand-made vases."[1] One
of them is shown in Fig. 204. Unlike the vases mentioned
above, these are made of a somewhat coarse red clay. Their
ornamentation consists of simple bands and wave-lines, given in
a dull dark purple on a dull ground of light green. These vases
belong then to the first great group with dull paint, but their
rough make certainly places them lowest in the scale of the
pottery found at Mycenæ. Were it not that one more vase from
grave II shows these peculiarities, we might believe that this

[1] *Mycenæ,* p. 162.

remarkable find on the slope of the rock had yielded us the
relics of a period preceding the pit-graves. The most recent
finds in the graves of the lower city have brought to light
similar examples. In many cases skeletons were laid in front
of the doors of these graves with meaner and ruder offerings,
though apparently buried simultaneously with the corpses lying

204.—TERRA-COTTA VASE FOUND NEAR GRAVE III (size 4 : 5).

inside. M. Tsountas is right in seeing here an illustration of
the Homeric custom, by which slaves or prisoners of war were
slain in honour of the illustrious dead and buried with them.
The skeletons above the pit-graves may be explained in the same
manner, only in that case, instead of belonging to the women's
grave III, they must belong to the men's grave IV, which is
close by.

6. The Second Grave

The second grave is the smallest of all. It only measures 9 feet by 10 feet. It contained only one corpse, which the whole furniture of the tomb shows to be that of a man; fragments of a bronze sword were found here, together with the spearhead of the same metal figured in Fig. 206. This spear-head terminates in a round socket, into which the shaft was fixed. On the side of the sheath is a ring, serving perhaps to fasten the curious object resembling a bag or a flag, which we see on the

205.—CUP FROM GRAVE II (size about 9 : 10).

spears in the great warrior vase (see below, Fig. 284). In this grave was found too the golden cup, Fig. 205, also beaten out of one piece of gold plate, and with its one handle riveted on. Around the upper portion runs an ornament composed of pointed arches; round the middle and the foot are double raised bands, whose slanting hatchings form the so-called herring-bone pattern.

As these objects prove beyond a doubt that a man was buried in this grave, we are at first somewhat astonished to meet with a gold diadem (Fig. 207). Its shape, however, is quite different from that of the diadems found in the women's graves. It is much narrower, and as it only broadens slightly in the middle, it resembles the fillets which we see round the brows of kings and poets in later and even the latest Greek art, and might quite well have been a masculine headgear. The other graves, however, will show us that these bands often lay in the grave in numbers far greater than there were bodies, and that some of them were found twisted round the bones of arms. It is probable, therefore, that they were armlets, and, moreover, that they were especially intended to be worn by men. For instance, the man riding on the bull in the Tiryns fresco wears such bands on his wrists and ankles, and also round his knees. It is noteworthy that in the decoration of this band the chief *motif*, the big circles linked together by tangents, with the small round bosses in the spaces near the tangents, recalls the system of ornamentation of the only terra-cotta vase found in grave III (see above, Fig. 203); only there the circles are filled by a palm leaf, here with a rosette composed of slanting leaves. Thus the second and third graves are probably closely related in time.

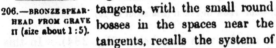

206.—BRONZE SPEAR-
HEAD FROM GRAVE
II (size about 1 : 5).

207.—GOLD DIADEM
FROM GRAVE II.

The other objects found in this grave are a small knife, three vases of the so-called Egyptian porcelain, and two painted vases. The shape of one of the latter is remarkable (Fig. 208). It has no handle, and terminates in a sharp point pierced with a hole, so that it may have served as a funnel. It is decorated with a reddish-brown varnish on the yellow ground of the clay. Round the neck, body, and foot are rows of bands. Both the intervening spaces are filled with large spirals somewhat

208.—TERRA-COTTA VASE FROM GRAVE II (size about 1 : 3).

carelessly drawn. The second painted vase is the one whose close analogy to those found on the edge of the third grave has already been noticed (Fig. 209). It is of coarse red clay, and hand-made. The whole surface has been washed over with a greyish yellow, and the ornaments, consisting of bands, a zigzag line, and a triangular pattern, are given in dull purple paint. In this grave we find the dull and the lustrous ware once more not only side by side, but related through the fact that both employ only the linear system of ornamentation borrowed from metal technique.

209.—TERRA-COTTA VASE FROM GRAVE II (size 1 : 2).

7. *The Fourth Grave*

The fourth grave was the largest, and in every respect the richest. The floor measures $16\frac{1}{2}$ feet by 22 feet; but the walls built against the sides and projecting 4 feet considerably diminish the area. In the grave "lay the bodies of five men; three of them were lying with the head to the east, and the feet to the west; the other two were lying with the head to the north, and the feet to the south."[1]

The graves we have considered up to now have shown us that the interpretation of many of the ornaments depends com-

[1] *Mycenæ*, p. 213.

pletely on the sex of the persons buried. The presence of certain objects exclusively pertaining to the one sex, and the absence of others belonging to the opposite sex, could always be satisfactorily explained by the answer that in graves I and III only women, in grave II only one man, were buried. In grave IV, however, the case is different, and therefore more perplexing. The great number of weapons of all kinds shows beyond a doubt that we are here chiefly concerned with men. On the other hand, various objects like hair-pins and a large massive bracelet have been found, which can only be regarded as articles of female apparel; yet the whole feminine outfit which we became acquainted with in graves I and III is far from being complete here; we notice more especially the absence of earrings and of the large breast-pendants.

The problem cannot be absolutely solved, though, after carefully weighing every circumstance, the conviction that three men and two women were buried in this grave gains upon us more and more.

Let us first consider the chief point on which the question turns. Dr. Schliemann enumerates as many as eight "diadems" as coming from this grave, and since the diadem which he puts down to grave III also belongs here according to M. Stamatakis's arrangement of the Museum, we get nine diadems in all. It is obviously impossible, since only five bodies were in the grave, that these should have all served as headgear, and it is unnecessary to discuss the ingenious theory by which Dr. Schliemann has tried to prove that perhaps several children's corpses were also buried in the grave, though every trace of their bones has disappeared. A band of similar shape to the one in Fig. 207, but of uniform breadth, and not tapering off at the ends, was found in grave V round the bone of an arm (see below, Fig. 257), and, as only men were buried in this grave, it can immediately be identified as a man's armlet. But bands of shapes different from this were also worn round the arm. In grave IV there was found round an arm a band, broad in the centre, and decreasing to a point at the sides, and finally terminating in a thin gold thread. It has the shape of the gold bands given in Figs. 148 and 149. We must then enquire which of the variously shaped "diadems" of the fourth grave can correctly preserve this name.

In the first place, we have two examples which are closely analogous to the large diadem with crest from grave III. The first, given in Fig. 210, also had a crest of small leaves riveted to it, but the crest, with the exception of a few fragments, has now disappeared. The second ornament in Fig. 211 resembles the first. It shows the same division into five fields by means of vertical bands, but in place of rosettes its three central spaces are filled with bosses of two sizes such as adorn the two corner spaces in Fig. 210, while in the corners a square pattern is repeated on each side. There is no separate crest, but the upper part of the diadem is itself shaped somewhat like a crest. This upper portion is adorned with three rows of small circular bosses.

Obviously these two bands were never intended to be worn round the arm. They are undoubtedly diadems, and it now only remains to decide whether they should be assigned to men or to women. Now we know that in this grave there were found thirteen gold crosses with arms shaped like laurel

210.—GOLD DIADEM FROM GRAVE IV
(size about 1 : 3).

leaves as in the crosses from graves I and III.   In the man's
grave II no such crosses
occur, nor in graves V and
VI, where it can also be
proved that only men were
buried. This seems to show
that these objects belonged
exclusively to female apparel.
Grave I taught us that some
five or six were found on
each body.   So that the
thirteen of this grave would
be correctly apportioned
between two female corpses.
Moreover, their patterns conclusively show that they
belong to the two diadems
(Figs. 212-214). They all
have circles and bosses, and
occasionally also they have
a leaf pattern recalling the
rosettes of the diadem with
crest of Fig. 210 ; they
even have the same oblique
hatchings along the edge.
The argument which proved
that the crosses always belonged to women's apparel
will therefore also apply to
the diadems, and can in
their case be strengthened
by the following circum-
stance. In grave II, with
the men's corpse, only one
small gold band was found,
and we have seen that it
was more probably worn
round the arm than on the
head. In the other men's
graves, V and VI, nothing

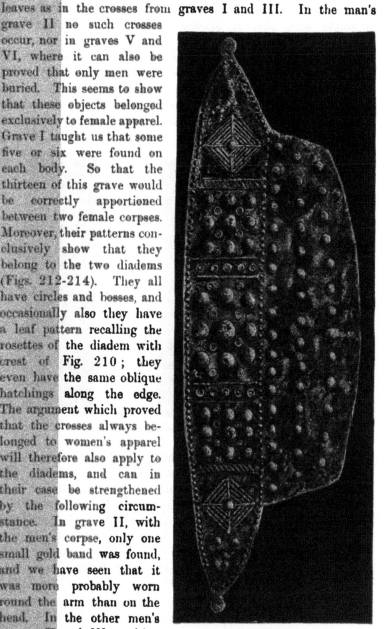

211.—GOLD DIADEM FROM GRAVE IV.

resembling a diadem has been found at all. Consequently
it would seem that at Mycenæ men were not buried with
diadems.

If we follow up these suggestions, and decide that two
women were buried in this grave, we are rewarded by finding
that a number of facts further support and strengthen our
conclusion. In the first place, we shall see that the ornaments in
Figs. 215-217 are hair-pins, and consequently portions of female
dress. The knob in Fig. 218 also probably belonged to a

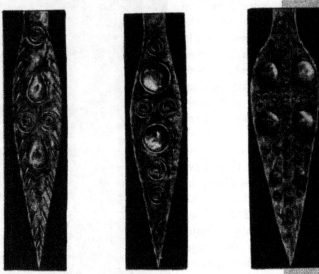

212-214.—ARMS OF GOLD CROSSES FROM GRAVE IV.

hair-pin; its upper point is finished off, but the lower point is
left open, and a gilt bronze pin was doubtless fixed into it. The
bracelet of Fig. 219, with its rosette of sun-rays set on a background of leaves, is very splendid. A comb has also been found;
its semicircular shape shows that it served to hold up the hair.
It is made of bone, but its back is covered with gold leaf. In
this grave tiny scales were again buried with the women. The
parts preserved are two thin fragments of gold plate, presumably
the outer coating of the scale beam.

To women's apparel belong further three of those same little
shrines with doves which we saw in grave III. These three new
instances are such exact replicas of the other two that they must

all have been cast from the same mould, or perhaps beaten out
with the same stamp; and this is an additional proof that these
two graves were closely connected in point of time.

Further, the necklaces, which were made of the countless

218.—GOLD HEAD
OF A HAIR-PIN
FROM GRAVE IV
(size 1 : 3).

215-217.—GOLD HAIR-PINS FROM GRAVE IV (natural size).

amber beads found in this grave, were certainly worn by women.
Finally, the two gold signet rings with the large and richly
carved intaglios (Figs. 220, 221) are so small that on a man's
hand of ordinary size they cannot be pushed lower than the
middle of the little finger, and must therefore have belonged

to women, although the exploits they represent are so thoroughly masculine.

On the first intaglio we see two men in a chariot hunting a stag. The chariot is of the shape we are familiar with from the grave *stelai*. Here also only one four-spoked wheel is given, behind which we must imagine the second wheel to be concealed. On the other hand, the chariot is distinctly drawn by a pair of horses. In it are two men, one of whom is leaning over to shoot at the stag. He holds his bow with his left hand, and with his right lets fly the arrow from the string. The other man stands erect; his hands are half raised to hold the reins, which, however, cannot be seen on the intaglio. Above the horses the stag is

219. —GOLD BRACELET FROM GRAVE IV (natural size).

bounding onwards and turning round its head. It must naturally be conceived as running in front of the chariot. As is often the case in the oldest art, the scene is compressed on account of the small space, and objects which should come one after the other are placed one above the other. Under and in front of the horses a waving line indicates the ground; along the upper edge of this intaglio, and still better in the second, we see leaf-shaped incisions, which may be intended for foliage or for clouds, or which more probably are merely brought in to fill up the space, like the spirals on the *stele*, Fig. 146, and the head of an ox and the foliage on the little gold plates given below, Figs. 260 and 261.

The second ring shows us a battle-scene. Four warriors are represented. The action culminates in the centre, where a warrior striding forward to the right has seized his opponent, who sinks on his knee before him, by the neck or by the hair, and is in the act of despatching him with his sword. The fallen man still tries to protect himself with his raised sword. From the right another warrior comes up to the rescue; he approaches under cover of his huge shield, and brandishes a long spear against the victor. On the other side of the group a fourth warrior sits resting on the ground, supporting himself on his right hand. His left knee is bent up close to his body, his right leg stretched out.

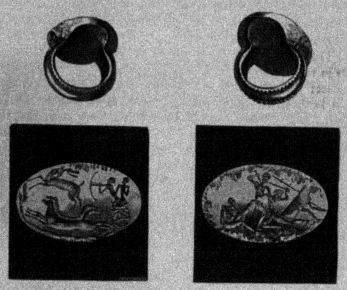

220, 221.—GOLD RINGS FROM GRAVE IV (natural size).

As on the former ring, so here, the men appear to be clothed only with aprons. But the warrior with the shield also wears a helmet, for the long plume can be distinctly recognised. The shield is not curved in at the sides, but quite straight; it is so strongly arched that it almost has the shape of a half-cylinder.

These rings complete the list of objects which we may safely allot to the two women buried in this grave. It would be satisfactory if it could be proved that these corpses were the same two which Dr. Schliemann found imbedded lengthways in the southern half of the grave, while the three others were lying crossways in the northern half. But the report of the find does not admit of this conclusion. Dr. Schliemann says: "Beginning the excavation of the lower strata of this tomb from the south side, I at once struck on five large copper vessels, in one of which were exactly one hundred very large and smaller buttons of wood, covered with plates of gold. . . . Close to the copper vessel with the gold buttons, I found a cow's head of silver with two long golden horns. . . . There were also found here two more cow heads of very thin gold plate, which have a double axe between the horns. . . . In further excavating from east to west I struck a heap of more than twenty bronze swords and many lances. . . . Some of the lance-shafts seemed to be well preserved, but they crumbled away when exposed to the air. . . . The two bodies with the head to the north had the face covered with large masks of gold plate in *repoussé* work." [1]

From this account it is clear that the two bodies with their heads to the north, with masks on their faces, and swords and lances close to their sides, were men, and that we must look for the women among the three corpses that lay with their heads to the east. This last conjecture is further confirmed by Dr. Schliemann's words: "I found with the three bodies whose heads were laid towards the east the two large golden signet rings and the large golden bracelet." [2]

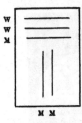

222.—THE FIVE CORPSES IN GRAVE IV.

A few other passages in the account of the excavations appear at first sight to challenge our supposition that two of the corpses were female, and to prove that only one woman was buried in this grave. The first point is easily disposed of. I assume beforehand that masks are especially characteristic of men's corpses. In this grave they covered the faces of both the bodies, which, to judge from the gifts of weapons, were certainly male; none are found in the women's graves I and III, and they reappear again in the men's grave V. Now Dr. Schliemann reports: "A third mask of much thicker gold plate (Fig. 223) was found covering the face of one of the three bodies which lay with the head to the east." [3] As the two skeletons lying north to south have been identified as men, this would then be the third male corpse, and the two remaining would be the women. However, the report proceeds:

[1] *Mycenæ*, p. 215.   [2] *Ibid.* p. 223.   [3] *Ibid.* p. 220.

y heavy gold mask was found at the head of
three bodies which had their heads turned to
closer examination we find that it represents
ead." A still closer inspection shows that this
had been fixed to a smooth surface by means of the
ontal plates projecting from the lion's head, and that it
ably served as a device for a shield. Anyhow, it is
a ogether improbable that this object ever covered the face of

223.—GOLD MASK FROM GRAVE IV (size about 1 : 3).

a dead person. If this difficulty may be considered disposed of,
we can provisionally return to our assumption of two female
corpses. Dr. Schliemann, however, says further: "The two bodies
which are turned with their heads to the east, whose faces were
covered with gold masks" (but one of these is the lion mask, which
had been previously stated to have been found "at the head"),
"also had their breasts covered with large gold breastplates. The

¹ *Mycenæ*, p. 222.

one is of massive gold, but without any ornamentation; the other is of a much thinner gold plate, and decorated with a *repoussé* work of borders of small circles, within which are five rows of shield-like ornaments with concentric circles. This latter breast-cover has at each of its extremities a hole for fastening it to the body."[1]

The breastplates also would obviously only be given to men; they are only found in this grave and in V. If two of the bodies lying crossways were really covered with breastplates, it would be difficult to grant that any but the last body was a woman's. But this difficulty has also received a satisfactory solution. The breastplate "without any ornamentation" which Dr. Schliemann speaks of is in the Museum among the other objects from this grave, the other is not to be found. Beyond the first breastplate, there is only one other belonging to grave V, but this cannot be the one meant in the description quoted above, for it has a totally different ornamentation (see below, Fig. 256). In conclusion, it is easy to recognise which is the object that was taken for a breastplate; it is nothing else but the second big diadem with the projecting upper portion in place of a crest (see above, Fig. 221). The "two borders of small circles," the division into five fields, the hole at each end, all these details are there. And if a further proof were needed to show that Dr. Schliemann really took this object for a breastplate, it is afforded by the small catalogue of the Mycenæ antiquities in Athens, where our diadem, which is labelled No. 274 in the Museum, is described as "petite cuirasse d'or très-mince avec ornement au repoussé."

What for an instant threatened to overthrow our theory of two female corpses now turns out to be its best support. The so-called breastplate which indicated a male body is now proved to be a large diadem, and can only have adorned a woman.

Moreover, the two women lay close to one another, for after the description of the last-mentioned object, Dr. Schliemann continues: "Close to the head of another body I found the beautiful golden crown"[1] (Fig. 210). He is certainly speaking of the same part of the grave, and of a head not covered by any mask. The net result is that three bodies had their faces covered with masks, and the remaining two had a diadem bound round their brow; the first were men, the latter women.

[1] *Mycenæ*, p. 228.　　　　[2] *Ibid.* p. 228.

Once certain that we are right in assuming that two women were buried in the grave, we can pass to the examination of the objects which formed the furniture of the three men buried in this grave. Among them the three masks are of the highest interest; in them the Mycenæan art rises for the first time beyond mere decoration, and attempts to solve the most difficult of artistic problems—the rendering of the human face. These masks show us a life-size human visage plastically modelled. The two which covered the faces of the bodies lying lengthways in the grave are so remarkably alike that only one of them has been figured here (Fig. 223). We see in it fairly regular features, a well-shaped nose of moderate size, a small mouth with full lips. The eyes are set close together and somewhat slanting. They are evidently closed, over the projecting eyeball a line marks the meeting of the lids; on either side of the line the eyelashes are rendered by small incised strokes; somewhat stronger strokes mark the brows on the projecting frontal bone.

All these characteristics are exactly reproduced on the second mask. The only noteworthy difference is that the ears are not quite so far from the eyes as in the first mask, and are more carefully shaped.

The third mask, which was found on the face of the man buried next to the women, has a totally different physiognomy (Fig. 224). The nose has 'been pressed out of shape, and is difficult to judge of, but the eyes are much bigger than in the first mask, almost spherical, and very prominent. As they are surrounded by sharp edges they give the impression of being wide open; however, as no inner markings are anywhere found in this mask, it is probable that the line marking the closed lids was only omitted through lack of skill. The eye-frame projects strongly, but the eyebrows are not marked. The mouth is rendered by a curved indenture, which goes off at each corner into a long line, so long that the ends can no longer be part of the mouth. Each end is joined by another line coming from the corner of the nose, and as the part thus enclosed seems somewhat raised, we probably have here the indication of a moustache, but the drawing of the separate hairs has been left out as in the case of the eyelashes and eyebrows. We must not imagine that the man wore only a moustache; he certainly had a full beard; however, since there is no trace of the latter on the mask, it may

have been quite slight, a fact which would mark the wearer of
the mask as young. The lower lip is very narrow. The ears are
completely misplaced, as the external cavity opens downwards
instead of to the front.

There can be no doubt that we have in these masks portraits

224.—GOLD MASK FROM GRAVE IV (size about 3 : 8).

of the deceased, chiefly on account of the closed eyes, which appear
once more in a mask of grave V. It is difficult to ascertain how
these masks were made. The plate is too thick to have been
moulded over the face of the dead, as was the case with the child's
mask from grave III; it is more likely that they were beaten out
on a wooden mould, like the numerous buttons and bosses found in

225.—GOLD BAND FROM
GRAVE IV.

this grave. These receive their patterns from
a bone core, which in several cases has been
preserved inside them. On it all the lines
which reappear on the gold plate have
previously been drawn.

The difference in the rendering of the
individual features between the two first
masks and the third is not to be attributed
merely to a different cast of countenance in
the persons portrayed. The dead man to
whom the third mask belonged had eyebrows,
lashes, and closed eyes as well as the other
two; but if these details are not expressed,
it is because the artist of the mask did not
understand how to do so. We may accordingly assume that this third mask belongs to
another and probably earlier period than the
other two, and that the man to whom it
belongs, namely the one who lay near the
two women, was buried before the other
men. The latter, to judge from the great
similarity of their masks, must have been laid
in the tomb at about the same period.

As I have already stated, if a mask
covered the face, it was hardly possible that
a band should go round the brow. As all
three men wore masks, and the two big
diadems have been appropriated to the
women, the remaining gold bands must have
been worn round the arm, as we have inferred in two other instances. In the
Museum, among the finds from this grave,
there is a gold band, each extremity of which
terminates in a gold thread; it is still clasped
round the bone of an arm. Now the question
arises whether these armlets were really worn
by men, or whether they ought not rather to
be attributed to the two women. The answer
to this is, first that a similar band was found
in the men's grave V, also bound round the

bone of an arm, and secondly, that there are several representations
of men with bands on their arms just above the wrist.   A further
argument in favour of some at least of these bands belonging to
the men is derived from their ornamentation.   The same pattern,
seen in the centre of the band given in Fig. 225, a rosette of
straight leaves with a rosette of slanting leaves on either side,
and laurel or olive twigs in the intervening spaces, reappears in
several objects undoubtedly pertaining to men's dress.   One of
these is given in Fig. 226.   It consists of a horizontal band
pierced at both ends ; from the centre of the band hangs a

226.—GOLD GAITER-HOLDER FROM GRAVE IV.

vertical strip strengthened by a rib down the middle, and
ending in a large round ring.   As one of these objects was
found round the knee of a corpse, it may be safely assumed that
they served to hold up the stuff or leather gaiters, which are the
predecessors of the greaves, and which we see on the warriors'
legs in the large vases we have so often referred to.   The
decorated band of these gaiter-holders was tied round the leg
just below the knee by means of a wire, and the vertical strip
hung down in front, and a button of the gaiter was fastened in
its loop.

The remaining gifts belong almost exclusively to one of the two great divisions, weapons and drinking-vessels. The weapons found are swords, daggers, spears, and arrows. We will take the swords first. Their blades are always of bronze; in fact iron has not been found in any one of the graves. They are all double-edged and of peculiar shape; they start with a considerable breadth, they gradually decrease along their great length, and finally end in a point. Dr. Schliemann had already remarked that they are much too slight in proportion to their length (3 feet) to have been used for the stroke. Several representations of combats have already shown us that the sword was always used for the thrust, e.g. on the intaglios of grave III and on the gold ring of grave IV (see Figs. 178 and 221). Some of the blades are decorated along their whole length with representations of running animals. One example from this grave has along each of its edges a long row of griffins, all exactly similar. They are worked in flat relief on the blade itself, and closely resemble the griffins of gold plate used as dress trimmings, from grave III (see above, Fig. 186). Dr. Schliemann could not mention these representations in his book Mycenæ; they were only discovered in the Museum, when the different objects were cleaned.

A still greater surprise was in store; when the dagger-blades, which were thickly coated with oxide, were cleaned, six of them revealed mar-

227. —AN INLAID DAGGER-BLADE FROM GRAVE IV.

vellous inlaid work. The first (Fig. 227) has a great lion-hunt on one side. On the left are five men, on the right three lions. The foremost man has been thrown on to his back by the furious onset of the first lion; his legs are entangled in his shield. The two men just behind are hurling their long spears against the forehead and into the jaw of the beast. The first man advances under cover of a large strongly-arched shield, curved in at the sides; the other man has a smaller rectangular shield slung on his back by means of a shoulder-strap. The fourth man is an archer; the fifth again a spearman, with a big notched shield slung behind him. Only the foremost lion stands his ground; he has already been wounded on the flank, and the two others have turned tail, and are running away.

This representation gives a great deal of interesting detail. We are already acquainted with the " bathing-trousers " costume of the men, but this is the first time that we have seen it clearly drawn. The two varieties of shields were also known to us before from the intagli and from gold coins. But the way in which they are slung is new, and throughout the whole of ancient art represented only here. Herodotos says that the Carians, a people who played a great part under Minos, the mythical king of Crete, were the first who invented handles for their shields.[1] Accordingly our dagger seems to belong to a period previous to that innovation. Further, it will be easy to detect many a calculated subtlety in the grouping of the figures. The men are represented in the most varied attitudes, and even the shields are allotted in such a manner that an oval notched shield alternates each time with a rectangular one. Quite as skilful is the treatment of the lions. The first one makes straight for his assailant, the second one has already taken to flight, but turns his head once more towards the scene of struggle, the third one has completely deserted the field and rushes away at full speed.

The effect of this powerful drawing is still further heightened by the use of colours; for the whole picture is formed by various metals inlaid on a thin bronze plate. This plate was then let into the blade. This method can be detected in all the blades of this grave and of grave V. The colours are apportioned as follows: the lions and the parts of the men shown as naked are inlaid in gold, the trousers and the shields in silver, while all accessories,

[1] Herod. i. 171.

such as shield-straps and devices and the patterns of clothes, are given in a black substance. The ground is coated with a dark enamel, on which the figures detach themselves admirably.

On the other side of this blade are represented a lion and five animals of the gazelle type. The lion has seized the hind-most, while the others are rushing away.

A second dagger found in the grave shows three lions running one behind the other. They are completely inlaid in gold, but their manes are rendered by a somewhat redder gold, and the lines on their legs and flank by a lighter gold than the remainder of the body; apparently the Mycenæans understood how to colour gold, probably by an admixture of copper in the one instance, and of silver in the other. The technique of this second sword varies from that of the first; the lions were first worked in relief on the bronze plate, which was inserted in the blade, and this relief was afterwards covered with the thin gold leaf. The lions detach themselves even better on the background than when they are merely inlaid.

The other daggers, which are no less remarkable, belong to grave V and will be discussed in their proper place. If we consider these objects, the care bestowed on the work, the life instilled into the scene, and the splendour of the colours, they give us a high conception of the civilisation which could produce them. There were plenty of discerning people, who held that the Homeric shields decorated with marvellous art, the splendid cups, the palaces of magical beauty, had not all been evolved out of nothing, but must have been suggested by things that actually existed. On the other hand, there were the faint-hearted, who held all this for idle phantasy and fable, because not supported by actual finds. Now we have the great civilisation of the Mycenæan period before our eyes, and can no longer doubt that this is the civilisation which underlay those Homeric descriptions, where every detail is so fondly dwelt upon. Our dagger-blades, for instance, show strikingly that these descriptions can only be thoroughly understood when we are in possession of their models. The shield of Achilles which Hephaistos cunningly fashioned, and adorned all over with bands of design representing town and country and vineyard, shepherd life and youthful dance, has been reconstructed countless times from Homer's description. Scene followed upon scene in neat circles, and

the whole was conceived after the fashion of the Phœnician
silver cups, the oldest *repoussé* work then known on Greek
soil.   But how the artists employed the various metals and
colours mentioned by Homer remained a mystery; this was mere
poetic phantasy on the part of the imaginative bard.   If, however,
we consider the shield to have been not in *repoussé* but in inlaid
work, then the meaning of the following verses immediately
becomes clear.

   " Also he set therein a vineyard teeming plenteously with

228.—SWORD-HILT FROM GRAVE IV   229.—GOLD POMMEL OF A SWORD-HILT FROM GRAVE IV
         (size 1 : 2).   (natural size).

clusters, wrought fair in gold; black were the grapes, but the
vines hung throughout on silver poles.   And around it he ran
a ditch of cyanus,[1] and round that a fence of tin." [2]

   " Also he wrought therein a herd of kine with upright horns,
and the kine were fashioned of gold and tin." [3]

   " Fair wreaths had the maidens, and the youths daggers of
gold hanging from silver baldrics." [4]

   Thus Homer is justified, and the Mycenæan daggers belong
undoubtedly to the art which inspired his descriptions.

   [1] See p. 117.   [2] *Il.* xviii. 561.   [3] *Ibid.* 573.   [4] *Ibid.* 597.

From the blades we pass to the hilts, the sheaths, and the baldrics from which they hung. The blade was fastened to a hilt by means of three or four rivets. The hilt is often of wood plated with gold. In this flimsy construction it would only be intended for the adornment of the dead. One example is given in Fig. 228. We can here clearly distinguish the three rivets, with scanty remnants of the blade, and the covering of gold plate with its rich ornamentation of spirals, rectangles, and dots. This hilt was assigned by Dr. Schliemann to grave V, but by M. Stamatakis to grave IV. The hilt ended in a pommel, which in the case of a gold hilt would also be of gold. In the majority of instances, however, these pommels are of bone or alabaster, and would then belong to a plain hilt wound round with thongs or hemp. Part of a golden pommel is seen in Fig. 229, and further on in Fig. 272. Those of bone or wood are of a hemispherical shape, and have on their flat side a socket into which the hilt was fixed (see Fig. 267). The annexed sketch (Fig. 230) is an attempt at showing what the sword-hilt with its pommel looked like. The shape is very similar to the one usual in the Middle Ages.

Only a few vestiges of the sheaths have been found. Like the core of the hilt they were of wood, or of leather, or sometimes, according to Dr. Schliemann, of thick folds of linen, particles of which have often been found stuck to the blades.[1] Dr. Schliemann is certainly right in assuming that a portion of the large round discs and buttons found in such quantities in this tomb served to decorate these sheaths. The largest were fixed on the broadest portion of the sheath, and they decreased in size down to the point. These buttons are interesting in various respects. In Fig. 231 the core, which in this case is of wood, and in others of bone, may be seen under the gold plate, which is partially destroyed. The pattern afterwards reproduced in *repoussé* by the gold plate was first carved in relief on this wooden core. Apparently the smooth gold plate was firmly attached to the core, and then pressed down hard, while the lines were followed with a

230.—SWORD-HILT
WITH POMMEL
(reconstructed).

[1] *Mycenæ*, p. 283.

pointed instrument until the pattern was fetched up to the surface. We may assume that this method of reproducing the pattern on the plate was not employed only in the case of the buttons; the masks, the diadems, the seven hundred gold discs of grave III, and many other objects, were almost certainly made in the same way.

There is a further point of interest in these buttons, namely, the large bosses which are always attached in groups of two or three to the angles of the lozenge. They are round discs, and their centre lies in every case outside the line of the lozenge edge. This makes their meaning clear; the discs represent the broad heads of the nails or tacks which fastened the lozenge-shaped

231.—LARGE POMMEL, OVERLAID WITH GOLD PLATE FROM GRAVE IV (natural size).

ornament to the object it was to decorate. The nails are never driven through the lozenge; accordingly, in the technique which served as models to the examples under discussion, the lozenge must have been made of a material which it was either difficult or dangerous to pierce. The materials known to us up to now from the grave-finds would suggest the material to be gems or amber, and it is possible that they were so used, though certainly not in ornaments as large as these lozenges. I therefore incline to think a third material, i.e. rock-crystal, was employed. The hilt given below (Fig. 250), probably belonging to a sceptre, is inlaid with small bits of rock-crystal. Large loose pieces of it have been found in this grave in great abundance. They are exactly of the size and shape of the notes of our modern musical glasses.

Their purpose has hitherto been problematical, as not one is pierced by a hole. I would suggest that, like the models of our gold plates, they were kept in place only by the heads of the nails, and were used to overlay sword-sheaths or caskets or similar objects.

Naturally in these gold plates only the idea of the nail-head set on the edge was borrowed from the stone or crystal ornaments, the design itself was derived from metal work. This is absolutely certain, now that the dagger-blades have thrown so satisfactory a light on the technique of the period. In Fig. 232, for instance, it is plain that the crosses within the border formed by two lines are meant to represent separate pieces laid on to a

232.—WOODEN POMMEL OVERLAID WITH GOLD PLATE FROM GRAVE IV (natural size).

darker background. So too the circle within the border has been filled up with a *swastika* or hooked cross, and each of the angular spaces between circle and border with a triple star of wave lines (the so-called *triskeles*). The same development which gradually replaced the inlaid work of the Homeric shield by chased work beaten out in one piece has also taken place here; the method is simplified, but the patterns remain constant. Moreover, as Dr. Milchhöfer has shown,[1] the ornaments of this example all reappear in Asia Minor—the cross on the façade of the so-called Midas tomb in Phrygia, the triple and quadruple star on Lycian coins.

In the grave were found three shoulder-belts or baldrics, one to each body. All three are of the same shape, and of approxi-

[1] *Die Anfänge der Kunst in Griechenland*, p. 25.

mately the same length. One has no ornamentation. The one
shown in Fig. 233 is the best preserved. It is 5 feet long,

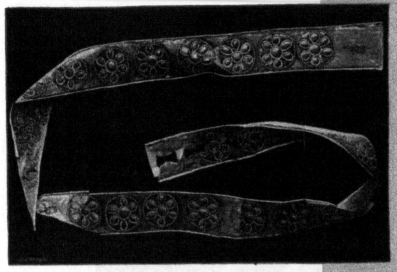

233.—GOLD SWORD-BELT FROM GRAVE IV (size about 3 : 16).

and about two inches broad, and is decorated with a continuous row of rosettes. At one end two holes have been cut.
Through these was passed a little golden bar suspended from a
small chain fastened to the other end.
There is little to be said about
234.—GOLD BAR SUSPENDED FROM the spears, arrows, and shields. The
THE HOLES IN THE SWORD-BELT chief portions of all these weapons
(natural size). were of wood, so that only very
scanty remains of them have been found. Dr. Schliemann says
that he saw several lances quite perfect just at the instant
of discovery, but that they crumbled away immediately the air
was admitted; now only their bronze heads remain. As many
as four come from this grave; they have the same shape as the
one given in Fig. 206, only there is no ring on the socket. It
is possible that the gold bands, like the one in Fig. 235, belonged
to the lances. There is a number of these bands of different
breadths; some are still bent into a ring, whose diameter approximately corresponds to the thickness of the spear-shaft. In

that case these gold plates would have been intended to imitate strong metal rings encircling the shaft.

The arrow-heads, thirty-five in number, are all of stone, the hard obsidian; bronze arrow-heads, so common in the *Iliad*,[1] are never found. The typical shape is that given in Fig. 236. The notched side of the head was evidently inserted into the slit of a wooden shaft. Absolutely no trace has been found of the bows, which must nevertheless have been placed in the grave along with the arrows.

Nor have any shields been found, but their presence in this grave may be safely inferred from several ornaments, which could only belong to shields, and from the fragment of an arched shield of wood with circular edge preserved in grave V. By the ornaments I mean especially the great mass of round gold buttons with a bone core, which I take to have been shield bosses. They are all unpierced, and must have been merely stuck on. We know how often Homer mentions "bossed"[2] shields,[3] and in the battle-scene on the intaglio, Fig. 178, we have already seen shields with borders formed by rows of dots, so that we can feel no hesitation in identifying those dots with our buttons and with the Homeric boss.

235.—GOLD BAND, PROBABLY USED FOR THE ORNAMENTATION OF A LANCE-SHAFT, FROM GRAVE IV (natural size).

These bosses probably also adorned helmets, called by Homer[4] "studded."[5] In the great warrior vase (Figs. 284, 285) they appear as light-coloured dots sprinkled over the dark surface of the helmet. However, the number of the bosses found is far too great to have served for helmets only; the greater part must have been used for shields. Another ornament, of which one example has been preserved

236.—OBSIDIAN ARROW-HEAD FROM GRAVE IV (natural size).

---

[1] *Il.* xiii. 650.　　　[2] Greek, ὀμφαλόεσσα.
[3] *Il.* iv. 448; xi. 34.　　[4] *Il.* v. 743; xi. 41.
[5] Greek, τετραφάληρος. See Helbig, *Epos*, p. 306, for the interpretation of this word as "bossed" or "studded."

in this grave only, must also be assigned to a shield. This is the lion "mask" (Fig. 237), which it was proved could not possibly have covered the face of a dead man, and which I hold to be the central device of a shield. Moreover, it must have been fixed to a flat surface. All round the head is a horizontal rim, the edge of which is perforated, and covered by a narrow deposit of green oxide, a proof that it was set in a bronze border which held the whole ornament in place.

237.—GOLD LION MASK FROM GRAVE IV.

The head is too badly preserved for us to judge of the workmanship. Still we can notice the sharpness of the edges, and the hard angular cast of the features, reminding us of Egyptian and Asiatic work. We know that at a later period a lion's head was one of the commonest shield devices. It may not be too much to assume that it was already adopted as such in the Mycenæan period. The shield of the foremost man who attacks the lion on the dagger-blade, Fig. 227, is adorned with three large ornaments resembling rosettes in outline, thus proving that

shield devices were already used at that time. Moreover, it is
precisely in the Mycenæan system of decoration that the lion
plays such an important part.

We now turn to the vessels of all kinds which are especially
numerous in this grave. Nine of them are gold cups, chiefly of two

238.—GOLD CUP FROM GRAVE IV (size 4 : 5).

shapes, which are also very commonly found in Mycenæan pottery.
One is the simple shape already familiar from the only goblet of
grave II, a plain cup without a foot, and with one handle riveted
on. Five of the cups found in this grave are of this shape.
They are decorated sometimes with vertical furrows or ascending twigs, sometimes with one or more horizontal hoops. The
cup with twigs is represented in Fig. 238.

The second typical shape is distinguished by the slender foot of moderate height which supports the cup. It occurs in three examples, one of which has no ornamentation, and corresponds completely to the goblets of red clay found in such numbers at Troy. The body of the second is adorned with hoops, and with rosettes affixed to it. The third and most interesting cup is of silver. It is adorned with inlaid gold work after the pattern of the dagger-blades (Fig. 239). In three places on the outer

239.—SILVER CUP FROM GRAVE IV (size 4 : 7).

circumference of the cup, namely, opposite the handle and to its right and left, is a low flower-pot. The outline of the ornamental bands and handles of the pot is seen in profile. In it plants are growing, and these are the lotus plants already seen in the large hair-pin of grave III (Fig. 172). Below these three designs is a ring of little inlaid round gold plates running round the cup. It has been remarked that these flower-pots point to a cultivation of flower-gardens which never existed in Greece, but which was highly developed in the countries of the Euphrates and still more in Egypt. We thus receive once more a hint of intercourse with distant nations beyond the sea; and to this intercourse we owe, if not the goblet itself, at any rate the model from which its ornamentation was borrowed.

A further development of this shape is seen in the cup with the doves (Fig. 240). It has approximately the form of the last wine-cup, the same high stand with a flat foot, and the same kind of handle; only instead of one handle it has two, which are further joined to the foot by a band of gold cut into thin strips. Two doves sitting on the handles have long suggested comparison with the Homeric description of the cup of Nestor,[1] "and beside

240.—GOLD CUP FROM GRAVE IV (size 3 : 8).

it a right goodly cup, that the old man brought from home, embossed with studs of gold, and four handles there were to it, and round each two golden doves were feeding, and to the cup were *two bottoms*.[2] Another man could scarce have lifted the cup from the table, but Nestor the Old raised it easily."

We may imagine the doves of Nestor's cup to have re-

[1] *Il.* xi. 632.
[2] δύω δ' ὑπὸ πυθμένες ἦσαν—tr. "and to the cup were two feet below," by Messrs. Lang, Leaf, and Myers.

sembled these. In other respects the cup must have had a very
different appearance; it was much larger, it had four handles
and two doves to each handle—and what the meaning of the
"two bottoms" is, or rather what the peculiar Greek word πυθμην
means, is still unknown.

The goblets without a foot, like those with a foot, sometimes have two handles, sometimes only one. Fig. 241 shows the
gold goblet with two handles. The shape of the body, however,
has been so far altered that the upper portion has a concave

241.—GOLD CUP FROM GRAVE IV (size about 5 : 8).

curve, while the lower portion is rounded. A terra-cotta vase of
the same shape has also been found in this grave. Both remind
us strikingly of those Trojan vases whose unique shape led Dr.
Schliemann to assume a separate settlement—the Lydian.

The most remarkable object, however, in this grave, and
perhaps in all the Mycenæan finds, is a large alabaster vase, which,
from its shape and technique, might come straight from a modern
drawing-room (Fig. 242). But on nearer inspection we see that
it is thoroughly in keeping with the Mycenæan system of shapes.
If we place the cup last described on the foot belonging to the

242.—ALABASTER VASE FROM GRAVE IV (size about 2 : 5).

243.—SMALL GOLD JUG FROM GRAVE IV (size 7 : 10).

silver cup, Fig. 239, we get the body of the alabaster vase. Three handles, curling at the top into spirals and curving out from the vase below, are fastened to it by means of fine pins.

In addition to these goblets and vases, two jugs have been found in the grave; the one, which is reproduced in Fig. 243, is a quite small golden jug; the other is of silver, and has much the same shape, but is without any ornamentation.

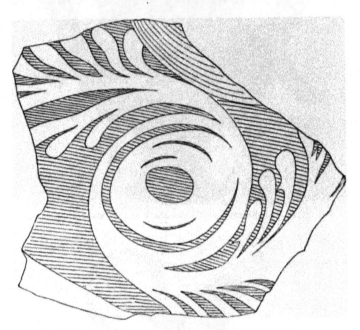

244.—FRAGMENT OF VASE FROM GRAVE IV (size 1 : 2).

Only a few fragments of terra-cotta ware have been found; among them are fairly large pieces decorated with sea-weed patterns, rendered in translucent white paint on the dark red ground (Fig. 244).

Next we have the large copper jugs and caldrons, of which thirty-four in all have been found in the grave. These seem to have been given to men as well as to women, for five were lying at the south end of the grave, at the feet of the two men whose faces were covered with masks; five others were found on the east side behind the heads of the other three bodies; further, ten were on the west side at the feet of these same corpses, and twelve were against the north wall. The exact place where the remaining two were found is not recorded. These vases again mainly reproduce two shapes; first we have the jug, such as we see it in Fig. 245, with a large upright handle uniting the neck to the body, and a second horizontal handle lower down, to tilt the jug up by when pouring out of it. Seven of these jugs were found. On the other hand, the shape of the large shallow

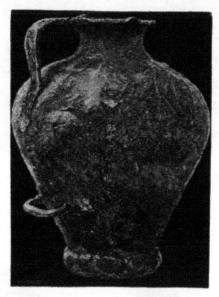

245.—LARGE COPPER JUG FROM GRAVE IV (size 1 : 8).

caldron of Fig. 246 was found in as many as twenty-two instances, sometimes with two, sometimes with three handles, sometimes with rounded and sometimes with straight sides. Of the remaining five, one is a pan with a tubular handle, into · which a wooden stave was fixed, the second an oval basin, the third and fourth large and deep caldrons, the fifth a tripod with three handles and a spout.

We must also reckon among the vessels a stag cast in an alloy of lead and silver. It has strong antlers, and from its back, which is hollow, rises a short funnel, which proves that

246.—COPPER CALDRON FROM GRAVE IV (size 1 : 8).

247.—VESSEL IN FORM OF A STAG FROM GRAVE IV (size 3 : 7).

248.—OX-HEAD OF SILVER FROM GRAVE IV (size about 7 : 20).

the animal probably served as a vase or oil-flask, or for some similar purpose. The work is quite coarse and clumsy (Fig. 247).

Finally, there remain a few objects to enumerate, the purpose of which is not always clear. First of all, there is the splendid large ox-head of silver with golden horns (Fig. 248). It is marvellously true to nature, especially in the rendering of the mouth. On ears, eyes, muzzle, and mouth are distinct traces of gilding. The gold was not plated straight on to the silver, but the silver first received a plating of copper, over which the gold was laid. On the forehead of the ox is fastened a large gold rosette, which likewise rests on a plating of copper. The horns are of thin

249.—OX-HEAD OF GOLD PLATE FROM GRAVE IV (natural size).

gold plate soldered together. The line of the solder can still be distinctly recognised, for one of the horns has split along it. On some Egyptian wall-paintings we see among the tribute brought by foreign nations to the Pharaoh the head of an ox, and on some other similar paintings we again meet with it, used this time as a weight in a scale. However, these analogies have as yet afforded no satisfactory explanation of this Mycenæan ox. Perhaps the head was hung up in the grave as a dedicatory offering. Small heads of oxen, with a double axe between their horns and cut out of gold plate, have been found in this grave to the number of about fifty-six (Fig. 249). The double axe again points to Asia Minor, where it appears as the device on Carian coins down to quite late times.

The pommel and sheathing of Fig. 250 have been referred to above. The cylindrical sheathing consists of four-petalled flowers united at their points, each petal being inlaid with a small piece of rock-crystal. The central part of the pommel is formed by a snake-like scaly body, whose separate scales are likewise rendered by bits of rock-crystal fixed into the gold. Heads of snakes or dragons, which are very much damaged, finished off the two extremities of the pommel. Judging from their technique, these

250.—INLAID POMMEL FROM GRAVE IV (size 3 : 4).

two objects belong together, but the round and narrow sheath makes it improbable that they served as a sword-hilt. Dr. Schliemann is nearer the truth in considering them to have adorned a sceptre. The presence of sceptres in the grave is made probable by other facts. A gold sheath about 40 inches long was found here broken in two: it can only have served as casing to a staff. Its upper and lower extremities are shown in Fig. 251. The lower end is decorated with the same triangular pattern which appears on the half-columns of the "treasury of Atreus," and the crowning of the sceptre reminds us to some extent of the capital of those same columns, the forerunners of the Doric capital.

Finally, we still have to notice the remarkable alabaster knot (Fig. 253) of which two complete instances and several fragments

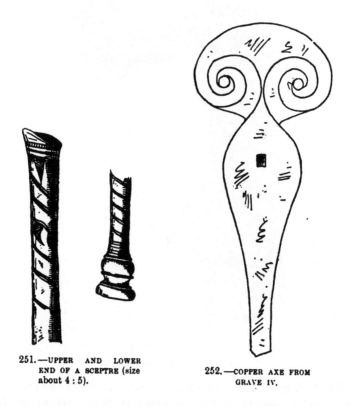

251.—UPPER AND LOWER END OF A SCEPTRE (size about 4 : 5).

252.—COPPER AXE FROM GRAVE IV.

have been found. The lower end is finished off by a fringe in very low relief, the rest of the knot is ornamented with a check pattern formed by white lines on a light green ground. At the back the surface is perfectly smooth, and this, as well as three perforations in the middle where the knot is tied, shows that it was affixed to some larger object; whether to a shield or to some other article, we cannot tell. It is noteworthy that on Egyptian wall-paintings and sculptures exactly similar objects are seen in the hands of kings or high priests, where they are usually interpreted as the symbol of initiation into religious mysteries.

253.—ALABASTER KNOT FROM GRAVE IV (size 2 : 3).

8. The Fifth Grave

The fifth grave has about the same dimensions as the first and third. In it were three corpses, about 3 feet apart, as in the other graves, and with their heads turned as usual to the east. "All three," says Dr. Schliemann, "were unusually large, and appeared to have been forced into the small space of only 5 feet 6 inches, left for them between the inner wallings: the bones of the legs, which are almost intact, are of unusual length."[1] While two of the bodies had large golden masks, the third one, which was between the other two, had none, and moreover

[1] *Mycenæ*, p. 295.

had hardly any gold ornaments. And as twelve gold buttons, small plates of gold, and countless objects of bone were found scattered at some distance above the bodies, Dr. Schliemann concludes that the grave had been opened long ago, and this one body plundered. Two of the corpses crumbled away immediately they were exposed to the air. "But of the third body, the round face, with all its flesh, had been wonderfully preserved under its

254.—GOLD MASK FROM GRAVE V.

ponderous golden mask; there was no vestige of hair, but both eyes were perfectly visible, also the mouth, which, owing to the enormous weight which had pressed upon it, was wide open, and showed thirty-two beautiful teeth . . . the nose was entirely gone. . . . Such had been the pressure of the *débris* and stones, that the body had been reduced to a thickness of 1 inch to $1\frac{1}{2}$ inch."[1]

[1] *Mycenæ*, p. 296.

From the size of the bones it would appear that three men were buried here. This is further confirmed by the offerings, which were of the kind attributed to the men in grave IV, whereas none of those destined to women were found.

Only a few of these offerings vary from those we are now familiar with from grave IV. This time the circumstances of

255.—GOLD MASK FROM GRAVE V.

the find allow us to allot each object fairly accurately among the two corpses, and the simpler furnishing of the one contrasts very sharply with that of the richer and more artistic adornment of the other.

For instance, one of the corpses had a breastplate without decoration, matched by a sword-belt, also without decoration. On its face was a mask, much less carefully worked than that of the

256.—GOLD BREASTPLATE FROM GRAVE V.

other, which had a breastplate covered all over with designs, and other rich gifts.

Most important of all are the masks. Over the face of the dead man who lay at the south extremity of the grave was found the bearded mask (Fig. 254). The features are well formed; the eyes are somewhat close together, the nose is long and delicate, and the lips thin. The eyes are encircled by a double rim, the line passing across them and marking the meeting of the lids show that they are closed. The eyelashes are not marked. The eyebrows and the full beard not only have their broad masses raised in relief, but are further made more life-like by inner markings produced by sunk lines.

Totally different is the appearance of the other mask, which covered the face of the body at the north end (Fig. 255). The face is beardless, and almost spherical, the nose is short and broad, the mouth is only indicated by a straight deep line, and the brows by a narrow raised ridge. The beardlessness, the shape of the face and of the nose, are of course characteristics peculiar to the individual portrayed. On the other hand, the method by which eyebrows and mouth are rendered, when compared with the bearded mask, distinctly betrays a lack of skill or of care on the part of the artist. Apparently in this case also the masks were not made by the same hand, and the bodies can scarcely have been buried at the same time.

To the body with the bearded mask at the southern end of the grave also belonged the golden breastplate of Fig. 256. It is about twice as wide at the top as at the bottom: on the upper portion the breasts are represented by oval bosses, the whole remaining space is ornamented with an artistic interlacing of spirals.

257.—GOLD BAND.

To the same body belonged the gold band adorned with rosettes and spirals (Fig. 257), which was still fastened round an arm-bone.

Near to it also lay a great number of perforated amber beads. Now seeing that this is the corpse with the bearded mask, there can be no doubt that at that time men as well as women must have used these beads, be it that they actually wore them, or that, along with perforated bones and boar's teeth, they were strung into neck-trappings for horses.

Near to this skeleton, again, were found thirty-seven circular

258.—GOLD LEAF FROM GRAVE V (natural size).

pieces of gold leaf, and twenty-one fragments of the same (Fig. 258). They exactly resemble the 701 gold leaf ornaments found in the women's grave III, and shown to be dress-trimmings. They belonged, however, as we now see, not only to women's, but also to men's apparel. The garment which they adorned had been, if Dr. Schliemann's observation be correct, drawn over the head of one of the bodies. He reports of the best preserved of the bodies at the north end of the grave: "The forehead of the man was ornamented with a plain round leaf of gold, and a still

larger one was lying on the right eye; I further observed a large
and a small gold leaf on the breast below the large golden breast-
cover, and a large one just above the right thigh."[1]

Near to the bearded man on the south side lay further two
broken silver vases, and a large vase of alabaster; inside it was

259.—GOLD SWORD-BELT FROM GRAVE V (half size).

a remarkable collection of thirty-eight golden buttons and a wedge-
shaped golden funnel.

The swords were about equally apportioned among the three
dead; they will be described together later on.

It has already been mentioned that a plain breastplate with

[1] *Mycenæ*, p. 296.

260-262.—GOLD PLATES OF A CASKET FROM GRAVE V (natural size).

sword-belt to match was found near to the body with the beardless mask at the north end of the grave.   Only the breasts are
indicated on the plain surface in the same way as on the breastplate, Fig. 256.   The sword-belt is given in Fig. 259.   One end
is still fastened to the end of the sword, and to the sword is also
still attached one of the round discs which decorated the sheath.
A great number of these buttons were found in this grave : Dr.
Schliemann counted as many as 340.   They all have the same
two shapes as the buttons of the previous grave (the circle or the
lozenge), but occasionally the patterns are different.   (See below,
Figs. 273 and 274.)

Very interesting are the twelve rectangular gold plates found

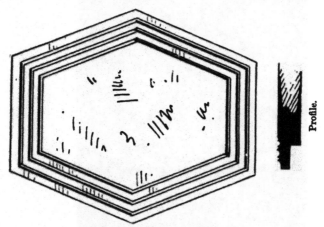

263.—WOODEN BOTTOM TO A CASKET FROM GRAVE V.

near the body at the north end of the grave.   There are four
replicas of each of the three examples given here.   On Fig. 260
a lion is furiously pursuing a stag, which is bounding away and
turning its head round.   The empty space above and below the
animals is filled up by the tops of palm-trees and other foliage.
Fig. 261 shows a similar scene ; but this time the lion is larger
and runs toward the left, and, on account of the diminished space,
the stag has been turned round, and is represented with his body
over the lion's head.   In addition to the foliage an ox-head with
huge eyes helps to fill up the space.   The third plate is somewhat
shorter (Fig. 262), and shows the pattern of intertwined spirals
which we have so frequently met with.

When at the Museum I perceived that these twelve gold plates had belonged to two small caskets whose hexagonal wooden bottoms are still in existence. These last have the shape shown in Fig. 263, with four long and two short sides. The long sides correspond exactly to the long plates, the short sides to the short ones. As Dr. Schliemann found the twelve plates to the right

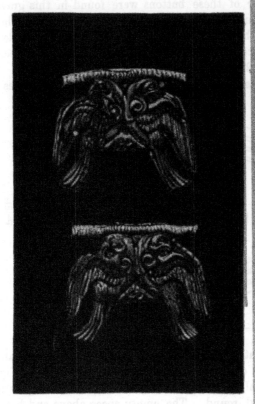

264.—DOUBLE EAGLES OF GOLD PLATE FROM GRAVE V (natural size).

and to the left of the body in question, we probably have here two caskets. The four long plates of Fig. 260, together with two of the small ones of Fig. 262, formed the one, while the four other long plates of Fig. 261, with the remaining two short ones of Fig. 262, made up the other.

It was on the face, breast, and loins of this same body at the north end of the grave that the five round gold plates

mentioned above were found.   Near to it also were five double
eagles of gold plate, similar to those from grave III.   These new
examples, however, had not been sewn on to the garments, but,
as is shown by a hollow tube fixed to their heads, they were
probably strung together to serve as a necklace.   Near to this
body again were found several vessels, namely, a large silver vase
and four silver cups, all of them much damaged ; then three gold
cups showing the two shapes which we now know to be typical

265.—GOLD GOBLET FROM GRAVE V.

for Mycenæan drinking-goblets.   Two have the simple cup shape,
narrowing towards the bottom, which is flat ; one has the rounded
shape with high slender foot ; all of them have only one handle,
which, as usual, is riveted on.   The first two examples are quite
simply decorated, the one with a row of high round arches, the
other with the usual interlacing spirals (see Fig. 265).   The
third cup, which is adorned with a frieze of running lions, is
given in Fig. 266, in order to show how dear this particular lion
scheme was to the Mycenæan artists.   Finally, to this portion of
the finds belongs a tall alabaster cup with perpendicular sides
and a foot.

We now pass to those objects which we cannot apportion
with any certainty among the separate bodies.   Among them are
two gaiter-holders, ornamented exactly like those of grave IV,
with three rosettes and a branch in each corner, as well as a few
fragments of armlets similar to the one given in Fig. 257, and
most important of all, a great number of swords (Figs. 267-269)
and daggers. Taking the fragments into account, there must have

266.—GOLD CUP FROM GRAVE V.

been some sixty of these swords in the grave. Several have
designs of extreme beauty. For instance, a long sword-blade has
a frieze of galloping horses worked in low relief on each side of
the central rib (Fig. 271). However, it is the dagger-blades
with their inlaid work which here also are the most remarkable.
The design on the blade in Fig. 270 is quite worthy of comparison with the lion-hunt from grave IV. On both its sides we
see arranged in very much the same scheme cat-like animals

hunting wild ducks in a marsh. On each side we have two cats or panthers and four ducks. The former are not, as in the usual lion scheme, running at full speed so much as creeping; the ducks in a sort of half flight are trying to escape, though some of them have already been seized by their pursuers. Between and under the animals is seen a winding river, in which fish are swimming and papyrus plants are growing. The cats, the plants, and the bodies of the ducks are inlaid with gold, the wings of the ducks and the river are silver, and the fish are given in some dark substance. On the neck of one of the ducks is a red drop of blood probably given by coloured, *i.e.* alloyed gold. The whole effect, both of drawing and colouring, is of remarkable power and beauty. The papyrus plants once more remind us that Egypt is the probable home of the original model.

267-269.—SWORDS FROM GRAVE V (size 1 : 3).

Another dagger-blade is adorned with separate blossoms, each with three inlaid stamens; similar flowers also adorn the gold plate which still covers the hilt. On a third, the well-known triple row of spirals of the *stele* Fig. 146 reappears with insignificant variations. However, the method of decoration differs in so far that here the pattern was not separately inlaid on the plate let into the blade, but the plate itself was a gold leaf, which only had to be engraved and then inlaid with *niello*.

No new shape of sword-hilt is found in this grave; one fragment, however, is so well preserved that it seems well to give it (Fig. 272). The handle was fixed to the round disc with the square hole.

Further, the remnants of a knot of Egyptian porcelain were also found here. Like the knots of grave IV, this also is smooth

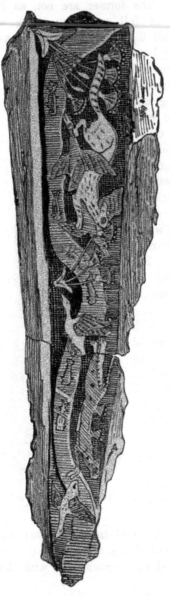

270.—INLAID BLADE OF DAGGER
FROM GRAVE V.

271.—DECORATED SWORD-
BLADE FROM GRAVE V.

at the back, showing that it was intended to be fastened to some
object. There were also a quantity of fragments of terra-cotta
vases and cups. One vase, which is well preserved, is given in
Fig. 275. It is a large-bellied water-jar with two handles.
The simple decoration of bands supporting semicircles is rendered
in white paint on the reddish clay.

Seven large copper vessels, which stood together on the west
side at the feet of the bodies, repeat the two shapes which this
kind of vessel had in grave IV. Two are large water-pitchers
like Fig. 245, with one handle joining the rim to the body, and
another lower down by which to tilt the vessel; five others are
caldrons like Fig. 246, with two or three handles attached to
the rim.

272.—HEAD AND CENTRE-PIECE OF A SWORD-GUARD FROM GRAVE V (size 4 : 9).

A large wooden object, which has been pieced together out
of many fragments, is of great importance. It is almost certainly
a portion of a shield (Fig. 276). Its flat face is curved to meet
the rim, which is formed by a projecting narrow horizontal border
of neat workmanship. It seems probable, therefore, that we have
here one end of a large shield pinched in the middle. In the
centre of the preserved portion is a round hole, which served to
fasten either a handle on the inside or a large device on
the outside.

Among the other objects found in the grave, we still have to
mention two little slabs belonging to a wooden casket; both have
the same design, worked in relief, of a lion and another animal
which is not so easy to identify. There were also found here a
number of oyster-shells and boars' teeth; all these were probably
used partly as horse-trappings, partly as decoration for helmets.

Finally, a genuine ostrich egg is of great interest; it has been most happily put together out of several fragments. Professor Landerer has analysed a tiny portion of it, and has proved that

273, 274.—GOLD KNOBS FROM GRAVE V.

275.—TERRA-COTTA VASE FROM GRAVE V.

we have here no imitation in Egyptian porcelain or the like; he writes: "The fragments dissolve in hydrochloric acid with effervescence, giving a light flocculent precipitate, which is due to the dried albumen that held the egg-shell together. The constituents of the fragment are accordingly carbonate of lime and albumen, which are the constituents of egg-shells." The egg is perforated at both ends, but this does not necessarily mean that it was suspended by a string; the holes would be required to blow the egg. Once again, and this time more strongly than ever, we are reminded of the active intercourse which must once have existed between Mycenæ and the land of the ostrich and the papyrus.

In conclusion, we must mention the analyses of the Mycenæan metals which were made for Dr. Schliemann at the Royal School

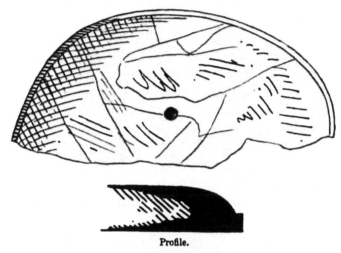

Profile.

276.—FRAGMENT OF A WOODEN SHIELD FROM GRAVE V.

of Mines in London. The gold contains a fair amount of silver, varying from 8 to 23 per cent in the different pieces of gold plate. The silver of one vase was pure, with the exception of 3 per cent of copper. With regard to the other metals, it was found that the large vessels consisted of almost pure copper (98½ per cent), while the swords contained 86 per cent copper and 13 per cent tin, i.e. the usual bronze alloy.

9. *The Sixth Grave*

It is well known that Dr. Schliemann only discovered the five graves hitherto described. A sixth grave was found, a year after his excavations, near the entrance of the circular precinct; its contents were removed by M. Stamatakis. The skeletons

277.—TERRA-COTTA VASE FROM GRAVE VI (size 1 : 4).

were better preserved in this grave than in any other. They were brought complete to Athens and set up in the middle of the Mycenæan room, just as they were discovered, with all their offerings around them. The two corpses are undoubtedly those of men. By the side of each are weapons in great number; at their heads are drinking-cups, and at their feet the large earthenware vessels. Neither masks, breastplates, nor armlets are found here. On the other hand, there is a pair of gaiter-holders, merely decorated by lines round their edges.

The weapons have the same shape as those from the first graves, but they have no decoration in relief, or inlaid work. They consist of swords, daggers, and spear-heads. The usual buttons for the adornment of the sheaths are plentiful.

Among the cups only one is of gold, with straight sides and a flat bottom. It is decorated with high round arches, exactly like one of the cups from grave V. A second cup of terra-cotta is adorned along its edge with plain segments of circles, rendered in dull paint.

278.—TERRA-COTTA VASE FROM GRAVE VI (size 1 : 4).

Neither copper kettles nor jugs appear to have been placed in these graves, but the number of terra-cotta vessels is all the greater. Their ornamentation shows several new details. With the exception of an insignificant little flask the big vase of Fig. 277 is the only one painted in varnish. The shape is the same as that of the beautiful vases, painted in varnish with a decoration of seaweed, from grave I. Here the ornaments are almost purely linear. Round the shoulder runs a pattern composed of curves and dots, round the body are several rings; then comes a band of spirals; next, after a few more rings, a wreath of ivy. All

the other vases are decorated in dull paint. Three have been
preserved intact. Two of these have the shape of the large
almost globular vase with the bill-like spout, from grave I (Fig.
166), which, it will be remembered, is also painted in dull colour.
The first is decorated with a plain hoop and a band of wave-
lines rendered in brown on a yellowish red. On the second
(Fig. 278) are various birds, also in brown on yellowish red;

279.—TERRA-COTTA VASE FROM GRAVE VI (size about 1 : 6).

their wings are marked with hatchings. The third vase, a
two-handled amphora (Fig. 279), shows a polypus with a head
similar to that of the griffins on the gold plates and on the
sword-blades of graves III and IV. Here they are painted in
white colour, outlined in brown on the yellowish red ground.

The terra-cotta vases show an exact correspondence between
this grave and the first: the same slim jug, which in grave I
was painted in varnish, reappears here; the bellied shape, which
in grave I was the only representative of the dull paint, is found

three times in this grave.   In grave VI there occurs an exception
to the general rule which Drs. Furtwängler and Löschcke
have established for the vases of the Mycenæan period, namely,
that the dull paint goes with linear decoration, while with the
use of the lustrous varnish we get imitation of natural objects;
except for the small ivy wreath, our varnish-painted vase is
decorated solely with linear ornaments, while two-thirds of the
bellied jugs with dull paint are adorned with animals.

10. Relation of the Graves to one another

The examination of the single objects from the tombs has
already proved abundantly that all the bodies cannot possibly
have been buried simultaneously, but that the burial-ground must
have come into existence by degrees.   It is particularly remarkable that the masks from one and the same grave differ strongly
from each other.   Now that we have examined the whole
material to our hand, the question next arises whether we can
determine the order in which the graves were formed, or the
length of the period during which they continued in use.   The
following points are the only ones which can be established with
any certainty.

Graves I, II, and VI on the one side, and III, IV, and V
on the other are closely related.   In graves III and IV we find
those little shrines of Astarte, which were apparently all made
on the same mould, and, in III and IV alone, the round
leaves which had served as decorations for garments.   Throughout
graves III, IV, and V gold and bronze predominate, whilst in
I, II, and VI by far the greater number of vessels are of
terra-cotta.   Hence it follows that the latter graves belong
to a simpler and less elaborate period than the former, and
a few further considerations point to the same conclusion.   If we
compare the women's grave I with the women's grave III, and
the men's graves II and VI with IV and V, we notice in each
case the much simpler furniture of the first group, I, II, and VI.
The gold objects in grave I, the diadems, pendants, and crosses,
have much simpler patterns than the similar objects from grave
III.   We notice, moreover, the absence of several ornaments, such
as earrings, bracelets, and amber beads.   In the same way, Nos. II
and VI are the only men's graves without masks, golden breast-

plates, or golden sword-belts; II, in particular, contained but few weapons. Accordingly I, II, and VI must certainly belong to a different period from III, IV, and V. The question whether this period precedes or follows the other depends entirely on whether the epoch we have to deal with was one of artistic development or of artistic decadence. The simplicity of the one group may have been a stepping-stone to the luxurious splendour of the other, but it may also have been an after refinement and modification, and there are various reasons for thinking this the more probable hypothesis. The terra-cotta idols from grave I, and the birds on the vase from grave VI, form links with the later finds from the citadel, which cannot be traced in the graves of the other group. An analogous case presents itself in the palace, where the older coatings of wall plaster are much more richly and elaborately painted than the later ones. Although, as far as general characteristics go, we can clearly divide the graves into two groups, yet when we come to details, countless small threads connect the one with the other and prevent us from assuming any considerable interval of time between the two. The massive breast-pendants of grave III are absent from IV, which is in other ways so closely connected with it, whilst they are to be found in I, which belongs to the other group. The design on the gold band from II—rings connected by tangents with small bosses near the tangents—is repeated on the glazed vase of grave III.

However, it is not merely the connection between the three graves in each group, which seems so close that no clearly defined chronological sequence is possible, but throughout we find no division between the groups wide enough to prevent all the graves from belonging to one period of culture, and that of no great extent. A century seems ample time for the development of the changes which come under our notice, and half a century would suffice to account for differences in furnishing between the earliest and the latest grave.

11. Dr. Schliemann's Finds outside the Precinct of the Graves

Dr. Schliemann's excavations on the citadel comprised, beyond the grave precinct, only a small tract to the south of it, close to the fortification wall. There he brought to light a labyrinth of walls built of quarry-stones and clay. It soon became apparent that they must have belonged to dwelling-houses. Subsequent excavations have laid bare similar buildings still farther to the south, as well as the chief rooms of the Palace, on the summit of the Acropolis, so that we are probably right in supposing the houses on the lower terrace to have been out-buildings for the accommodation of the suite and the menials.

The great find in the complex of buildings laid bare by Dr. Schliemann was made a few days after the conclusion of his excavations. The engineer, M. Drosinos, who had remained on the citadel to revise the plans and maps he had made, thought he saw to the south, close to the outer edge of the circular precinct, the vertical walls of a grave. He sent for the royal commissioner, M. Stamatakis, and there they found a great number of golden vessels, cups, signet rings, and spiral rings. At that time Dr. Schliemann thought that this was the site of a grave, and described it as such in his book, relying on the fact that the surrounding walls were built in the same style as those of the shaft-graves inside the precinct. At the same time he was much astonished that the grave was not hewn in the rock, but was enclosed on two sides by walls with a filling of _débris_ at the back, and that at two of the corners these walls projected beyond the area of the grave.

As a matter of fact we shall see that the contents are not of the kind found in graves. Even though the objects closely resemble the golden finds from the shaft-graves, it is very evident that not one of them was fashioned only for the use of the dead, as were the tinsel plates of the graves and the other objects covered with the thinnest possible coating of metal. Here everything is made of solid gold, and each article has served some purpose in real life. Another reason against the grave theory is that all the objects, as Dr. Schliemann himself says, were contained " in a space not more than 2 feet long and 8 inches broad." They must therefore have lain in a chest like the great treasure at Troy, and been stored here in the cellar of the house.

The most prominent objects in this find are four beautiful golden goblets, with curving cup and a high stem, like the silver goblet from grave IV, but with two handles instead of one.

These handles are solid, and are finished above by dogs' heads, whose open jaws bite into the rim of the vessel.

The most important object is a gold ring ; on its large signet is a highly interesting design (Fig. 281). In the foreground we see a woman sitting under a tree with her right hand in her lap and holding up a bunch of flowers in her left hand.[1] In front of her stand one small and two large female figures. Behind her another small figure is gathering something from the tree. Each

280.—GOLD GOBLET (size 1 : 2).

of the two small figures stands on a heap of stones. The women have long projecting noses and enormous eyes, and their costume is most curious. The dress fits tightly over the bosom and is girt round the hips, but below the waist it falls away from the figure so as to form a deep fold, and ends in a crescent line round the ankles. The skirt shows four or more bulging horizontal folds or tucks, and in two instances at least the flat space

[1] The cut represents the impression from the seal, not the seal itself, so that "right" and "left" are interchanged in the description.

between these tucks is filled in with a scale pattern. The heads
seem to be adorned with a diadem, from which rises a curious
ornament resembling a cluster of three flowers. A tress of hair
hangs down behind. It is not easy to discover what the tree
may be. As the small figure is gathering something from it, it
must bear edible fruit; and we most
likely have here a clumsy representation
of a vine. In the background are seen
a sun and a crescent moon; the two
wavy lines below them probably represent the sea. Farther down still is a
double axe of the same shape as the axe
in gold plate found in grave IV. Above,
on the right, is an idol, armed with a

281.—DESIGN ON A GOLD RING
(natural size).

great bipartite shield of the well-known notched shape, only the
feet showing below it. The idol holds a lance in its left hand,
which is slightly raised. A tress of hair seems to flow from the
head. On the right, near the edge, the space is filled up by six
heads of animals turned full to the front.

Starting from the holy symbols represented above, Dr.
Milchhöfer would interpret the figures in the foreground as a
group of divinities, viz. Mother Rhea receiving fruit and flowers
from her nymphs. Thus the chief gods of primitive Greek
religion would be grouped together here. "The double axe is
the sign of Zeus, the son of Rhea; the armed man represents her servants the Curetes or Corybantes, who do honour
to the mountain mother by orgies and sword dances." But it
seems strange that some of these divinities should be represented
by mere symbols, others by an idol, and the third by the living
form. For these reasons I believe that Dr. Milchhöfer's theory
must fall to the ground. It is just because in the background
divinities are represented by mere symbols and figures that we
cannot suppose them to have a human form in the foreground.
These figures of the foreground are doubtless ordinary mortals.
Nor can I assent to the theory, now generally adopted, that these
are necessarily engaged in an act of worship. The small tablet
from the palace (Fig. 288 below) shows how totally different
was the representation of sacrifice and prayer, and how completely
in accordance it was even at this time with later Greek customs.
On this ring I see only women and children innocently amusing

themselves with fruit and flowers in a purely human and natural fashion. The holy symbols do not necessarily stand in any relation to the scene represented; they may very well serve only to fill up the space, and have none but a decorative significance, like the shrines and images of Aphrodite sewn on garments.

On the signet of a second somewhat smaller ring are four heads of animals, similar to those along the edge of the great ring, together with three unmistakable heads of oxen, with long curved horns (Fig. 282).

There are five plain gold rings and one of silver belonging to this find. In addition to these, there are eleven spiral rings, some of which are of round and others of quadrangular wire. The larger of these doubtless served as armlets, the smaller as finger-rings. Dr. Schliemann thought he saw an analogy to the

282.—DESIGN ON A GOLD RING (twice natural size).

gold rings on Egyptian wall-paintings, and that like them the Mycenæan rings possibly served as a medium of exchange.

To judge from certain details of form, the objects in this find are of somewhat later date than those from the shaft-graves. The dogs' heads on the cups, in particular, recall similar heads attached to the handles of the great "warrior" vase, which we shall examine presently. Spiral rings and gold beads were not found in the graves; but in spite of these small discrepancies the cup and the rings have broad and undoubted resemblances both in workmanship and in shape to the objects found in the shaft-graves. This find of gold is certainly of slightly later date than that of the graves, but it belongs to the same period of artistic development and national supremacy.

Among the other objects found in the maze of buildings discovered by Dr. Schliemann, two stone moulds claim our attention; the larger one is made of granite and the smaller of basalt. Two sides of the former are engraved and four sides of the latter. These moulds cannot have been used for ordinary casting where the ornament to be moulded, whether of gold or of molten glass, is cast solid between two moulds fitting one above the other. No traces of any such method are visible; we find neither a smooth surface in the parts which are not engraved, nor any means by which the two moulds could be fastened together, and there is no channel for pouring in the molten flux. As small balls which would just fit into the mould engraved on one side of the smaller

283.—FRAGMENT OF A VASE (natural size).

stone have been found in fairly large numbers, and as they are, moreover, made of highly-baked clay covered with a leaden varnish, it is clear that these moulds were used not for casting but for moulding, and also, no doubt, for embossing ornaments. It is probable that the small golden objects from the graves were made in this manner. The eagle on the second stone, for instance, recalls the small eagles of gold plate found in the graves.

The mass of the find consisted of terra-cotta female figures, similar to those of which fragments were found in grave I, of figures of animals generally meant for cows, and lastly of vases. The greater number of these vases show signs of a later period than those found in the graves, a natural consequence of our having to deal in the one case with a restricted, and in the other with an undefined period of development. Seaweed and polyps are rare, geometric ornamentation with rings and concentric circles is the rule, while birds, walking solemnly one behind the other in single file, are almost the only representatives of the animate world (Fig. 283). In one instance alone is the human form represented, on the great "warrior" vase, so often referred to, which is the most important example not only at Mycenæ, but in the whole range of Mycenæan vases. This vessel has the shape of a large amphora. Round the body runs a broad band of figures : on the one side (Fig. 284) five warriors are sallying forth while a woman watches them depart ; on the other (Fig. 285), which is unfortunately much destroyed, is a combat of several warriors. All the figures have long pointed noses, and grotesquely big eyes. The warriors on the obverse apparently wear a close-fitting coat of mail over a chiton, which reaches with its fringes half-way down the thigh. The legs, from the knee downwards, are protected by gaiters, and the feet by pieces of cloth or leather bound round with bands or thongs. The rings above the knee and the wrist served not merely to fasten or draw in the garments, but had also an ornamental purpose, and therefore probably consisted on occasion of gold bands like those found in the men's graves. The head is covered by a helmet with two projecting horns in front and a plume hanging down behind ; the white dots sprinkled over the helmet probably represent glittering bosses. On the left arm they carry a shield, which is quite round but for a small segment cut off at the bottom. In the right hand they carry a long lance, with an object resembling a bag fastened to it just below the point. Dr. Furtwängler and Dr. Löschcke consider this object to be a knapsack ; others think it was a gourd-shaped bottle, such as the soldiers of Saul carried on their spears. The woman behind the warriors is raising her hand to her head, in token of distress at their departure. In the battle-scene on the reverse the men's equipment is somewhat different. They wear a skin cap instead of the helmet, the shield is a perfect circle, and there is nothing attached to the lance : perhaps we have here the enemies of the warriors who are sallying forth on the other side.

The fastenings of the handles are shaped like dogs' heads ; two geese, of the type common on the later vases, fill up the space below the dogs. The connection of this vase with the

284.—WARRIORS SETTING OUT.   DESIGN ON A LARGE VASE (size about 1 : 4).

285.—WARRIORS FIGHTING. DESIGN ON A LARGE VASE (size about 1 : 4).

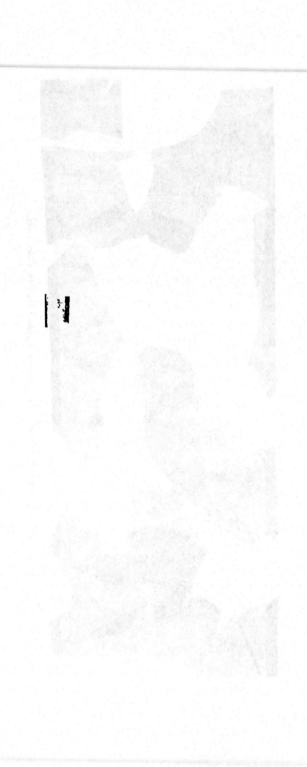

later Mycenæan, as well as with the dipylon vases is also marked by three concentric circles used on the reverse to fill up the space, where in the earlier Mycenæan style we should have expected spirals. The whole design is carried out in dark brown varnish on a ground which is painted yellow. The interior of the vase is painted red. The clay of the vessel is rather coarse, another mark to show that it belongs to the later period. Here, as in Tiryns, an important example bridges over the transition between the Mycenæan and the later style of vase-painting. The large notched shields of the old Mycenæan period disappear, and the helmets no longer have a bee-hive shape (Fig.

286.—BLOCK OF PORPHYRY (size 1 : 4).

198). There is much that recalls the vases with stirrup handles (*Bügelkannen*) on the one hand and the dipylon vases on the other; but the whole style of the drawing most resembles the Melian vase-paintings, the precursors of the pure Greek manner of later ages.

Besides a few stones engraved with figures of animals, little bronze wheels and keys, bone pegs, and other objects of minor importance, we need only mention the curious fragment of a porphyry block (Fig. 286), which leads us to consider the buildings whence all these objects found outside the graves are derived. The porphyry block is oblong in form, with a rectangular section, and is of about equal depth and breadth.

The upper and under surface are smooth beds, but the exposed surface is ornamented by a curious pattern in relief—an elliptical rosette, cut into two halves by a broad band passing over the middle. The stone beam was apparently adorned with this pattern along its whole length, for there are traces of more rosettes both to the right and to the left. Further, we notice that on the left, where the block ends at the edge of the band that traverses the rosette, the surface of the side is so worked as to show that it joined on to another block decorated in the same manner. How and where these stones were employed remained a problem till the excavations at Tiryns disclosed precisely the same system of ornamentation on the great alabaster frieze in the palace. Soon after, the buildings to which alone the beautiful porphyry block could have belonged were discovered at Mycenæ.

12. The Greek Excavations in 1886. The Palace

In 1886 the Greek Archæological Society undertook fresh excavations at Mycenæ. They uncovered a further portion of the labyrinth of buildings near the citadel wall. Most important of all, they found on the summit of the citadel the ancient palace of the kings, with the same ground-plan as at Troy and Tiryns, where the correspondence had already excited such wonder and interest. The Ephor, M. Tsountas, one of the most promising of the younger Greek archæologists, superintended the excavations, and has since published the results in an excellent essay. Not only would it be impossible nowadays to omit these important later discoveries in any description of Mycenæ, but they form as it were the crown of all Dr. Schliemann's researches, for no previous discoveries could afford such undeniable confirmation of the theories put forward by the illustrious explorer. Accordingly, we feel justified in including them in our account of his work. Our description is naturally based on M. Tsountas's article.

Massive ancient walls had long been known on the summit of the citadel; they seemed to enclose a great rectangular building, and they appeared in this form on Captain Steffen's map. During the excavations these walls turned out to be the foundations of a Doric temple belonging to the sixth or seventh century B.C. The temple lies almost due north and south, and

forms a rectangle measuring 65 by 140 feet. The only architectural remains found were a slab of the cornice and two
fragments of metopes, with a few scant remains of figures on
them. On the north side the foundations rest on the rock, but
on the south side they rest on a layer of *débris* as much as 10
feet deep. It was within this *débris* that walls of two different
ancient periods came to light. Those at the south-west corner
of the temple are slight, and consist of small stones bonded with
clay mortar. The others are built of much larger stones, and in
parts of dressed blocks; just at the south-west angle they
enclose a room with a pavement of lime concrete that stretches
under the walls mentioned above. Accordingly, the stronger and
better built walls must be the earlier, and the less strong the
later. On further excavation the earlier walls were found to
yield exactly the same ground-plan which the finds at Troy and
at Tiryns had shown to be the typical one for the main divisions
of the Homeric palace, viz. a large hall with two ante-rooms, a
stately courtyard, and several smaller apartments; the whole was
surrounded by a wall of great strength, and approached from the
lower city by two roads. We now proceed to a detailed
description of the separate parts.

The main road, certainly intended for carriage traffic as well,
ascended in zigzags from the precinct of the graves to the great
flight of steps, which lies to the south, close under the courtyard
of the palace (between I and K). These steps were evidently
protected by a gateway, of which only a few fragments of walls
and pillars remain. At the bottom of the stairs, in room I, a
bench of masonry ran along the northern and western sides.
The staircase itself is 7 feet 10 inches broad, and has twenty
steps, which are in good preservation. Each is 4 to 5 inches
high and 14 to 18 inches deep. The breadth was not got with
a single stone, but as many as three or four had to be employed;
this, however, was not visible to the eye, as the whole staircase
is overlaid with a coating of plaster some $\frac{3}{4}$-inch thick. The top
landing has been destroyed, as also the entrance, which doubtless
led through a second gateway into the palace court or Aulé.

The courtyard (L) is 37 feet 9 inches broad, and is paved with
a lime concrete. Under this concrete may be seen in places the
traces of an older pavement, which had been made with more care
and with finer materials. The north wall of the courtyard is

still standing to a height of 7 feet 10 inches, and comprises six courses of dressed blocks; between the lowest course and the one immediately above it is a horizontal beam similar to that found in the palace walls at Troy and Tiryns. This support is a survival from the old method of building, which employed quarry-stones and clay; in ashlar masonry it would naturally be dispensed with. The same construction is found in the west wall of the courtyard.

To the right of this open place of meeting comes the ante-room of the men's apartments (M). Two columns stood at the entrance between two antæ. These were all of wood, and stood on stone bases. The depth of the ante-room is 10 feet 3 inches, the floor is paved with limestone slabs.

Next comes the second ante-room (N); at its entrance (6 feet 5 inches broad) is a stone threshold with great square holes on each side, into which the door-posts were sunk. On the edge of this threshold is cut a groove (6 inches broad), in which the door moved; at the right-hand extremity is a round hole, which, as at Tiryns, held the bronze pivot for the door-hinge.

The floor of this room was paved round the walls with slabs, measuring 3 feet 4 inches by 3 feet 10 inches; but in the centre there was a limestone concrete. From it we pass into the living room—the megaron (O). At its entrance we again find a threshold with holes for the door-posts, this time, however, without the round hole for the hinge. As in the megaron at Tiryns, there can have been no door here, and a simple curtain sufficed to shut off the room.

The megaron is the largest room in the whole palace, and measures 37 feet 9 inches by 42 feet 5 inches. The roof was supported by four wooden pillars which stood on stone bases. These are sunk $\frac{3}{8}$-inch below the concrete floor, as it has appreciably gained in depth through frequent restoration. In the centre, between the columns, stands the great circular hearth, of which about a third remains. It is raised only $5\frac{1}{2}$ inches above the floor by two shallow steps, and shows as many as five superimposed layers of stucco, which had all been painted.

The design of the third and best-preserved layer is figured below after Dr. Dörpfeld's drawing (Fig. 286). The vertical surface of each step is decorated with spherical triangles; the one set is coloured grey and white, the other red and white, each of the white fields being filled up by a small star.   The horizontal surface connecting the two is coloured blue.   At the top a band of spirals, painted white with blue dots in the centre and enclosed by red and blue lines, runs round the hearth.

The floor of the megaron, like that of the ante-room, is paved with slabs along the walls, while the centre has a concrete pavement, with a chequered pattern corresponding almost exactly to that in the megaron at Tiryns.   The whole south-east corner of the living room has been destroyed by a landslip; at this point the hill descends abruptly to the ravine of the Chavos.

Returning to the great court, we find on its west side another room (P), which is not in direct communication with the court, but is approached through an ante-room.   A second opening led to a room adjoining it, but neither entrance had a door.   Against

286a.—PAINTED DECORATION OF THE HEARTH IN THE MEGARON.

the north wall of this room is a remarkable square hearth, $31\frac{1}{2}$ inches broad by $41\frac{1}{2}$ inches deep, and 2 inches high; under the floor was a conduit, built with square earthenware pipes.

To the north of this room a passage leads straight from the courtyard to the western portion of the palace, which is now entirely destroyed.   At the entrance leading from the courtyard lies a threshold which had no door above it; on the right are three stone steps, forming the lower portion of a staircase which led to the upper story.   The two lower steps measure 6 to 8 inches in height and 12 to 14 in depth; the third is a landing 3 feet 4 by 3 feet 7, from which the staircase turned to the left, and was continued in wood.   The space under the staircase must have been utilised, as it could be approached from the other side.

On the north of these stairs is a long broad passage (R), to the west of which lies a great threshold with the hinge-hole for a single door.   The continuation of the passage on this side doubt-less led to a second gate, directly accessible from the Lions' Gate by means of a steep footpath.   Unfortunately the boundary wall of

U

the palace is so completely destroyed at this point that the disposition of the gate can no longer be made out. On the left of a
person coming from outside, and just behind the great threshold,
entrances led from this same passage to further apartments which
were closed by doors. In the other direction, to the east, the
passage is covered by the foundations of the temple, but it must
have led to the different small rooms (S, etc.) traces of which are
still to be found near the megaron, and which probably served as
women's apartments, treasure-houses, and sleeping-rooms.

What applies to the ground-plan applies also, as separate
instances have already proved, to the construction—everywhere we
find the most remarkable resemblance to the palace at Tiryns.
Floors, doors, posts, thresholds, and roof all correspond. The
only difference is in the more advanced technique observable in
several details, such as the employment of dressed blocks for the
walls, and in the freer use of wall-painting, traces of which are
found in and near the megaron, in the courtyard, and in room P.
We undoubtedly have here one and the same period of civilisation, and M. Tsountas has abundantly proved by his observations
during the excavations that this period is that of the so-called
Mycenæan vases. In his account of the find in the great
court, on whose pavement rise the poor clay walls of the later
houses, he writes : " Even before any connection could be made
out between the different walls, whose upper part we first laid
bare, I noted in the journal of the excavations that between the
walls, which were soon after proved to be of later date, only fragments of vases of the geometrical style with designs of quadru-
peds and birds were found, while below, on the limestone concrete,
and wherever there were no later walls, all finds belonged to
the Mycenæan class." This is a clear and interesting result,
which may yet be of the greatest service to us, when we try
to determine what was the period of time corresponding to the
great building epoch at Mycenæ, and who were the race who
then inhabited the citadel.

The excavations lower down, close to the wall of the
Acropolis, brought to light a group of smaller buildings which
may be probably regarded as private houses. Among the medley
of walls of different periods we note especially a chamber belonging to the oldest period, with a square hearth in the centre.
This must be the megaron ; in front of it, to the west, is an

ante-room, and farther on a courtyard with traces of a sacrificial pit in the centre. At this point the ground falls rapidly from north to south, so that the suite of rooms running parallel to those just described is one story lower, and is reached by a staircase.

287.—WALL-PAINTING FROM THE GROUP OF BUILDINGS ON THE SOUTH WALL (size 1 : 2).

These lower rooms must have been dark and hardly habitable. They were the cellars of the building; from the general plan we gather that the women's apartments were over them.

288.—WALL-PICTURE FROM THE GROUP OF BUILDINGS ON THE SOUTH WALL (size 1 : 2).

Very interesting fragments of wall-painting were also found in this group of buildings; the "women sacrificing" (Fig. 288) were discovered in a room on the north side of the room with the hearth, and three figures with asses' heads (Fig. 287) on a wall to the south, near the stairs. These are by far the most important specimens of the kind found in Mycenæ; from the megaron and the adjoining sleeping-apartment we have only a very few fragments with portions of men and horses, showing no peculiarity except that round the knees and ankles of the men are bands similar to those worn by the warriors on the great vase, and also by the acrobat on the bull at Tiryns.

On the first of the new fragments are traces of three figures, which, to judge by the long ears, have asses' heads. The upright point in front of the ears can only be the tuft of hair on the forehead. These creatures must be the same as the demons which belong to the earliest religious conceptions of the Greeks, and which Dr. Milchhöfer has treated in so exhaustive and suggestive a manner. Even down to later times the lesser forces of nature subordinated to the greater powers, the spirits of wood, hill, or stream assumed a form half human half animal; satyrs, Tritons, river-gods, centaurs, and the minotaur are classical examples. These beings were of far greater import-ance in earlier times, for it every day becomes more and more certain that Greek religion originated in monotheism, i.e. in the worship of a supreme Zeus, to whom all other natural forces, represented under the form of these composite beings, were subject. Such forms are found especially on the gems of the Mycenæan period—the so-called island stones; they almost always have the legs of birds, one figure only having the legs of a lion; frequently they carry on their shoulders, as in our specimen, a pole, with their slaughtered prey hung on the ends

289.—ISLAND STONE FROM CRETE (nat-ural size).

(Fig. 289). We are therefore justified in assign-ing birds' legs to the figures on our wall-painting, and in supposing that the pole was used to carry the spoils of the chase. The figures with their long tongues hanging out are scarcely conceived in a serious spirit, and are somewhat of the nature of caricatures. The Homeric poems do not shrink from occasional satire, even on the greater gods; accordingly, the temptation to treat their attendant gnomes and goblins in the same way would be still much stronger.[1]

---

[1] [A quite different explanation of these curious figures has recently been given by Winter (see "Arch. Anzeiger," *Jahrbuch des k. d. Instituts,* 1890, p. 108). He regards them as Mycenæan attempts to reproduce the Egyptian hippopotamus

The colours in this picture are still remarkably fresh. The ground is blue-grey; the figures are flesh-coloured in front, but their backs are painted blue, with inner markings in black, yellow, and red.

The second fragment (Fig. 288) is a separate limestone tablet about 1 inch thick, intended doubtless to hang on a wall. The design, which is unfortunately much damaged, develops from the centre towards the sides, which correspond exactly. From the traces left we can make out the central figure, especially as the altars on either side afford us a clue—it was an idol, similar in form to that on the great gold ring (Fig. 281). The outline of the large notched shield shows plainly, and above it is the remainder of a head, apparently with flowing locks; in front are traces of an outstretched arm holding a lance. To the right is an altar, and behind it a woman, while from several traces we may assume that the design was repeated on the left. The shape of the altar is known to us from the relief of the Lions' Gate, where two similar bases are set side by side to form a support for the pillar. The woman stands upright, both hands raised above the altar, and her clothing corresponds in every particular to that of the women on the gold ring mentioned above. The upper part of the body is covered by a close-fitting garment; while a skirt cut up by several tucks flows down from the waist. It is clear that the bosom was not bare, as Dr. Milchhöfer maintained in the case of the figures on the gold ring, because only the hands and face are white, while the bosom is coloured yellow and matches the skirt that covers the lower part of the figure. To the left is a woman in the same attitude, and of course there must once have been an altar on this side also. The upper part of this figure, with a diadem and a necklace, is still to be seen. We may interpret the whole picture as a scene of sacrifice offered by the two women to the idol in the centre. We need scarcely conclude, with M. Tsountas, that this picture, which is the only representation of a religious subject in Mycenæan art, was not made on the spot, but imported. It shows the same blue-grey ground, and also the same colours and technique which are found in the wall-paintings.

goddess Thueris. We should thus have another piece of evidence to prove that the inlaid dagger-blades are native imitations of Egyptian work, and not themselves imported.—W. L.]

Among the finds in the palace was a scarabæus bearing the name of Queen Ti, and archæologists hoped that they were at last in possession of a definite point by which to fix the dates of the Mycenæan monuments.   Unfortunately their hopes were only very partially realised.   Professor Erman, to whom an impression was sent, pronounced it indeed to be genuine Egyptian work, but added that, in the first place, there had been many queens called Ti, and in the second, that even if it did refer to the most famous of them, the wife of Amenophis III (thirteenth century B.C.), the scarabæus might belong to a later period, for the names of celebrated royalties continued to be engraved on amulets long after their death.

At any rate, we may infer from this discovery that the palace must have been inhabited after the thirteenth century B.C.

13. Graves of the Populace in the Lower City

The indefatigable Greek Archæological Society undertook during 1887 and 1888 fresh excavations in the lower city, where M. Tsountas opened fifty-two graves.   Both the position and the contents of these graves threw light on several difficult points in Dr. Schliemann's discoveries, as well as in the whole question of Mycenæan civilisation.

In addition to the six bee-hive chambers already known, in which no further investigations were made, a seventh came to light, but unfortunately it had already been completely plundered in past ages.   The rest of the graves were not domed, but were simple chambers hewn in the rock.   A horizontal approach through the rock, usually some yards long, led to the square burial-chamber; this was sometimes fitted with niches, and in some few cases a second chamber, approached by another short passage, lay behind the first.   The roof is almost always of gable form, and only occasionally hewn into an irregular vault.   The chambers are generally from 10 by 13 to 13 by 16 feet in area, and reach a height of 6 to 8 feet at the sides, and of 8 to 10 feet in the middle, under the gable.   These graves do not form a cemetery, but lie in scattered groups more or less everywhere among the ruins of the lower city.   South of the bee-hive tomb 3 lie seven graves; to the north of No. 4 four, and six more to the south of it; eight are found near No. 5; about ten minutes to the north of the Kokoretza, at a place called Asprochoma, lay twenty-two graves, in addition to two groups of six and four respectively, at the foot of Mount Elias. The graves in one group generally correspond both in size and in the nature of their contents; the larger ones are more richly furnished with implements of ivory and costly metal, while the smaller ones are more humbly decorated with terra-cotta figures, and, oddly enough, with great numbers of the so-called "island stones"; the roughness of the designs clearly shows that these stones represent the commoner manufacture, as compared with the objects made in more costly material. From all this it follows that each group of graves must correspond to some division of the people, and M. Tsountas is certainly right in supposing that we have in these groups the graveyards of separate families or clans, each having its burial-place on the boundary of its own district. This is why the groups near the vaulted tombs 3 and 4 are in the midst of an inhabited region; they lay between two clan districts.

It is well known that the walls of the lower city only enclosed a small portion of the inhabited level tract; the greater part of the population lived in open villages. To live in such communities, and to bury the dead within the precincts of the communities, was in accordance with an ancient Greek custom, surviving down to historical times among the Spartans, who were the most careful to maintain ancient customs. "The Spartans," says Thucydides,[1] "live in open villages" (κατὰ κώμας);[2] and Plutarch[3] still knows that they buried "within the town," and certainly with the same division as the Mycenæans, for we know that the graves of the Agiadæ lay to the south, and those of the Eurypontidæ to the north of the city. This was also the custom at Athens in very early times; many graves have been found there within the inhabited area, and this fact had already led Plato[4] to the conviction that the ancient Athenians buried their dead in their houses. After this there is nothing remarkable in the presence of a graveyard on the Acropolis at Mycenæ. The Acropolis was the strongly fortified district of the ruling clan, and they, like the communities of the lower city, had their burial-place within their own precincts.

On special points, too, the finds from the new graves offer interesting and overwhelming evidence. Not one of the corpses

[1] ii. 10.　　[2] See Curtius, *Peloponnesos*, ii. p. 225.　　[3] *Lyk.* 27.　　[4] *Minos*, 315.

seems to have been cremated, though traces of ashes were
found, which, as in other cases, must have come from the funeral
sacrifices.   After the burial of the last corpse, the doorway of
the grave was walled up, with the exception of a small gap
under the lintel, and the path in front was blocked up with
earth.   Finally, the gap itself was closed with stones.   In
the blocked-up path in front of the entrance human bones were
often found, and in one case as many as six bodies, which to
all appearances had been buried at the same time; we can but
assume, with M. Tsountas, that slaves or prisoners of war were
occasionally slain at their lord's funeral, just as Achilles slew
twelve Trojans at the pyre of Patroklos.   In this way we can
also explain the strange group of bodies which was found above
the third shaft-grave (see above, p. 210).

Among the offerings to the dead a great many female idols
of terra-cotta were found, especially in the poorer graves.   They
certainly do not always represent the same divinity.   The greater
number wear a royal diadem, and may well be images of Hera,
but others with bare neck and large necklace appear to portray
Aphrodite.   Only one of these figures was found here.   There is
a third class of these figurines carrying a child.   These are found
only in a few instances; we may perhaps interpret them as images
of Demeter Kourotrophos, by analogy with the numerous images
of Demeter of a later period which have been found at Tiryns.

Many of the objects found in these graves are characteristic
of genuine Mycenaean art; such are the cups with stirrup handles.
This indeed is the shape characteristic of the vases of this find,
which it thus proves to belong to the later stage of the Mycenaean
period.   On the other hand, there are a few objects which at
present are isolated examples of their kind in the finds of this
civilisation; for instance, several razors, fragments of a small
glass vase, and many round metal mirrors with ivory handles,
adorned with figures carved in relief.   Iron is met with for the
first time in the form of a few finger-rings, which show that this
metal was considered costly and only worked into trinkets.   Of
great importance, finally, are three bronze safety-pins, for up to
now one was forced to believe that the Mycenaeans, contrary to
Homeric and Greek custom, only wore sewn garments, and on
this ground their connection with later Greeks was questioned.   The
pins found are of the most primitive shape,—a wire is twisted

twice in the centre to form a spiral, then the lower end is turned back to meet the upper end, and is hooked into it. This discovery teaches us that towards the end of the Mycenæan period, even as in Homeric and later Greece, garments were formed by square pieces of stuff wrapped round the body and pinned over the shoulders.

The object which shows the greatest artistic skill is a silver cup decorated with inlaid and enamelled work. Its shape is flat, almost like a saucer, and it has a handle. Round the upper rim, and lower down round the body, run rows of inlaid gold leaves; the space between these bands and the rim is occupied by twenty-one men's heads, one behind the other. They show a well-marked Greek type; forehead and nose form a straight line, with only the very slightest depression at the root of the nose; and this line is almost vertical, instead of oblique, as on the warrior vase and on the gold rings. The heads wear pointed beards, as on Greek vases of the sixth century B.C.; the drawing and proportion of the eyes are also similar. Three locks of hair fall on the neck and are twisted into curls below. Similar curls are also seen on a roughly-painted vase found in these graves. This had evidently been made on the spot, whence M. Tsountas concludes that the cup was also made at Mycenæ.

It is now only necessary to add a few words respecting the mutual relationship of the earlier finds, especially between the shaft-graves and the palace. The general opinion was that the shaft-graves were the oldest stratum in Mycenæan soil, and represented a different period and a different race from those of the bee-hive tombs, etc. They certainly represent an earlier period; but the development to be traced from them to the palace and the graves of the lower city is unbroken and uniform. The clay idols so common later on are found, though sparsely, in the shaft-graves; the vases, though differing in ornamentation, are of the same fine clay and have the same varnish; the gold beakers of the graves were also found in the dwelling-house near the burial precinct—of finer workmanship, it is true, and with dogs' heads on the handles, but still in the same hammered work; while the wonderful inlaying of the silver vase from grave IV and of the dagger-blades from graves IV and V finds its closest analogy in the new vessel from the lower city. There can be no doubt that shaft-graves, palace, and lower city belong to one and the same great and connected period of civilisation.

We see from the Acropoleis of Tiryns and Troy that only the rulers dwelt there. At Athens likewise there was no room in the Acropolis for the populace. The Cyclopean circumvallation walls of the Athenian citadel had long been known, and since 1887 the remains of the old palace have been discovered beside the Erechtheion and the Parthenon. The Acropolis at Mycenæ is certainly larger, but the space was none too large for a whole ruling clan with their numerous retainers and servants. We must therefore imagine the rulers as living there, and find in this fact the easiest explanation of the presence of a graveyard on the citadel mound, which roused so many scruples, and which first suggested doubts as to the Greek character of the Mycenæans; just as in the lower city each family or clan had its own graveyard within its own boundaries, so too the rulers, shut in within their fortress, had their royal graves on the Acropolis. It was only later, when the simple shaft-graves had given way to the colossal bee-hive tombs, that the Acropolis no longer sufficed for such burial and the lower city had to come to its assistance.

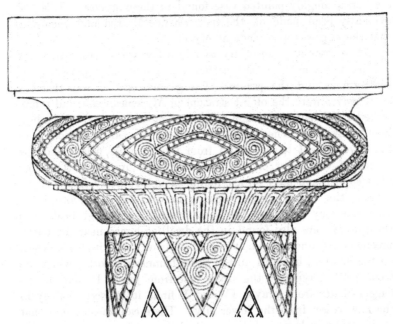

289*a*.—RESTORATION OF THE CAPITAL FROM THE TREASURY OF ATREUS.

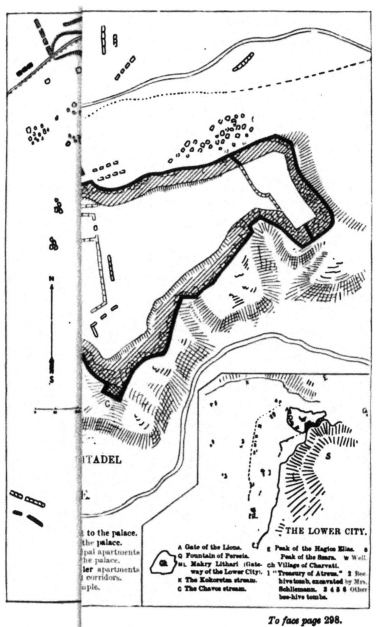

ITADEL

to the palace.
the palace.
pal apartments
he palace.
ler apartments
l corridors.
ple.

A Gate of the Lions.
Q Fountain of Perseia.
ML Makry Lithari (Gate-
　way of the Lower City).
K The Kokoretza stream.
C The Chavos stream.

THE LOWER CITY.

g Peak of the Hagios Elias.
　Peak of the Saara. w Well.
ch Village of Charvati.
1 "Treasury of Atreus." 2 Bee-
　hive tomb, excavated by Mrs.
　Schliemann. 3 4 5 6 Other
　bee-hive tombs.

To face page 298.

CHAPTER V

1. Orchomenos

DR. SCHLIEMANN'S excavations in Orchomenos were undertaken at different times—in November 1880, in the spring of 1881, and again in the spring of 1886. They form an important addition to the picture of Mycenæan civilisation, inasmuch as the chief monument brought to light, the great bee-hive tomb of Minyas, is in some essential points better preserved than even the "Treasury of Atreus" at Mycenæ, and these points carry our view far beyond the region of the bee-hive tombs themselves.

These excavations take us over to Bœotia. In the very centre of the country lies the great lake Copaïs, at the end of a vast and fruitful plain; it has no natural outlet to the sea, and at times, when the artificial drainage fails, it is a great source of danger, as it exposes the district to inundation and pestilence. In past ages several excellent channels joined it to the Euripos, the strait between the mainland and Eubœa. However, as all such undertakings were neglected under Turkish rule, and as the young Greek kingdom has not yet quite completed the great work of laying out new channels, the whole country has a bad reputation for fever.

The first Acropolis of Orchomenos apparently lay on the east side of this lake, some 6 or 7 miles distant from the Euripos, at a spot where giant Cyclopean walls are still visible on the heights of Goulás. The choice of this site accords with the custom, usual in early ages on the coasts of the Archipelago, of placing the capital of a seafaring nation at some little distance from the sea, though not too far.

is formed, on which, as in the Atreus grave, were fastened bronze rosettes. "Almost in the centre of the treasure-room was a long hole in the level rock 9 inches deep, 15 inches broad, and 19 inches long, which must have served to secure some monument."

A door (6 feet 11½ inches high, 3 feet 9 inches broad above, and 3 feet 11½ inches below), whose posts, to judge from the indentations still left, were richly adorned with bronze ornaments, leads from the vaulted room to the square chamber adjoining it. This second chamber rouses keen interest from the peculiarities of its arrangement and its beautiful internal decorations. It measures 12 feet 3 inches by 9 feet, and is 7 feet 10¼ inches high. On all four sides rise the vertical walls of native rock; but this chamber was sunk from above like a shaft, and not hewn out in the rock with the vaulted room as a starting-point. "The ceiling seems to have fallen in only about 1870 under the pressure of the superincumbent mass of rubbish," says Dr. Schliemann; "because all the villagers agree that at that time the earth suddenly gave way with a great noise precisely above the place where the chamber is, and a deep hole was then formed." The interior construction of the chamber is as follows. Walls of small quarry-stones bonded with clay were built against the sides, while at a height of 8 feet above the floor green schist slabs 16 inches thick were laid across from one wall to the other to form the ceiling. The exact construction of this ceiling is not clear. It seems that in order to relieve it a cavity, practically a second story, was constructed; it was formed by walls hewn in the natural rock and overlaid with slabs; then above this followed the mass of *débris* reaching up to the top. The slabs of the ceiling are most exquisitely sculptured on the inner side with a pattern composed of rosettes and spirals. The conjecture that this design was copied from a carpet pattern seems correct. Just as in textile fabrics, first comes a centrepiece, formed by interlacing spirals, from the corners of which spring palmettes; round this is a frame consisting of a double row of rosettes. Then follow more interlacing spirals and palmettes, framed by another border of rosettes, which is edged on the outside by the familiar dentils.

The walls had been revetted with marble slabs, some of which still remain in their original place. They exhibit the same pattern as the ceiling; above and below runs a row of rosettes,

To face page 302.

and the remaining space is filled with spirals and palmettes. We see at a glance that this style of ornament is thoroughly Mycenæan: the rosettes are found on the alabaster frieze at Tiryns, the interlacing spirals on wall-paintings from the same place, and the border of dentils is frequent enough both at Tiryns and Mycenæ. Even if the architecture of the building did not proclaim its connection with similar buildings in Mycenæ, the wall-decorations would settle the question. A further point of special interest is that the second chamber affords a new link in the transition from the "shaft" to the "bee-hive" tombs. The latter were merely a magnificent development of the former. The tomb at Orchomenos is identical with the shafts at Mycenæ: it is sunk straight into the rock, lined with rubble walls and closed with stone slabs. The only difference is that the round chamber for the cultus of the dead, which in the Mycenæan Acropolis was above the graves, is here beside them. The desire to gain easier access to the actual grave, no doubt, inspired the splendid innovation of the "bee-hive" tomb.

2. Ithaca

The investigations undertaken in Ithaca by Dr. Schliemann and others have been mostly of a topographical nature. They serve not so much to further our knowledge of the civilisation of the heroic age of Greece, as to explain the relations between Homer's descriptions and the landscape which inspired them. The observations we made on this point with respect to the Troad receive· here interesting confirmation. It is obvious that the singer of the *Odyssey* had no mere general acquaintance with the island, but was absolutely familiar with its local features.

Dr. Schliemann visited Ithaca as early as 1868, and described his journey in his first archæological work, *Ithaca, the Peloponnesus, and Troy*. Ten years later he went again and corrected some of his original impressions in the biographical sketch prefixed to *Ilios* (1881). An English traveller, Sir William Gell, is the most important of Dr. Schliemann's predecessors, and may be considered the discoverer of the Homeric Ithaca. Since his time different writers have advanced most contradictory theories. Especial mention should be made of R. Hercher, who denies here as in the Troad all connection between Homer's pictures and the reality. In the following pages we shall chiefly follow the account of Dr. Emil Reisch, the last scholar who has visited Ithaca with a scientific object; he has kindly placed at our disposal his MS. notes. Parts have already appeared in Baedeker's *Greece*, for which the account was written.

There is no doubt that the Ithaca of Homer is identical with the island which now bears that name. Its proximity to Cephalonia, which is also called Samos, is often insisted on. The sway of Odysseus extended as far as there, for he set Philoitios over his cattle "in the land of the Cephallenians."[1] Moreover, in *Od.* xx. 187, Philoitios had to bring over the ferry which lies between the two banks, "a barren heifer for the wooers, and fatted goats; and ferrymen had brought them over . . . who send even other folks on their way, whosoever comes to them."

In the neighbourhood of Ithaca there is one special landmark; a couple of miles to the west, about half-way between Ithaca and Cephalonia, lies a small islet, now called Daskalion; evidently it is the very islet on which the suitors lay in wait to slay Telemachos on his return from Pylos and Sparta.[2] The description of Homer runs: "Now there is a rocky isle in the mid sea, midway between Ithaca and rugged Samos, Asteris, a little isle; and there is a harbour therein with a double entrance, where ships may ride. There the Achæans abode, lying in wait for Telemachos."[3]

It follows from this passage that as Telemachos had to sail up the strait between Cephalonia and ·Ithaca to reach the city, this city must have lain on the strait, *i.e.* on the west coast of the

[1] *Od.* xx. 210.

[2] [This is hardly correct. The little rock-ledge called Daskalió or Mathitarió—both names mean "schoolhouse"—is two miles from Ithaca and hardly 600 yards from Cephalonia, as will be seen on reference to the map from the Admiralty Charts given in Appendix III to Merry and Riddell's *Odyssey*. No one has admitted more frankly than Schliemann himself the absolute impossibility of identifying it with Asteris. "Its length is 586 feet; its breadth varies between 108 feet and 176 feet. On account of these small dimensions it cannot possibly be identified with the Homeric Asteris, which, as the poet says, had two ports, each of them with two entrances" (*Ilios*, p. 46. See also *Ithaque*, p. 75). Schuchhardt omits to explain also how a poet personally acquainted with Ithaca could have described it as "furthest towards the darkness" (*i.e.* the west), while the neighbouring islands "face the dawning and the sun" (*Od.* ix. 25, 26). Ithaca is overshadowed by Cephalonia immediately to the west. The following identifications must therefore be accepted only with great reserve.—W. L.]

[3] *Od.* iv. 844.

island; there is a general consensus of opinion on this point, but the precise spot was disputed. The most popular view was that the Homeric settlement had been situated in the north, at a spot called Polis, which lies on the only fruitful and important valley in the island; but Dr. Schliemann declared that the isolated height there called Kastro (City), and supposed to be the Acropolis of the old town, was merely a natural rock fortress, and had no ruins to show. Like Gell, he believed that the old settlement was farther south on the narrow neck of land which connects the north and south portions of the island. Here rises Mount Aëtos, a conical hill about 650 feet high; quite at its summit is a small plateau surrounded by a Cyclopean wall, which is still standing to a height of 20 to 25 feet; while lower down are two other circumvallation walls. Dr. Schliemann placed the palace of Odysseus on the summit, and thought he had discovered the remains of about 190 Cyclopean houses between the two lower walls.

To this theory Dr. Reisch makes the following objections: "Even though the nucleus of the fortification walls undoubtedly dates from very early times, this stronghold cannot possibly be taken for the Homeric city; for, granting that the descriptions in the *Odyssey* borrow only the most general outlines from a real background, yet the city cannot have been situated on an inhospitable rock 650 feet high. There was no room between the blocks on the narrow plateau for a palace even of the very smallest dimensions, nor for a town on the steep declivities of the rock.[1] The only possible site for a settlement is on the slopes to the north and south-west of Aëtos, and yet the excavations undertaken here by Dr. Schliemann have produced practically no result. Nevertheless, in the ruins of the 'Palace of Odysseus' we have a fortress of great age and strength, which in times of danger served as a refuge to the dwellers round about, and was of the utmost importance for the defence of the whole island; for it commanded not only the landing-places to the south-east and north-west of Mount Aëtos, but protected the only means of communication between the north and south parts of the island."

While the theories of Gell and Schliemann break down

---

[1] Dr. Schliemann himself says: "The slopes of Mount Aëtos rise at an angle of 35°, and are therefore 7° steeper than the upper cone of Vesuvius."

owing to special local conditions, our attention is once more irresistibly drawn, by the story of the suitors' ambush, to the valley of Polis. Their ambush on the island of Asteris is only comprehensible if Telemachos had to journey up to Polis, not if he had already landed close to Aëtos.

Now we find that evident traces of a very archaic settlement are to be seen in the valley of Polis: on the hill of Castro, the northern headland of the bay, said by Dr. Schliemann to be nothing but a rock, Dr. Reisch saw remains of a terrace-wall of great roughly-hewn blocks preserved for a length of 30 paces, and below, from the bay "right up the hill, as far as the present village of Stavros, stretched an important settlement, whose existence can be traced by means of the extant remains from the seventh century B.C. to the time of the latest Roman Empire."

Ruins were also found on the other side of the village of Stavros, to the north. "There, among olive trees and vineyards, is situated the little church of St. Anastasios, which rests on an ancient platform (26 × 16 feet) made of large carefully joined blocks, and still from 6 to 10 feet high. Other ancient foundations in the immediate neighbourhood show that we have here the remains of a great settlement. An ancient staircase, cut in the rock, leads from the church to a little plateau, where rectangular niches hewn in the smoothed rock walls seem to point to an ancient place of worship. This place (or, according to another version, the platform of the church) has been known for the last hundred years as 'Homer's School.' A little lower down is an ancient well, discovered in 1886 by the priest of the church, and near it a rock tomb; 30 yards farther on, among the vineyards, is an interesting old subterranean well-house. A passage of roughly-hewn stones, about 3 yards long, descends to the entrance, where a few steps are still preserved; the small inner chamber, the floor of which is covered with water, has a vaulted roof of roughly-hewn blocks."

Not far from these ruins gushes out a spring called Melan-hydro. It has been identified with the Homeric "shady spring," by which Eumaios pastured his swine. This spot should, however, be sought for elsewhere, as we shall see. The place where the Phæacians landed Odysseus, and the pastures of Eumaios, to which he then went, are precisely the two spots which are easiest of identification.

We know that Odysseus was not taken straight from Phæacia to his city, but was placed ashore in a bay, and that when he awoke he did not immediately recognise his native land. Only when Athene comes to his aid does the mist fall from his eyes. She tells him the name of the haven where he was set on land, and shows him the vast cave of the nymphs on the hill, and in the distance the high mountain Neriton. Nothing, however, is said of the town, which must therefore have been far out of the range of vision. The close description can leave no doubt as to where we must look for the landing-place. Homer describes it as follows : "There is in the land of Ithaca a certain haven of Phorkys, the ancient one of the sea, and thereby are two head-lands of sheer cliff, which slope to the sea on the haven's side and break the mighty waves that ill winds roll without, but within the decked ships ride unmoored when once they have attained to that landing-place. Now at the harbour's head is a long-leaved olive tree, and hard by is a pleasant cave and shadowy, sacred to the nymphs, that are called the Naiads. And therein are mixing bowls and jars of stone, and there, moreover, do bees hive. And there are great looms of stone, whereon the nymphs weave raiment of purple stain, a marvel to behold, and therein are waters welling evermore. Two gates there are to the cave, the one set towards the north wind, whereby men may go down, but the portals toward the south pertain rather to the gods, whereby men may not enter : it is the way of the immortals." [1]

There can be no doubt that the "haven of Phorkys" must be looked for at some spot on the Gulf of Molo, for to the south of it, at a height of 160 feet, lies a great cavern, which certainly suggested the Homeric description of the grotto of the nymphs. An entrance (6 feet high and 12 to 20 inches broad) leads to a small outer chamber, which gives access to a large damp inner chamber, about 45 feet in diameter. From the roof as well as on the walls hang wonderful stalactites, which a poet's imagination fashioned into the great looms of stone and the bowls and jars of the nymphs. A carefully-hewn block of stone (30 by 20 inches wide), with a hole in its upper surface, lies at the back of the cave. It must have served as an altar, and shows that the cavern was used as a place of worship, no doubt in honour of the nymphs.

[1] *Od.* xiii. 96 *sq.*

It has further been disputed whether the deep bay of Vathy itself, or a small harbour called Dexia on the west of the entrance, is the real haven of Phorkys. The question is of little importance. The cave is equidistant from either spot. One would naturally conclude that the larger well-defined bay of Vathy was meant, but Dr. Schliemann thinks that "the two headlands of sheer cliff, which slope to the sea on the haven's side" of the Homeric description, may be identified precisely in front of the little haven of Dexia. Possibly his view is correct. In any case the region about the Gulf of Molo can account for every detail in the Homeric picture, and is above all consistent with the account of the visit paid by Odysseus to Eumaios.

The pasture-grounds of the goodly swineherd must have lain to the south of the island, for when Telemachos is returning from Pylos (i.e. from the south) to his home Athene's advice to him is : "When thou hast touched the nearest shore of Ithaca, send thy ship and all thy company forward to the city, but for thy part, seek first the swineherd who keeps thy swine, and is loyal to thee as of old"; [1] but for Odysseus the way to Eumaios lay in the reverse direction, and is thus described : "But Odysseus fared forth from the haven by the rough track up the wooded country and through the heights, where Athena had shown him that he should find the goodly swineherd, who cared most for his substance of all the thralls that goodly Odysseus had gotten. Now he found him sitting at the front entry of the house, where his courtyard was builded high, in a place with wide prospect." [2]

Two other landmarks help to the belief that the pasturage lay to the south of the island, and on a hill "with wide prospect" -the Korax rock, and the black water "of the spring Arethusa": "Him shalt thou find sitting by the swine, as they are feeding near the rock of Korax and the spring Arethusa, and there they eat abundance of acorns and drink the black water, things that make in good case the rich flesh of swine." [3] Odysseus says to Eumaios, with reference to the Korax rock, "But if thy lord return not according to my word, set thy thralls upon me, and cast me down from a mighty rock," [4] so that there must have been a high, steep cliff here. All these conditions are fulfilled in the great plateau to the south of the island. There we find "a wide prospect," there is a deep spring, now called Perapegadi, and

[1] Od. xv. 36.   [2] Od. xiv. 1-6.   [3] Od. xiii. 407-410.   [4] Ibid. xiv. 398.

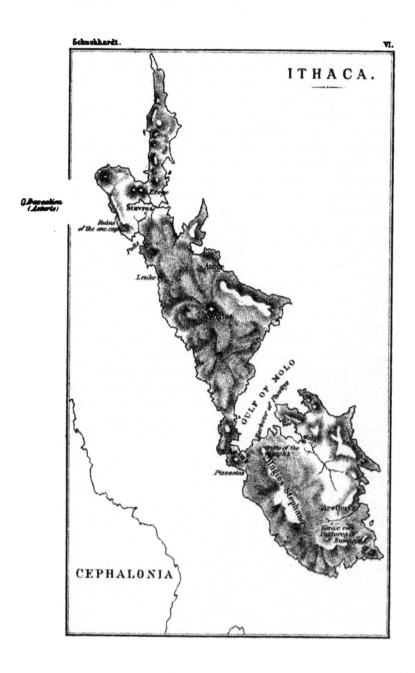

ITHACA.

CEPHALONIA

there rises a rocky cliff, which corresponds absolutely to the
" Raven cliff." Here then lay the pasturage of Eumaios.

These are the principal points in the ancient topography of
Ithaca, which can be clearly recognised in the modern conditions :
still more has the general character of the island remained
unchanged. Athene says of the country : " Verily it is rough
and not fit for the driving of horses, yet it is not a very sorry
isle, though narrow withal. For herein is corn past telling, and
herein too wine is found, and the rain is on it evermore, and the
fresh dew. And it is good for feeding goats and feeding kine ;
all manner of wood is here, and watering-places unfailing are
herein." [1] All this can be still said of Ithaca at the present day.
Wine is still a great industry, though it is not yet largely
exported. On one point only do we notice a striking difference ;
you may look in vain for " all manner of wood." Athene says to
Odysseus on his awakening : " This hill is Neritos all clothed in
forest." [2] Neritos is generally supposed to be the highest
summit of the Anoge range, just in the centre of the northern
half of the island, but even if we identify it with St. Stephanos
in the southern half, it is certain that neither is any longer
" clothed in forest." We have here another proof of what may
so often be noticed on classic ground, that the mountain ranges
were not bare in ancient times as they are now, and that their
present condition is only the result of centuries of bad cultivation.

[1] *Od.* xiii. 242-247.   [2] *Ibid.* xiii. 349.

CHAPTER VI

HISTORICAL SURVEY OF THE HEROIC AGE OF GREECE

SOMETHING of the same excitement which greeted the arrival of the Æginetan sculptures at Munich in 1830 was experienced when the treasures of the Mycenæan shaft-graves were brought to Athens. People shook their heads at this unprecedented style of art, and were unable to detect in it any single Greek characteristic. Now, however, just as then, discovery after discovery has helped to bridge over the gulf between the once solitary island of Mycenæan civilisation and the *terra firma* of known Greek art. Yet dispute is still rife as to whether the island belongs to this or to the other shore.

Dr. Schliemann believed, as we know, that he had discovered the civilisation of Homer's Achæans in the graves at Mycenæ. Dr. Köhler,[1] on the other hand, tried in 1878 to prove that these graves belonged to the Carians. These two opinions, reinforced by various fresh arguments, still confront each other.

It must be acknowledged that Mycenæan civilisation differs very considerably from that which is reflected in the Homeric poems, and from that of later Greece. The advocates of the Carian hypothesis lay special stress on the difference in the mode of burial. The bodies found in the shaft-graves were buried, and, as Helbig maintains, they are even embalmed.[2] In Homer, on the contrary, as in the dipylon graves, which may certainly be regarded as Greek, cremation is universal. The earlier custom, it is said, presupposes the Egyptian belief, "that the life of the soul is bound up with the preservation of the body, while to the Homeric Greeks the body is nothing more than a blot on the sunlight, and must be purified by fire, so that the gates of the lower

---

[1] Kohler—*Kuppelgrab von Menidi.*   [2] Hom. *Epos*, p. 53.

world may be opened to the liberated soul." Resemblances to Egypt and Asia Minor occur to us at once. The people who ruled in Mycenæ and Tiryns must have been a powerful seafaring race accustomed to distant voyages, while the Greek legend " still makes Orestes travel on by land, and Menelaus reaches Egypt only through being wrecked in a storm." Mycenæan civilisation held sway on the east coast of the Greek mainland only; it did not penetrate into the interior. It centred chiefly in the islands of the Archipelago.

In everything a sharp contrast to the Homeric picture world was evident. As this contrast extended even to details, as the sewed garments pointed to a purely Asiatic costume, and the absence of iron marked an incredibly early period, it was thought that all connection between Mycenæan civilisation and Homer must be abandoned, and that this civilisation must be referred to people who, coming originally from Asia, flourished long before the Achæans, and then gave place to them. This early race would most probably be the Carians, who, according to Herodotos[1] and Thucydides,[2] were for a time the most important people on the islands, and transmitted to the Greeks many inventions, such as the use of escutcheons and handles for their shields, and of plumes for their helmets. They were conquered by Minos, who was the first to put a stop to piracy, and were specially employed in fitting out vessels. Thucydides further relates[3] that in his time old graves were found in Delos, which, to judge from " the equipment of weapons buried with them," must have belonged to the Carians. This last passage, more especially, was readily connected with the Mycenæan graves, which were found filled with weapons. Dr. Dümmler, who with Dr. Studniczka further developed Dr. Köhler's hypothesis in 1887, was familiar with some of the oldest burying-grounds on the Cyclades. As " a dagger or a spear-head are only very occasionally " found in them, he concludes that these island-graves must have been pre-Carian, and the Mycenæan shaft-graves Carian. A few minor points appear to lend further support to this hypothesis. The double axe, which is found between the horns of the heads of oxen from the shaft-graves, is still the symbol of the Carian Zeus on later coins; a burial-mound near Megara is called Car; the family of Isagoras in Athens, down to Herodotos's time, sacrificed to the Carian Zeus,[4] and so on.

---

[1] i. 171.   [2] i. 4.   [3] i. 8.   [4] Herodotos, v. 66.

We now have to consider whether the results of the excavations compel us to accept this theory, or whether some alternative view has more to commend it.

The most important fact about Dr. Schliemann's excavations is that they invariably confirm the former power and splendour of every city which is mentioned in Homer as conspicuous for its wealth or sovereignty. In Mycenæ, Tiryns, and Orchomenos one and the same "Mycenæan" age of civilisation meets us; in Troy most of the remains from the chief stratum are different and obviously older, but towards the end of that great period the Mycenæan style appears there also, and this establishes the connection in time between the two points. The second city at Hissarlik had come into contact with Mycenæan civilisation shortly before its downfall. In all these places the chief stratum represents the one great period of the city, after which there comes practically nothing of importance either at Mycenæ or Tiryns, while at Troy, after a long period of village settlements, the only city of any size built on the spot belongs to Hellenistic times. It follows from this alone that Homer's conceptions about his heroic age of Greece are founded on the tradition of the golden eras of Mycenæ and of Troy. In many cases it is plain that not mere tradition but thorough knowledge is at his service, and this is all the more striking in various points where Mycenæan usage differed entirely from that of later periods.

Foremost in this connection are the strongly-fortified citadels which do not reappear after this period either in Greece or in Asia Minor. Sparta is typical of the custom universal among the Dorians of leaving their cities unwalled. According to Thucydides the Greeks of Asia Minor up to the time of the Persian invasions had no walls round their settlements. But Homer knows exactly about walls and towers and gates. His description of the Skaian gate with its great platform, from which women and aged men witnessed the fight on the plain, exactly answers to the oldest city gate uncovered at Hissarlik. He knows too how things look within the walls. The great court, surrounded by porticoes, with the altar to Zeus in the midst, and the central hall in which Odysseus is to find the queen of the Phæacians as "she sits at the hearth in the light of the fire, her chair leaned against a pillar," are proofs of it.

The wealth of metals in this period of youthful display is also distinctly reflected in Homer. The vaults of the tholos buildings gleam with the shimmer of brass like the walls of the palace of Alkinoos. But for the golden treasures of the shaft graves, Homer's tales of chased goblets like the cup of Nestor, of inlaid shoulder-belts, and the golden dogs that kept watch before Alkinoos' door, would still be treated as bold flights of fancy, as was in fact the case before the excavations.

The most striking and important correspondence, however, between the Mycenæan discoveries and Homer is that shown by the inlaid work on the dagger-blades, and on the cup of the fourth grave (p. 240). Nowhere else in Greece has work of this sort, complete pictures in inlaid metals, been discovered. Yet Homer had a very clear conception of this kind of workmanship, for he describes in detail how, on Achilles' shield, vineyards were represented with purple grapes on golden stems, surrounded by a hedge of tin, and later on speaks of youths wearing golden swords hung from silver baldrics.

It is enough to enumerate these leading points of agreement. They are sufficient proof that for certain parts of his descriptions Homer can have had no other models before him but those of Mycenæan art and civilisation. We know, however, that Homer is only a collective name, that his epics were pieced together at a comparatively late period, from songs which had gradually come into existence during a period that extended over centuries. Therefore, although there survives in the oldest parts of these songs a clear conception of the actual conditions of the Mycenæan age, yet many of the later ones arose when that great civilisation had already decayed, and we must not be surprised if they often represent another world. Iron, for example, which only appears in ornamental work near the end of the Mycenæan period, is in Homer almost always used for tools and weapons. In Homer, again, the custom of wearing garments not sewn but merely pinned together with fibulæ is general, whereas at Mycenæ only scanty traces of it can be detected quite at the end. In the same way we must explain the new mode of interment by cremation, in place of the Mycenæan burial. Although the two customs originally betokened a difference in religious belief, such beliefs change with time and other conditions. In the dipylon graves cremation is the rule, corresponding to the Homeric custom. But among later Greeks there still lived a tradition, kept alive perhaps by occasional discoveries, that their ancient heroes, like Perseus and Theseus, had not been burnt, but buried, and in Hellenistic times the two customs were again practised side by side.

Thus it is not as impossible to bridge over the chasm which separates Mycenæ from the Greek life, of which Homer is considered to be the first distinct representative, as the Carian hypothesis assumes. Of course, when that hypothesis arose, most of the striking coincidences which have guided us were still wanting. Dr. Köhler wrote his treatise in 1878, when the Mycenæan shaft - graves had only just been discovered. The palace of Tiryns, which taught us to recognise the palace at Troy, was not brought to light till 1884, that of Mycenæ in 1886. The inlaid work on the dagger - blades was only discovered in 1881, and the doubts aroused by the total absence of iron and of fibulæ in the Mycenæan period did not entirely disappear till 1888.

Though the correspondence between the discoveries and the epic descriptions is sufficient to prove that by his Achæans Homer meant the representatives of Mycenæan civilisation, we must not over - estimate this correspondence, as many do at present, and ascribe this civilisation to the typical Greeks after the great migration, the Dorians. It is astonishing to find this view insisted on in the latest historical works of Busolt and of Pöhlmann. It must be most decidedly rejected. How could the Dorians, who knew of no instruments but axe and saw to fashion their roofs and doors with, who used nothing but iron, even as a medium of exchange, who despised fortifications and lived in cities without walls, have anything in common with the refined ornamentation, the profusion of gold, and the astonishing architectural activity of the Mycenæan period? To ascribe to the Dorians the culture of the Mycenæans we must either entirely ignore the high development of the latter or else assume that the Dorians at their very first appearance had reached a height of culture and art, of which they never showed themselves capable in the whole course of their after-history.

We must not forget that for all the resemblance there are numerous differences between Homer and Mycenæ, and that the people whom he calls Achæans may have been quite unlike what we have hitherto imagined from his poems.

Traces of Mycenæan civilisation have hitherto been found all along the east coast of Greece from Lacedæmon (Amyclæ) through Argolis (Mycenæ, Tiryns, Nauplia) and Attica (Athens, Spata, Menidi) to Bœotia (Orchomenos), and as far as Thessaly (Dimini, near Volo). It extended, besides, over the whole Archipelago, where in Cos, Calymnos, Carpathos, Syra, Thera, and above all in Crete and Rhodes, finds have been made. On the coast of Asia Minor also its traces are cropping up. We have repeatedly mentioned the gold work of Mycenæan style found at Troy; Mycenæan vases have lately been found at The-angela in Caria, and similar ones, including the stirrup-handled cup, are said to have been lately discovered by Mr. Flinders Petrie in Egypt.[1]

This civilisation extended accordingly over a very wide area. It is highly improbable that the vases were all made in one place, as some have supposed, and then exported all round. It is true that M. Fouqué believes, from an analysis of fragments found at Mycenæ, that this pottery was made in Thera. Many would conclude on this account that an island, perhaps Thera or Crete, was the centre of Mycenæan civilisation. But as regards Mycenæ, it is certain that nearly everything found there had been made on the spot. This is absolutely certain in the case of the *stelai*, the masks, and all that was only required for the furniture of the tomb; M. Tsountas has now made it probable that this was also the case with the inlaid work. How then should they have imported such ordinary objects as earthenware vases? The finds of vases in Mycenæan style are accordingly not the product of a single commercial town, which monopolised for a time the trade of the Archipelago with its exports, but they bear witness to a population that spread over all that region, and was united by a common civilisation. And this civilisation must assuredly have lasted for centuries. The walls of Tiryns are considerably older than those of Mycenæ. The Mycenæan walls themselves represent the period that extended from the first laying out of the Necropolis till it was closed, and its precinct

---

[1] [See his article on "The Egyptian Bases of Greek History" in the *Journal of Hellenic Studies*, vol. xi. pp. 271-277. Mr. Petrie there states that the age of the Mycenæan vases found in Egyptian tombs can be definitely dated, with an error of not more than one hundred years. The most primitive forms, with linear decoration, belong to 1400 B.C., the later, with natural objects, to 1100 B.C. Gold and bronze fibulæ were found and dated to 1900-1200 B.C.—W. L.]

levelled up and surrounded by the circle of slabs. But even with the latest shaft-grave we are still in an older period than that represented by the oldest objects in the finds from the rest of the citadel, such as the golden goblets and rings found in the house near the burying-ground. Finally comes the repairing of the town wall, which is carried out in polygonal, or genuine Greek masonry. For all this development we must not allow less than from two to three hundred years.

The representatives of Mycenæan civilisation must thus have held long and firm sway in Mycenæ. It is only in this way that we can explain their fortresses, built with such vast resources, and the unparalleled wealth displayed in their tombs.

The time to which this civilisation belongs cannot yet be fixed with any accuracy. In Thera (the modern Santorin) bits of Mycenæan pottery were buried under a layer of ashes, which, geologists say, must have been thrown up by the volcano about the middle of the second millennium B.C. Geological calculations, however, always allow a few hundred years' margin, so that this assertion really teaches us little. The scarabæus found in the palace at Mycenæ, with the name of the Egyptian queen Ti, only proves that the palace was in existence after the thirteenth century B.C. At Rhodes also, among Mycenæan objects, a scarabæus of Amenophis III was found. The Mycenæan vases discovered quite lately in the Fayum were lying with twelve cartouches of Amenophis IV and of Ramses II (1500-1400 B.C.) Here too the objects need not be contemporary with the kings whose names they bear, but fix the fourteenth or fifteenth century as the farthest limit to which they can date back. Finally, in the grave of Aa Hotep, the mother of Ah Mose, who freed Egypt from the Hyksos (about 1600), a sword was found, worked in relief with four locusts and a lion pursuing a bull, exactly in the style of the Mycenæan blades. Since model and copy cannot be very far apart, we thus get the fifteenth or sixteenth century B.C. as the earliest date for this Mycenæan work.

This period, from about 1400 to 1000 B.C., would exactly suit for the Homeric Achæans. Its end would coincide with the date at which, by general agreement, the Dorians entered the Peloponnesus, seized the Achæan strongholds, and crushed their ancient glory. But the territory over which Mycenæan

civilisation holds sway does not coincide with that which the
Achæans of Homer possess.   The poet includes under their
name all the Greek tribes, and makes all the inhabitants of the
opposite coast, including even the Carians, allies of Troy.
Mycenæan civilisation, on the other hand, only spreads along
the eastern coast of the Greek mainland, but on the other hand
encroaches upon Asiatic soil at different points.   It may be said
that in the west, at the places named by Homer,—Olympia not
having attained importance till later,—no satisfactory excavations
have yet been undertaken, and that the same civilisation may
yet be found there.   But this civilisation is too closely connected
not merely by its geographical distribution, but also by its
essential qualities, with the eastern sea, with Asia and with
Egypt, to allow of our attempting to bring it into harmony on
this point with the Homeric conception.

The style of art shows in numerous details its dependence
on Asiatic motives.   One need only mention the continually
recurring lions and palms, the double axe of the Carian Zeus,
the sitting female figure on the little gold plate, which exactly
resembles the mother of the gods on Mount Sipylos; the pointed
shoes of the men on the gold cups of Amyclæ, which correspond
to those of the so-called Sesostris at Nymphi on Sipylos; the
vaulted shape of the graves, which is probably to be traced
back to the Phrygian style of building; and the masses of gold,
which can only have been procured from Phrygia or Lydia.
That there was an active trade with Egypt is proved by the
ostrich egg and the scarabs, the papyrus plants on the dagger-
blades, and the flower-pot on the silver vase, the inlaid work
and the whole shape of the swords, the pattern on the ceiling at
Orchomenos, the fresco from Tiryns, and many other minor
details.

Owing to these striking resemblances, which were not as yet
counterbalanced by any affinities to Homer and Hellenic culture,
Dr. Köhler had conceived of an Asiatic race, the Carians, as
representatives of Mycenæan civilisation.   But these Asiatic and
Egyptian influences need not astonish us.   The later Greeks
themselves had a clear tradition which frankly admitted their
existence.   Perseus, who comes from the islands, and Pelops,
who comes from Lydia, to the Peloponnesus, are successive
kings of Mycenæ.   And in the person of Danaus, who immigrates

from Egypt, is embodied everything which the Hellenes thought
they owed to the land of the Nile.

It has never been assumed that the Greeks were the original
inhabitants of their mainland. Their migration from Asia
cannot be doubted. A people, however, who inhabited the islands
and only laid claim to the coast of the mainland must certainly
have come from Asia by sea, and that at not such a very remote
time, as they were still half Asiatic in their ways of life, in their
architecture, their art, and their dress. They had been a seafaring
people, and had not, like the Greeks of the following period, given
up to the Phœnicians all commercial intercourse with each other
and with Egypt, but had carried it on themselves. The commercial
supremacy of the Phœnicians in the Archipelago began in the next
period. We have learnt that from the Cyprus Necropoleis, where
pottery of the Trojan make precedes all Phœnician productions.

The violent displacement and change experienced by
Mycenæan civilisation at the time of the dipylon vases is most
simply explained by the appearance of the Dorians. They won
the Peloponnesus by force. As they came from the north out of
the interior, we may presume that the style of art they introduced
was that which continued to prevail long after over the whole of
Central Europe, the geometrical style of the dipylon vases.
These vases took the place of Mycenæan pottery on the mainland. But on the islands the Mycenæan style underwent a
regular development, first in the so-called vases of Melos and
afterwards in those of Rhodes, which, along with the closely
allied Corinthian fabrics, strongly influenced later Greek vase-
painting from the sixth to the fourth century B.C. The vases
therefore afford us evidence of an unbroken chain of development
from the Mycenæan to the purest Greek style. In many other
points the relations between the two sides may be observed.
The Mycenæan capital is the first step towards the Doric; the
latest restoration of the Mycenæan city walls shows Greek
polygonal work. The recent excavations have yielded figures of
different female goddesses, which we may call by Greek names.
They have also for the first time come upon iron, fibulæ, and
mirrors of the type on which the later Greek shape is based.
Indeed, in these excavations heads have been found as devices on
a gold goblet, with a type of face hardly to be distinguished from
that of the sixth century B.C.

We must not call the Mycenæan style Greek, for Greek style and Greek character, from all that we can observe, did not develop into full individuality till the seventh century, when the name " Hellenes " first appears.   Mycenæan civilisation gives us rather a glimpse of the seething mixture of elements out of which later Greek life emerged.   We see there Phrygian, Carian, Egyptian, and above all " island " elements, but everywhere the tendencies to a new individual growth are noticeable.   It can hardly be supposed that the name of the Achæans prevailed wherever this civilisation spread.   We know neither what race first bore this name, nor how Homer came to apply it to the whole of the Greeks.   Argolis is specially named Achæan, but Achæans are also mentioned in Crete and Thessaly.   With them we must think of the Minyæ as settled in Bœotia, the Ionians in Attica, and the Carians on the islands.   Mycenæan civilisation was thus peculiar to no single race, but was developed through lively intercourse among all the tribes dwelling in and around the Archipelago.   A temporary political union of these different races may possibly have aided still further the equal spread of their civilisation.   We are involuntarily reminded of the empire of Minos, who, with Crete as the centre of his power, exercised a great naval supremacy.   He subdued the Carians and exacted tribute from the Greek coast.   This is attested as regards Athens by the regular tribute of youths and maidens paid by the Athenians and abolished by Theseus.   But within such an empire, whether its capital was in Crete or at Mycenæ, or first in the one and then in the other, a number of races must have shared the same civilisation.   To which of these was it indebted for its existence ? To the Carians ?   Partly, no doubt.   They were, according to Herodotos, a skilled seafaring nation ; they invented devices and handles for shields, and plumes for helmets.   Mycenæan civilisation has therefore been influenced at many points by Carian custom.   But more numerous resemblances point to Lydia and Phrygia.   From these countries may have come the chief influence ; perhaps, too, the majority of the immigrants.

From the mixture of the different foreign elements a new whole was formed on the new soil.   The influence of the old inhabitants in the different regions also contributed to this result. On the Greek mainland Mycenæan civilisation prevailed on the east coast only.   Farther inland dwelt those whom the legend calls Pelasgians, and who may also have consisted of a number of different races.

With this picture the Trojan war finds its explanation. The chief condition for the establishment of Minos's naval supremacy was the abolition of piracy, and this was attained by the subjugation of the Carians. The extension of Mycenæan civilisation affords a striking proof of the peaceful and prosperous conditions of the whole Archipelago. But the previous disturbers of the peace need not have been Carians only. The rape of Helen from the European coast to Troy has now long been regarded as a figurative expression for an act of piracy. The town of Troy must moreover have been all the more dangerous an adversary to powers striving for order, because, as is shown by her favourable position on the straits between two seas, and by the finds made there, she was then the most powerful city on the Asia Minor coast. The "Achæans" may accordingly have required all their strength and resources in order to conquer this foe of the new civilisation and power, and thus the overthrow of Troy came to be regarded as the greatest achievement of the "Achæans."

To judge from the discoveries, the second town upon Troy, representing the only great and important period of its history, came to a sudden end in the midst of the period of Mycenæan prosperity. The explanation is not far to seek; the end was brought about by the advance of Mycenæan civilisation. Thus the Trojan war finds a far more real foundation than the last half century has been willing to concede, and Homer appears in quite a new light. The Homeric poems represent, for the greater part, Greek conditions after the Dorian migration. Hence it was concluded that the poems had arisen among the Achæans after they had been exiled by the Dorians, and had fled for the most part to Asia Minor, and that in the Trojan war we had the picture of the battles fought by the newcomers on the new soil. But apart from the fact that the fugitives, defeated and scattered at home, would hardly have begun by making conquests and besieging towns, such an explanation was always especially unsatisfactory, because it was difficult to understand why the poets made their heroes return home after the war was over. This led to the assumption that the poets had invented a taking of Troy by the ancestors of the fugitives, in order to celebrate in its story the deeds of the descendants. Now, however, facts show that, while we have no ground for assuming any great achievements for the descendants, the expedition of the ancestors may well be an historical reality. It is this, then, which we must regard as the basis of the poem.

It is improbable also that the earlier portions of the Homeric poems should have arisen in the troubled conditions of life of the fugitives in Asia Minor. The development of poetry always goes hand in hand with a development of creative art; and neither can well be conceived without an advanced political and specially monarchical power. Now that we know those centres of monarchical power on the Greek coast, and see how splendid was the art that developed there for centuries, it is impossible to allow that during all that time no singer appeared to enliven the monarch's table, and that the emigrants' tongues were first unloosed in the miserable struggle for a new existence. If we realise that in the older portions of the Homeric songs there lives a clear conception of the conditions of life which were destroyed by the Dorian invasion, that the palace and walls and gates of the fortress and the inlaid gold and silver work are described, our view will certainly not be considered too bold.

To sum up briefly. Mycenæan civilisation prevails on the east coast of Greece, and over the islands to Asia Minor. It bears a strongly Asiatic stamp, yet its analogies to Homer are important enough to prove that by the Homeric "Achæans" the representatives of Mycenæan civilisation are meant. It is to be concluded that these Achæans were a mixture of several tribes, Minyæ, Ionians, Carians, and perhaps other immigrants. The uniform distribution of the civilisation is explained by the temporary welding together of the different races into one kingdom, which, after the subjugation of its opponents, especially of Troy, established for the first time peaceful commercial relations in the Ægean.

Speaking broadly, this civilisation covered the years 1500 to 1000 B.C. It was destroyed by the Dorian invasion. The greater part of the "Achæans" migrated to the islands and to Asia Minor, where the further developments of Mycenæan art may be traced.

The earlier portions of the Homeric poetry belong to the meridian of Mycenæan civilisation. Its continuation and revision followed after the Dorian invasion, so the epic bears, almost throughout, the stamp of this later time.

The discoveries of the coming years and decades will certainly establish still firmer connections between Mycenæan and later Greek art on the one side, and between the older civilisations of the south and east on the other. We shall then understand with increasing clearness the origin of the Greeks, the conditions of their heroic age, and the relation of Homer towards it.

APPENDIX I

PREFACE

MY dear husband had intended to resume the interrupted work at Troy on March 1st of this year, in the hope of completing the excavations which had been begun more than twenty years ago.

God has willed it otherwise! He was suddenly snatched away in the midst of his ceaseless activity and plans, before he had had the satisfaction of putting the finishing touch to the great work which had been the dream of his youth.

I now consider it my sacred duty to carry on the excavations at Hissarlik, and to complete them as my husband had intended. The present short account of the excavations at Troy during the year 1890 had already been sent to press during my husband's lifetime, and I have thought it incumbent on me to publish it in the form he contemplated.　SOPHIA SCHLIEMANN.

ATHENS, *January* 26, 1891.

1. BY DR. H. SCHLIEMANN

I had thought that with the excavations of the year 1882 described in *Troja* (1884), my work at Troy was for a time at an end, and that I could turn my attention to Crete, where I hoped to discover the original home of Mycenæan civilisation. This plan was, however, frustrated by various difficulties, and finally by the recent disturbances in Crete, which made excavation there impossible, so that I decided on resuming the Trojan work. This seemed all the more

---

[1] *Bericht über die Ausgrabungen in Troja in Jahre* 1890. *Von Dr. Heinrich Schliemann. Mit einem Vorwort von Sophie Schliemann und Beiträgen von Dr. Wilhelm Dörpfeld. Leipzig, F.A. Brockhaus,* 1891. The translation is in parts abbreviated and condensed.

desirable as both Dr. Dörpfeld and myself had been persistently attacked for six years by Captain E. Bötticher, who had maintained in several articles, and especially in his book *La Troie de Schliemann une nécropole à incinération,* that Hissarlik was merely a fire necropolis ; he accused us of having purposely done away with the cross walls of the furnaces destined to cremation, and consequently of having falsified the plans we had published.

With the courteous assistance of Herr v. Radowitz, German ambassador in Constantinople, the necessary firman for continuing the excavations was obtained from the Turkish Government in October 1889. The work was resumed on November 1, and by the end of the month a conference took place, to which Captain Bötticher, after repeated invitation on my part, at last consented to be present. Professor Niemann of the Academy of Fine Arts at Vienna and Major Steffen, well known for his maps and plans of Mycenæ, were the witnesses.

Although the result of the conference was to prove to the complete satisfaction of both the witnesses [1] the absolute veracity and fidelity of our plans in all points, yet Captain Bötticher refused to do more than withdraw his imputation of *mala fides* against us, and in other respects maintained his former position.

The excavations had to be broken off in the middle of December on account of the winter. They were resumed on March 1, when I had the advantage of two tramways, which greatly facilitated the removal of the *débris,* and enabled me to enlarge the extent of the excavations in a way that would have been impossible under ordinary conditions. From the beginning of May onwards, three tramways were at work.

As Captain Bötticher continued to attack the results of our excavations in the newspapers, and to explain the Pergamos as a fire necropolis, I felt obliged to invite a second larger international conference for the end of March. Arrangements were made to accommodate as many as fourteen guests, among whom were the eight following *savants :—* Professor Rudolf Virchow, of Berlin ; Dr. W. Grempler, of Breslau ; Dr. von Duhn, Professor of Archæology at Heidelberg ; Dr. K. Humann, Director of the Berlin Museum ; O. Hamdy Bey, Director of the Constantinople Museum ; Mr. F. Calvert, American Consul in the Dardanelles, to whom half of Hissarlik belongs, and who is well known through his excavations in the Troad ; Dr. C. Waldstein, Director of the American School of Classical Studies in Athens, delegated by the Smithsonian Institution in Washington ; and M. C. Babin, by the Académie des Inscriptions et Belles Lettres in Paris. These eight gentlemen, after a thorough inspection of the ruins, drew up the following report.

[1] See *Hissarlik-Ilion*, Protokoll der Abhandlungen zwischen Dr. Schliemann und Hauptmann Bötticher, 1-6 December 1889. Als Handschrift gedruckt.

Conference at Hissarlik, March 1890.

The undersigned were invited by Dr. Schliemann and Dr. Dörpfeld to investigate the excavations at Hissarlik, and have spent several days in a careful inspection of the ruins, having previously made themselves acquainted with the writings of Captain Bötticher on the character of the buildings discovered there, and especially with the book *La Troie de Schliemann une nécropole à incinération.* The conclusions drawn from this inspection are as follows—

1. The ruins of Hissarlik lie on the extreme end of a ridge running from east to west, which extends into the plain of the Skamander. This point, which commands a view of the plain and of the entrance to the Hellespont beyond it, seems well suited for the site of a fortress.

2. Walls, towers, and gateways can be seen there, constituting fortifications of different epochs.

3. The circuit wall of the second settlement, coloured red in *Troja,* Plan VII, and in *Ilios,* Plan VII [1] (French edition), consists of a substructure of limestone, the face of which is usually scarped ; on this is raised a vertical wall of unbaked bricks. At some points in the circuit wall the plaster on this brickwork is still preserved. Three towers of this wall have been recently discovered, which still preserve the superstructure of clay bricks : they stand on the east side at the point where the stone substructure was lowest, and where in consequence it was least necessary to strengthen the wall with buttresses.

4. A cutting made through this wall, in prolongation of the trench XZ, proved the non-existence of the supposed corridors. As far as the brick walls are concerned, the only example which could be quoted for assuming corridors in the walls, is found in the walls of the buildings A and B, which lie close to one another. In this case, however, the two walls belong to two different buildings.

5. The hill of Hissarlik never consisted of a series of artificial terraces, in which each stage was smaller than the one below ; on the contrary, each successive layer of building nearer to the surface occupies more space than the one immediately below it.

6. An inspection of the different layers of *débris* has resulted in the following conclusions : In the lowest layer nothing is to be seen but walls lying almost parallel to one another, in which there are no traces that point to the burning of corpses. The second and most interesting layer contains ruins of buildings, the most important of which resemble the palaces of Tiryns and Mycenæ in every respect. The layers immediately above this consist of dwelling-houses, which were built on each other's ruins at different times ; a great number of them contain large vessels (*pithoi*). In the highest layer are found foundations of Græco-Roman buildings, and numerous fragments of masonry of that epoch.

[1] See coloured plan above, p. 92.

7. The numerous *pithoi* discovered in the third layer were still in their original upright position, some alone, some in groups. Several of them contained large quantities of wheat, pease, and rapeseed, more or less carbonised, but never human bones, whether burnt or not. The sides of these *pithoi* bear no traces of unusual exposure to fire.

8. In general, we affirm that in no part of the ruins have we found any signs that point to the burning of corpses. The traces of fire to be found in different layers, and above all in the second, the "burned town," arise generally from the violence of the conflagration. The strength of the heat in the second layer was so great that the bricks of dried clay have been partly baked, and even vitrified outside.

We also wish to state definitely that the plans in *Ilios* and *Troja* correspond accurately to the existing remains, and that we fully share the views stated by Messrs. Niemann and Steffen in their report of the conference of December 1-6, 1889.

PROFESSOR RUDOLF VIRCHOW.
DR. W. GREMPLER.
DR. F. VON DUHN.
DR. K. HUMANN.
O. HAMDY BEY.
F. CALVERT.
DR. C. WALDSTEIN.
C. BABIN.

HISSARLIK, *March* 30, 1890.

The judgment of the ten archæologists and scholars of the first rank, who were present at the two conferences at Troy and signed the reports, will, it is to be hoped, convince every unprejudiced mind that at Hissarlik we have to do with a fortified place, which has been inhabited for thousands of years. We are also encouraged by the fact that during the spring and summer we were visited by more than a hundred other scholars and antiquarians, who all rejected the theory of the fire necropolis, and several of whom have since made their views known both by speaking and writing. Should Captain Bötticher continue to explain the Pergamos as a fire necropolis, and raise a suspicion in the mind of any sensible man that the world of learning is wrong and Captain Bötticher alone is right, we invite such a doubter to visit us at Troy while the next excavations are going on, that is, between March 1 and August 1, 1891, and to convince himself of the facts on the spot.

Among other distinguished personages and scholars who came to Hissarlik was Dr. Joseph Durm of Karlsruhe, who has since published his views in an essay on the "Trojan War" (*Centralblatt der Bauverwaltung*, x., 1890, No. 40, p. 409). His remarks on the small dimensions of the Pergamos and his comparison of the different acropoleis and citadels are most interesting. In spite of the small size of the citadel of Ilios he does not find anything improbable in the view that Priam found room for himself and his kin on the hill of Hissarlik. No doubt the common people here as elsewhere lived outside the citadel, which might therefore enclose a smaller space than one would naturally have expected.

A very close parallel to this is found in the town of Lachish (Λάχεισα) recently discovered and partly excavated by Mr. Flinders Petrie. Lachish, now called Tell Hesy, is situated in Palestine in the district of Daromas ; it was an old Canaanite royal seat, and was taken by Joshua (Joshua x. 3, 31). Mr. Flinders Petrie in the *Contemporary Review* describes the site as a hill 60 feet high composed of towns built one upon another, containing an area of 40,000 square feet, *i.e.* only two-fifths as large as the Pergamos of the second town of Troy, which has an area of 100,000 feet.

As the river which flowed at the foot had carried away some of the ruins, a vertical section of the mound of *débris* was exposed. In the upper part Mr. Petrie found archaic Greek pottery of the 5th and 6th centuries B.C. ; half-way or three-quarters of the way up he found Phœnician terra-cottas, which his Egyptian experience enabled him to date 1100 B.C. The most important town of all is the lowest, which he dates 1500 B.C. Its circuit wall, like that of Troy, is built of unbaked bricks, merely dried in the sun ; it is 28 feet 8 inches thick, and still 21 feet in height. The house walls are of the same material. Just as in the Pergamos of Troy, settlement followed upon settlement in the royal city of Lachish, and the method of building was the same. New buildings were erected on the ruins of the old ones, and in the course of centuries a mass of *débris* accumulated, which is even greater than that at Troy.

The last excavations at Hissarlik lasted from March 1 to August 1, 1890. Although the full account of the work and the detailed plans are reserved till after the thorough completion of the excavations, yet it seems desirable to give a brief account at once of the results of the first year's work, and to add a plan of the citadel.

Plan VII in *Troja*[1] shows that in the previous excavations of 1882 the citadel inside the circuit wall of the second town, which had been destroyed in a great catastrophe, had already been excavated in several places right down to the house walls. In many places, however, these were still covered by the walls and *débris* of the third settlement, while here and there, as for example east of the gate OX, the mound of *débris* had not been disturbed at all. Our intention was to expose all the house walls of the second settlement, a work which required great care, and was only completed by the end of July. On the west we left standing the buildings of the third settlement marked HS in the plan, but even here we laid

[1] See coloured plan, p. 92.

bare enough of the house walls of the second town which lay beneath to make a plan of them. It was also possible to fix exactly the alterations made in the buildings during the different periods of the second settlement.

The great resemblance between the Trojan buildings and the prehistoric palace of the kings of Tiryns, excavated in 1884 and 1885, should be carefully noticed. It is most striking in the two buildings A and B, the plan of which is almost exactly the same as the plan of the palace at Tiryns.

We also discovered at Troy a ramp ascending at the side of the fortress wall, like the one excavated at Tiryns.[1] The wall marked BC on the coloured plan of Troy, which we once took for a wall of the lower city, proved to be this ramp. It is built, like the one at Tiryns, of great unhewn blocks of stone, bonded with clay. There must, as at Tiryns, have been a gate in the north wall at the top of the ramp, and this gate we hope to discover in the course of next spring. The steps found at the bottom of the ramp are of the highest interest.

A second and apparently much older ramp was discovered in front of the great south-east gate (OX on the coloured plan). It is constructed of small stones bonded with clay, and forms an approach like a flight of steps. It proves that on this side too the citadel was separated from the plateau of the lower city by a fall in the ground. We have carefully excavated this south-east gate down to the level of the ground, and in so doing have proved that it was altered at different times. It originally had two flanking towers that projected equally ; later on the gateway was made narrower, and the flanking towers strengthened by new walls.

For thousands of years the chief ascent to the Pergamos was on this spot, and to this day we can see high above the south-east gate the remains of two *propylæa* dating the one from Greek, the other from Roman times. Several marble fragments of Corinthian columns belonging to the Roman *propylæum* have been found.

In addition to this big south-east gate and to the gate which, as mentioned above, we conjecture to have existed at the top of the ramp in the north wall, the Pergamos of the second city had three other gates, *i.e.* the big south-west gate excavated in 1872 (RC on the coloured plan), from which a road paved with large stone slabs and protected by lateral walls led down to the lower city at an inclination of 1 in 4. Next came the south gate, discovered in 1882 (NF on the plan), and further a gate on the west side, discovered during this last campaign. It is situated near to one of the big towers that project from the walls, and apparently belongs to the first period of the second city. It entirely corresponds both in shape and masonry to the south gate (NF), which also belongs to the first period of the second city. When the

[1] See plan of Tiryns, p. 161.

south-west gate (RC on the plan) was made, those two gates belonging
to the first epoch had already been walled up and blocked.   Near to
this newly-discovered west gate we discovered at the foot of the
substructure a very well-preserved postern gate about 7 feet 10 inches
high and 3 feet 11 inches broad, through which a narrow way gave
access to the interior of the citadel and led up to the summit of the
Pergamos.   The side walls of the gate were protected by wooden posts,
of which we found large fragments in a charred condition.

In the side walls of the gate may be seen the holes for the bolt
which served to fasten it.   We propped up the lintel by means of an
iron beam, so as to secure it in its present position.

One of the most important operations of the year was to undertake
the excavation layer by layer of the large mound of earth which had
been left quite untouched on the west and south-west side of the Pergamos.
This excavation has had important results for archæology, for in the
centre of the Acropolis the Romans had destroyed the walls of the
houses of the preceding layers in order to form a plateau, while
here, outside the Pergamos of the second or burnt city, and nearer to
the citadel walls of the Roman Acropolis, the house walls are preserved
to an average height of 4 feet, with their foundations.   These
are the walls of four distinct settlements, which followed one upon
the other after the downfall of the last prehistoric city, and below
them again are the house walls of three consecutive prehistoric
settlements before we reach the level of the second city.   We have
left a few house walls of each of these seven strata standing, in order
that visitors may examine and study them.

The Roman is by far the most extensive of the upper settlements.
The foundations of its buildings often reach to a depth of 16 feet.
The pottery found here is very coarse ; occasionally it has received an
inferior black varnish, but the greater quantity is not coloured ; lamps
and vases shaped like bottles are numerous.   All this pottery was
undoubtedly made on the spot.   Two wells built of regularly hewn
blocks are specially deserving of notice in this Roman settlement.
They pass through all the lower layers and reach down to the native
rock ; the many earthenware waterpipes by means of which the water
was brought from the upper Thymbrius to the fortress of Ilion are also
interesting.

The theatre excavated in 1882 on the north side, which
would hold more than 6000 spectators, belongs likewise to this
Roman city ; so too does another theatre-like building, found this year,
which could accommodate about 200 spectators.   The ground-plan
of this second building differs considerably from that of a theatre ;
possibly it is neither a theatre nor an Odeum, but the place of assembly
of some body of citizens, perhaps the Βουλή.   The roof has fallen in ;
otherwise the building is well preserved with the exception of the
upper rows of seats, which were supported by the massive blocks of

the circuit wall and are now missing. It consists of hard limestone, only the lower tier of seats is of marble. Two life-size marble statues were discovered here ; one probably represents Tiberius, for close by were found two inscribed marble slabs, one of which can be dated in the seventeenth year of this Emperor's reign, while the other is perhaps a year or two earlier.

South of the circuit wall and quite close to it nine huge *pithoi* stand upright in a group. They belong to an older period, probably to the fourth or fifth settlement counting from the top. Such jars, however, are also found in the Roman settlement, and are very common in all the other historic and prehistoric strata. They are always found in an upright position, and they are almost invariably covered with a stone slab. They served to store oil, wine, water, fruit, and grains. Similar jars were used for the same purpose in the oil and wine shops of Pompeii and Herculaneum, and to this day in Asia Minor and in Greece, where there are no cellars. It will be remembered that at Rome, during the reign of Domitian (81-96 A.D.), the Monte Testaccio, which is 165 feet high and over 325 feet in diameter, was completely formed of broken wine-jugs. This proves how general the use of these *pithoi* was for the storage of wine. The vegetable products which the Hissarlik jars contained were several sorts of grain and pease. One large jar alone contained more than 440 lbs. of these pease.

A kind of pottery very superior to the Roman is to be found in the second stratum from the top, which belongs to the Hellenic period. Here, among other fragments, are some with black varnish ; they are frequently decorated with white or red ornaments, though it should be noted that these are not always reserved on the ground, but are sometimes painted over the black varnish. We will not enter into the question whether this pottery was manufactured on the spot or imported from Greece. We must suppose the first to be the case at any rate with the numerous vases of red clay decorated with figures of animals, more especially of water-birds, for vases with similar painted decorations are found everywhere in the Troad.

Archaic Greek pottery appears in the succeeding stratum, which scarcely contains any native fabric, except perhaps the peculiar cups, whose irregular colouring in their upper portion has been caused through dipping the cups into the colour.

Beautiful Attic red-figured vases are characteristic of this stratum, as well as Rhodian vases decorated with figures of animals, with plants or with geometric designs, and Corinthian or proto-Corinthian vases with friezes of running animals.

Most noteworthy, on account of its buildings made of huge dressed blocks, is the fourth settlement from the top, in which was found the curious grey or black monochrome pottery, which I formerly held to be Lydian. Every single house belonging to this colony within the citadel had been cleared away by the Romans, and there remained only pottery, which was found at a depth of some 7 feet below the surface. Here, however, on the west side, beyond the Trojan Pergamos but within the Roman and Greek Acropolis, and nearer to the walls of the latter, we struck at a depth of some 23 feet below the surface upon this remarkable settlement, which itself reaches to a depth of 7 feet. As the same monochrome pottery in yellow, grey, or black, which is very abundant here, has also been found in all the so-called "heroic tumuli," as well as in the older settlements on the Bali-Dagh behind Bunárbashi, on the Fulu-Dagh, on Kurschunlu-Tepé, and in Kebrenc, there can be no doubt that this pottery is a native manufacture. Along with it, however, there appears a great deal of painted pottery belonging to what we usually regard as the most ancient Greek type.

Among these we should specially note the Mycenæan cups with stirrup handles, painted with parallel bands. Their shape is that most usually found at Mycenæ and Tiryns. Similar vases have also been found by Mr. Flinders Petrie at the pyramids of Ilahun, in the Fayoum in Egypt, in graves of the time of Rameses II (about 1350 B.C.) Next in order of interest are the numerous vases of Mycenæan type, decorated with plants or with concentric circles and spirals; then come the painted Mycenæan cups (see Plates I and II; Figs. 5-17). I cannot feel certain whether these ancient types of vases were imported from Greece or not. We know that in Hellas proper, the civilisation to which these types belong was brought to an end in the twelfth century B.C., through the Dorian invasion or the so-called return of the Herakleidæ, and practically disappeared without leaving a trace. The Dorian invasion, however, gave rise to the Æolian migration to Asia Minor, and especially to the Troad, and it is quite possible that the potters took part in the migration and introduced their art in Ilion.

As regards the native grey, yellow, or black monochrome pottery, it should be noticed that almost all its types are found abundantly in this settlement, but not in any of the five lower prehistoric strata, —for example, the large vases and cups with horned projections;[1] the cups with long handles bent into an elliptical curve, and running up into a point;[2] the vase handles in the form of snakes, or of heads of horses or oxen;[3] the big dishes with two or four handles.[4] Vases with two vertical tubular projections, which in the lower prehistoric settlements appear in such great numbers, are exceedingly rare in this stratum; since the beginning of the excavations in Ilion in 1871, perhaps four may have been found. The idols found in this stratum are of terra-cotta, and are much coarser than any found at Mycenæ (see Plate I, Nos. 1-3).[5] As in the five lower prehistoric strata,

[1] See *Ilios*, Figs. 1369-1377.   [2] See *Ilios*, Figs. 1379-1381.
[3] See *Ilios*, Figs. 1391 and 1399-1405.   [4] See *Ilios*, Figs. 1363-1365.
[5] See *Ilios*, Figs. 1412, 1413·

the decorations on the vases in this curious native pottery are either scratched [1] or indented.[2]

In this settlement some knives and other instruments of bronze are found, but at the same time there are a great number of stone implements, such as axes and hammers of diorite, pestles of granite or basalt, saws of silex, knives of obsidian, hand-mills of trachyte.

We were able to draw a plan of one of the buildings of this settlement constructed of large dressed blocks. It is given in Fig. 4 (p. 348). We have here the ground-plan of the old megaron as we discovered it in Tiryns and in the second or "burnt" city at Troy. Whether this ground-plan represents a house or a temple cannot as yet be decided.

We have left this interesting structure quite untouched, and we should like to request all visitors to Troy to study it with the help of our plan. Several fortification walls were also discovered, which most probably belonged to this settlement.

The three strata with traces of house walls, which lay below the one just described, correspond according to the pottery they contained to the fifth, fourth, and third cities in the interior of the ancient Pergamos.

Up to this time no trace of iron had been found in any of the five prehistoric Trojan settlements, nor in any of the excavations at Mycenæ, Orchomenos, and Tiryns, so that I was led to believe that this metal was completely unknown in prehistoric times both in Asia Minor and in Greece. Now, however, when the house foundations in the interior of the Pergamos came to be cleared, more particularly those of the great building to be seen within the square G5 of the plan, there were found two lumps of iron. On one side they were much deteriorated by the rust, on the other they were in good preservation. One of them has a large square hole on its better-preserved side, and it very possibly served as the handle of a staff. It is therefore certain that iron was already known in the second or burnt city; but it was probably at that time rarer and more precious than gold. Together with the pieces of iron were found four large stone axes and other small objects, which will be described fully in the large publication.

It was only when we cleared the walls of the second city, and excavated beneath them, that we fully understood how long the duration of this settlement had been, and for what centuries its golden era must have lasted. Not only could we distinguish three periods of building in the house walls, but we also found, beside the older and the more recent fortification walls marked c and b on the coloured plan, a still older circuit wall of the Pergamos. We have laid it bare at various points. Both the wall and its towers are scarped at a low inclination and are well preserved. Here also the superstructure

---

[1] See *Ilios*, Figs. 1359, 1373, and 1397.
[2] See *Ilios*, Figs. 1365-1369 and 1374-1376.

consisted of unbaked bricks, the mass of red or yellow brick *débris* that lay in front of the wall can leave no doubt on that point.

The discovery of the ruins of the first period of the second city has made it possible to distinguish the pottery of this settlement more closely. In the first period is still found a glazed monochrome black pottery, which bears a very close resemblance to that of the first Trojan city. The plates and dishes have exactly the shape of those of the first city, only here there are no horizontal tubes. Just as in the first city, so here the vases have projections at the side with two vertical holes for suspension. It was only later, and little by little, that the vase shapes which we find in the third and last period of the second city were developed.

In the four upper prehistoric settlements was found, as before, an abundance of vases, brooches, hammers, knives, handmills, moulds, door-sockets, etc. With the exceptions of a few vases which bear some resemblance to the so-called funeral urns, not one of the many thousand objects in the Trojan museums at Berlin and Athens has any connection with the cultus of the dead. The vases shaped like the human face, of which some sixty in all have been found, cannot be taken into account in this connection. Funeral urns with human faces are certainly occasionally found in graves in Germany, and the number of these found up to now possibly amounts to one hundred; they are, however, large and bulky, while the Trojan vases with human visages are exceedingly small, many of them might be described as liliputian. Only one was found that was 2 feet high. They were always found in houses, and without any trace of ashes or bones; they must accordingly have been household utensils. Vases with human visages for purposes of burial could only occur in graves; not a single grave, however, has been found within the citadel.

We scarcely worked at all this time in the stratum of the first settlement, for excavation there is quite impossible without disturbing the much more important and interesting ruins of the second city that lie above it.

On the south and east side we have uncovered the walls and towers of the third period of the second city almost along their whole extent.

Our excavation on the west side laid bare the whole south and south-west citadel wall of the second city. Its strongly scarped substructure is well preserved to its full height of 28 feet. The countless heaps of brick *débris* which were found in front of the scarped wall show clearly that this wall had a superstructure built of sun-dried bricks. Two towers were discovered on the west side; their lower part is very well preserved; they project 8 feet from the walls. When the great Trojan wall was still standing intact, even if we reckon the height of the brick wall to have been only 20 feet, and that of the upper gallery 6 feet 6 inches (such a gallery is now known to have existed in the walls of Themistokles at Athens, and has been discovered in the wall of Tiryns), it must have reached to the height of 55 feet, and with its huge towers must have presented a very imposing appearance here on the west side. It is therefore conceivable that its building should, in accordance with the legend preserved to us by Homer, have been ascribed to Poseidon and Apollo.

It had been my intention to excavate here on the south side a great portion of the lower city; but the difficulties that presented themselves were almost insurmountable, as the mass of *débris* is more than 50 feet deep, and each one of the numerous house-walls had always to be cleaned before it could be photographed and then cleared away. Unfortunately much valuable time was lost in this way, and in spite of all my efforts I have only been able to lay bare a very small portion of the lower city belonging to the Pergamos.

At some distance from the Pergamos, but outside the Roman circuit wall of the lower city, we found a great number of graves. Some were built with slabs, some were shafts hewn in the rock, and from the objects found inside them, appear to belong to the first centuries of the Christian era. We also excavated a whole row of Byzantine graves.

The cone-shaped tumulus south of Ilion, excavated by Mrs. Schliemann in May 1873, and popularly called Pasha Tepé, was excavated afresh. I discovered here a human skeleton—but without any offerings to the dead—and a stone stair which formerly led up, in the east side, to the apex of the tomb. It had been covered with earth through the gradual washing away of the tumulus by the rain of centuries.

We have sunk trenches 325 feet long at the foot of the citadel on the south and west sides, and have discovered within them the walls of the massive buildings of Ilion, and many Corinthian columns. However, the work of laying bare the lower city of Troy is so difficult, on account of the great mass of *débris* which has to be cleared, that we had to put it off to next year.

In the layer of ruins where the vases of Mycenæan type were found together with the native ware of monochrome grey or black, *i.e.* in the sixth settlement from the bottom, I found the whorl shown in the annexed illustration. It is of brown terra-cotta, and has letters that were scratched on it while the clay was still wet. I sent this whorl to Professor Sayce, who reports on the inscription as follows: "The inscription is one of the finest and clearest I have ever seen, and a splendid instance of Cypriote epigraphy. The reading is Πα-το-ρι Τυρι. According to Hesykhios there was a word Πάτορες with the meaning 'owners.' If the inscription is Greek, we must translate 'To the owner Tyris.' But it seems to me more probable that the language is Phrygian, and in this case we can consider Πατορι to be the equivalent of the Greek πατρι, for Tyris is the divinity from whom the name of the Phrygian city, Tyriaion, is derived. Accordingly the translation of the two words would be 'To the father Tyris.'"

In addition to the two inscriptions of the age of Tiberius, mentioned above, and to several Hellenistic inscriptions, there was

1.—TERRA-COTTA WHORL.

found built in a Roman wall of Ilion a marble slab, 2 feet 6 inches long and a little over 17 inches broad, inscribed on both sides with a list of proper names.   It seems to be a fragment of a full list of the burgesses of the town, and is interesting because of the frequent occurrence of Homeric names in it.   Instances are Skamandrios, Teukros, Memnon, Glaukos, Menestheus, etc.   These names seem to point to the fact that the Ilians were proud of the deeds of their Trojan ancestors, whose renown had been immortalised by the divine poet.

2. By Dr. Dörpfeld

The Buildings of Troy

In the first portion of this report Dr. Schliemann has given a general account of the buildings and fortifications discovered in the year 1890.   It only remains for me to enter in somewhat greater detail into the shape and construction of separate buildings.

It will be most convenient for the reader to have them described, not in the order in which they were uncovered, but in the order of the several superimposed settlements, beginning with the lowest stratum, and working gradually up to the uppermost Roman settlement.   However, a complete description of all the buildings discovered will not be attempted.   It will be best to reserve this till the completion of the excavations.   In this preliminary report I shall rather confine myself to a description of the newly-discovered buildings, and lay special stress on the alterations and additions which the recent excavations have necessitated in the plan of the Trojan ruins, as given in the former publications.[1]

[1] I do not wish to lose this opportunity of expressly stating once more that I will not condescend to publish any sort of answer to Captain Botticher's recent libels.—*Jan.* 1891.

In order to make the explanation clear, a new plan of the Trojan citadel is given on Plan III. Like Plan VII in *Troja*[1] it only shows the Acropolis of the second stratum, and contains almost nothing beyond the buildings of this important settlement. The walls and buildings of the upper settlements, as well as those of the lowest stratum, are left out, so as not to overload and confuse the plan. Plans, sections, and photographs of these other buildings will be given in the complete publication after the close of the excavations. The plan has been divided into squares of 65 feet, each marked with a letter and a number, so that every spot mentioned on the citadel may be quite easy to identify. The walls of the separate strata and periods are distinguished on the plan by different cross-hatchings (see explanation on the plan). The numbers marked on several parts of the plan give respectively the height above (+) or the depth below (−) a level which I have fixed at the lowest point of the rock within the citadel in D3.

(1) *The First and Oldest Stratum*

The only walls known as belonging to the oldest settlement, which lay directly on the rock, are those which are disclosed in the great trench dug from north to south. On the coloured plan these walls are given in yellow and marked F. As the recent excavations have practically added nothing to this part, I have only marked the trench on the new plan and left out the walls, so as to show the building A more clearly. The only excavation made in the lowest stratum took place while Professor Virchow was at Troy. He was anxious to lay bare a fresh portion of the lowest and most ancient settlement, and he accordingly had the big trench widened somewhat towards the west. A cross wall was thus discovered, which connects several of the thin longitudinal walls together, and like these consists of small quarry-stones and clay mortar. Professor Virchow recently read a report before the Anthropological Society of Berlin,[2] on the significance of these walls and on the objects found between them. I completely share his opinion that these walls can only represent dwelling-houses. Some of the divisions, however, may very well have been left uncovered and have served as stalls for cattle.

No cause has yet been found for the destruction of this oldest settlement. It cannot have been destroyed by fire, for neither charred wooden beams nor any of those other unmistakable traces, which we invariably find in buildings destroyed by fire, are to be met with here. The walls are still standing to an average height of 3 feet; their upper portion has fallen down and partly filled up the spaces

---

[1] *i.e.* the coloured plan, p. 92.
[2] See the *Transactions* of this Society, 1890, p. 338.

between the walls.   Specimens of the style of work will be published later.

The north and south boundary of the first settlement was already known.   Though this year's work has not shown how far it extended from east to west, yet the shaft in C4 showed that the first settlement did not probably extend on the west far beyond the portion already excavated.

(2) *The Second Stratum, the Pergamos of Troy*

As the buildings of this stratum are the most important and also the largest, with the exception of the Hellenistic and Roman buildings, our chief endeavour during the recent excavations was to free and uncover it further.   Large portions of the fortification wall have been brought to light and examined, the ground-plan of several of the edifices already discovered within the citadel has been substantially added to by the discovery of new walls, while some buildings have been uncovered for the first time, through the clearing away of the later walls built upon them.   The great alteration which has thus been effected in the ground-plan of the citadel can be best appreciated if we compare the new plan on Plate III with the old coloured plan.

A third and older citadel wall has been discovered in addition to the two which were already known.   Accordingly we can now distinguish three periods within the second stratum, all three of which we shall afterwards find represented in the dwelling-houses within the citadel.   These various buildings of the second city do not represent separate settlements, but merely new buildings and alterations that took place in the same layer.

The level of the second settlement only altered very little during these three periods.   In most of the divisions the floor of the older period is found only a few inches under the later pavement.   In some places indeed there was no increase at all.   On the other hand, the difference of height between the floors of the different strata is generally from 3 to 6 feet, and sometimes reaches as much as 16 feet.   For this reason we speak of three periods the same stratum, not of three different strata or "cities."

Thus the citadel of the second layer received three different circuit walls, and its circumference was extended twice.   The older circuit wall, which was unknown up to now, came to light in the trenches in the south-west portion of the citadel.   On Plan III it is given by a dotted shading, and marked *d*.   The circuit wall of the second period was already known.   On the old Plan VII it was coloured grey, in the new plan it is shown by a broad cross-hatching.   Like the older wall, it has up to now only been uncovered on the south and west side of the citadel.   The wall of the third period, formerly coloured red, is given in the new plan by means of a narrow cross-hatching, and is

z

marked *b*. It has been traced on the west, south, and east of the citadel.

The earlier description of the city walls can only be supplemented for the present by a few further remarks on the construction and shape of these three walls. A large portion of the oldest wall (*d* on Plan III) on the south-west side of the citadel, in the square C6 to F6, is surprisingly well preserved. One can still see the stone substructure which was erected as an outer supporting wall of the citadel mound; it reached up to the level of the citadel. The outer face is scarped at a low inclination, for the wall was built of small stones and clay mortar, and could not otherwise have withstood the pressure of the earth. The thickness of the wall at its upper surface is 9 feet. We have found two towers separated by an interval of about 35 feet. They are about 10 feet wide, and project 6 feet 6 inches from the line of wall. One of these towers (*da*) is under the later south-west gate (FM), the other (*db*) is farther to the east. Still farther to the east there was presumably a third tower, which was probably destroyed by the great north trench.

The existence of these towers and their excellent preservation is specially valuable because doubts have been expressed concerning the presence of towers. Such a doubt is no longer possible. It is absolutely certain that these projections served a military purpose, that they were real towers and not buttresses, because the wall on account of its thickness and low inclination did not need any additional support. From the builder's point of view these towers were an actual disadvantage, for their projecting angles merely weakened the wall's power of resistance to the effects of the weather. With the small stones available, it must have been very difficult to construct the right-angled or even slightly acute-angled corners of the towers. A wall without towers was much easier to build and also to keep in good condition, but for purposes of defence a wall with numerous towers was to be preferred.

This ancient circuit wall has two gates: in the south the gateway FN, which projects like a huge tower (in square E7), and in the west the somewhat smaller gate FL (in square B5). The first of these was already known. We assigned it to the second period of the second city, *i.e.* to the circuit wall *c*. A closer examination has, however, proved that it is older than this wall. This may be verified by looking at the plan, where it is seen that the gateway is at right angles to the wall *d*, whereas it cuts the wall *c* at an acute angle. The second gate (FL) was uncovered this year for the first time, when the west wall of the citadel was entirely disengaged from the outside. It is only preserved along the lower course of stones; the upper portions, which up to this time were the only ones excavated, were in the line of the later circuit wall. Both gates, although of different dimensions, have the same plan, and differ materially from the gates of the later periods. For instance, the later gates are situated on the upper edge of the citadel, and a ramp or else a road with steps led up to them; while the older gates are at the foot of the citadel, the road that passes through them is covered by a huge tower, and the ascent to the citadel plateau is thus within the citadel (cf. the altitudes in the gateway FN). These long gateways are also considerably narrower than the later ones; they are respectively 11 feet and 8 feet 6 inches broad, while the later gates are respectively 23 feet and 17 feet. Apparently the breadth of the gates was about doubled in the later period.

The great tower, 59 feet broad and over 65 feet deep, which covers the larger south gate FN, has been proved by thorough investigations to have been considerably smaller at first, and to have been strengthened at a later time, though probably still during the first period of the second stratum. On the west wall it is even possible to trace a double enlargement. The complete description of this alteration must be deferred till next year, as the southern end of the gate has not yet been completely disengaged.

While the citadel wall of the first period has been completely brought to light between the two gates FL and FN, only two small portions of it have been found on the other side of the gate. We know nothing of its further course on the north and east sides of the citadel. We may probably reckon on finding at least a few separate portions when the excavations are continued. The upper portion of this wall no longer exists, any more than the superstructure of the gates; they probably both consisted of unbaked bricks. It is only on this supposition that we can explain the masses of clay bricks burnt a red colour, which have been found in the gateways and in some places also in front of the citadel wall.

As the wall was partially destroyed through some mishap, and the remaining portion covered with *débris*, a new citadel wall was built well outside it; it is rendered on the plan by broad cross-hatchings, and marked *c*. This wall is preserved along its whole distance between the two gates described above, and was provided on the outside with one entire and two half towers (*ca, cb, cd*). North of the gate FL another piece with the great tower *ce* is known; the complete construction of this tower can unfortunately no longer be made out. At the western end of the citadel, in especial, there are many walls, the purpose and date of which are not yet fixed with any certainty, and the description of which had therefore best be postponed for the present. It is therefore impossible to give a definite answer to the question, whether a wall of the lower city joins the citadel wall at this point. Farther to the north, in the square B4, another small piece of the wall *c* has been found, but it almost immediately disappears beneath the later wall that lies above it. On the north side there is nothing to be seen of this wall. Possibly Dr. Schliemann destroyed a great portion of it at the time of his earlier excavations on the north slope of the hill, yet we hope still to find remains of the lower layers, when we sink new trenches.

The scarped wall on the north-east (in G3-H4), which has long been known, may possibly belong to this period, but no definite conclusion can be arrived at until its further course has been ascertained. The wall BC, which is also on that side, and which we formerly conjectured belonged to the lower city, has been further disengaged, and proves to be a ramp, *i.e.* the supporting wall of a road, whose eastern extremity has been uncovered. We were anxious to make out the western course of this ramp, and whether a gate existed at its upper extremity, as one may venture to suppose; but the question remains uncertain, and can probably only be decided by clearing away the great lump of earth that is still standing in the squares F3 and G3. The shape and disposition of this second circuit wall on the east side is equally uncertain, as the wall which has been discovered there presumably belongs, along with its numerous towers, to the third period.

Soon after the building of the circuit wall *c* the two older gates probably fell into disuse, and the two new gates FO and FM were built in their place. One is inclined to believe at first that this took place simultaneously with the building of the wall *c*, yet this is scarcely possible, for there is much to prove that the old gates continued in use for some time, and that the two new ones were not built till later. The new gates lie symmetrically next to the older ones: the large main gate FO east of the earlier main gate, and the smaller gate FM at exactly the same distance east from the older FL. This symmetrical arrangement leads one to conclude that both the old gates were replaced at the same time.

The two gates FM and FO have already been thoroughly described in *Troja*;[1] when the detailed plans are published it will be possible to show what little new has been found. Just a few indications will suffice here. Both gates were flanked with massive towers during the second period, when the wall marked on the plan with open cross-hatchings was built. The well-preserved lower portion of these towers is marked on the plan by the same open cross-hatchings. Whereas the south-west gate (FM) presumably only had one portal at first, the south-east gate seems to have had two from the beginning.

In addition to these two main gates, a small postern gate (FK) was also built close to the old west gate. A view of it is given in Fig. 2 below. The postern is at the foot of the high wall of the second period; its excellent preservation can only be ascribed to the fact that it was blocked up at an early period. The gate was covered by a wooden beam and had a wood frame; large pieces of burnt wood still remained *in situ*. After the burning of the beam a portion of

---

[1] See Schuchhardt, p. 47 ff.

the wall fell down.   A narrow way led through the postern to the
great gateway FL.   When the gate had been blocked it probably went
up to the upper plateau by means of a stair.

2.—POSTERN GATE.

The city wall of the second stratum was almost entirely rebuilt a
third time.   The lower part of the old wall which ran to the north-west
of the south-west gate was retained, and only the upper part of the
stone substructure was renewed, together with the whole of the brick
superstructure, but between the south-west and south-east gates a
perfectly new wall was built, which ran farther to the south, and so
enlarged the area of the citadel once more.   The new wall is traced on
the plan (Plate III) with close cross-hatching and marked *b*; it has no
towers on its outer side, but its whole substructure, like that of the
old walls, is scarped at a low inclination.   The scarping was particularly
necessary here, as the stones of the wall were even smaller than those
of the older circuit-wall *c*.

It appears that the superstructure of sun-dried bricks did not
originally form a very thick wall; foundations still remaining rather
tend to prove that being a thin wall it was supported by buttresses
on the inside.   These buttresses appear again in other old walls
of sun-dried bricks (*e.g.* at Olympia in the Heraion and in the old
building which has been transformed into a Byzantine church); they
are on an average 4 feet wide, and stand out about 5 feet.   As the

high stone substructure of the wall, which could only have been climbed
by an attacking force with the greatest difficulty, made it impossible to
use any engines for destroying the brick wall, it was therefore unnecessary to make this brick superstructure as strong as at those
points where the substructure was low and it could easily be reached.
In spite of this the wall was strengthened later on by a much thicker
brick wall built without buttresses.   This is distinguished on the plan
by a simple hatching with dots.   Portions of the brick wall can still
be seen standing in places where the upper layers of *débris* and the sun-
dried bricks have not been removed by mistake during previous
excavations.

On the east side of the citadel only one wall of defence has been
found, which certainly belongs to this last period of the second stratum.
The walls of the two earlier periods may possibly be laid bare in
future excavations ; they must be looked for farther to the west.

As the citadel was connected with the yet steeper plateau of the
lower town on the south-east, and was only separated from it by a dip
in the ground, it did not need a high scarped wall of defence on this
side, and the brick wall with vertical face was merely raised on a substructure of stone about 3 feet high.   This was not scarped, and was
partly sunk in the earth to serve as a foundation, partly left uncovered as a socle.   Such walls of defence, built of brick with a low
substructure of stone, were in use at every period of antiquity, as
we see among other examples in the brick walls of Eleusis, which are
still well preserved, and in the town walls of Athens, of which some
fragments are still to be seen.   As the substructure of the citadel
wall on the east side was so low, an enemy could easily have reached
the part which was built of sun-dried bricks, and have tried to destroy
it.   To prevent this, the wall was made almost 13 feet in width
(compared with 9 feet in the wall at Eleusis, and 8 feet in the
Themistoclean walls at Athens), and besides this it was strengthened
with a number of towers.   Three of these have been discovered,
and others are probably still under the earth.   They are 10 feet 6
inches in breadth and project about 7 feet 6 inches from the face of
the wall.   Both the stone substructure and the brickwork above it
remain to the height of several feet, and in some places the original
plaster which covered the outside is still to be seen.   The distance
between the towers was only about 31 feet 6 inches from centre to
centre, giving about 21 feet clear width, so that even with simple
means of defence the wall was most effectively flanked.   Towers
with very similar proportions and measurements are also found in
fortresses of the middle ages, as J. Durm has shown in the case of the
fortress of Arques.[1]   The space between the two towers *br* and *bd* was
filled with a stone wall later on, when the brick wall began to need
repairs.

[1] *Centralblatt der Bauverwaltung.* 1890, No. 40.

To the north-east the citadel wall has been destroyed in earlier excavations, and only its stone substructure has apparently been preserved in divisions G3 and H4 of the plan. We can infer that here too there was a superstructure of brick raised on the stone wall, as farther south, where the earth above has not been removed, the brick wall is still standing, about 6 feet 6 inches in height, and baked quite red. Although the stone substructure has not been laid bare right down to the rock, it here has a height of about 26 feet. The ramp BC, which is built of large blocks of stone, and led up to the scarped wall of the citadel at this point, has been described above (p. 328).

No traces of the citadel wall of the third period can now be seen on the whole length of the north side, and its course is therefore only marked with a dotted line. It must have run rather more to the north than it does in the old coloured plan, as the buildings inside the citadel extend rather farther to the north than we had imagined. It is to be hoped that further excavations may disclose some remains of this wall. A very small portion of the substructure would be enough to indicate the line it followed.

Two gates have been found in the citadel wall of the third period, the buildings FM and FO mentioned above (p. 340). They both had double gates and chambers behind them. A ramp paved with large slabs of stone led to the smaller gate FM, while the gate FO was approached by a road rising in steps, several of which remain in G7. This gate was originally provided with only two flanking towers, but later on it was strengthened by several walls and towers built out in front of it. At the same time the opening of the gate, which was found to be too broad, was partly built up and made narrower. The existing remains of these buildings are distinguished on Plan III with simple hatching and dots.

The building RP above the south-east door, left white on Plan III, consists of the foundations of a Roman gateway of the Acropolis, already described in *Troja*, p. 23.[1] Inside this propylon the single wall which is not hatched is the last remains of a Greek gateway, which must also have stood on this spot high above the old gate.

Next to the walls of the fortress and its gates the great buildings inside the citadel claim our interest. Here also we find three distinct periods in the second stratum alone, corresponding in all essentials to the three periods of the circuit wall. The shafts that had been sunk during former excavations had already brought separate older walls to light beneath the level of the second layer. We have continued sinking shafts with more success. Numerous walls have been discovered whose connection can be clearly made out at various points.

The three superimposed groups of buildings are marked on Plan

[1] Cf. above, p. 83.

III, like the three circuit walls, by different cross-hatchings; by this
means the different periods can be distinguished, and to a certain
extent a picture of each may be formed.   In each of the three periods
a great complex of buildings, with a more or less similar ground-plan,
stood on the citadel.   The latest buildings are the best preserved.
Their walls are marked on the plan with close cross-hatchings.

In front of the south-east gate lies a small gate in E5.   It leads to

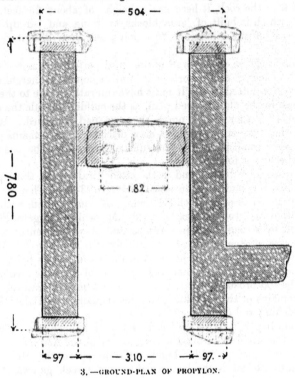

3.—GROUND-PLAN OF PROPYLON.

an inner court which gives access to the most important buildings of
the citadel.   I have already pointed out in *Tiryns* (p. 254)[1] the great
resemblance between the plan of these buildings and the king's house
at Tiryns.   At that time, however, one could do no more than conjecture, though with every probability, that the building C was a gate.
Now further excavation has brought to light the two missing anta
stones of the propylon, so that its purport is now absolutely certain.
The ground-plan of the propylon is given in Fig 3.   It consists of the
gate proper, whose massive threshold, formed by a single block, is still
in situ, of a vestibule adorned with two antæ, and of a somewhat shorter

[1] Cf. above, p. 50.

inner vestibule. If we except the disengaged columns, which do not yet appear here, we already have in this gate building the prototype of the magnificent Propylæa of Athens.

The walls of the inner court come up to the right and left of the gate; at NO there are two walls which clearly belong to different periods. These walls have received buttresses which probably supported a far-projecting roof. We may therefore assume that the court was surrounded with porticoes as at Tiryns. It should be remembered that similar buttresses appear in the Heraion at Olympia as supports for a roof and as forerunners of a colonnade. Unfortunately the extent of the courtyard cannot be exactly ascertained; its length seems to have been about 88 feet, whilst its breadth measures about 33 feet on the narrowest side.

The buildings A and B, which lie opposite the gate, were discovered in 1882 and described in *Troja*.[1] The few points in which this description has to be corrected or completed are best reserved till later. The walls of sun-dried bricks with horizontal wooden beams laid at regular intervals will then be thoroughly discussed. I shall only point out here that neither building was a temple, but that as I conjectured in *Tiryns* (p. 254)[2] they must be explained as dwelling-houses. The building A would be the chief apartment, or megaron of the palace.

To the right of A and close to it lies the narrower building B. It appears that an almost similar building E, of which only one small portion on the north-east remains, existed on the left of A and was likewise parallel to it. The greater portion of this building was destroyed along with the half of the megaron A by the great north trench of the year 1872. The preserved portion shows that this building probably had the same breadth as B, and that it had a hall or opisthodomos at the back. As a similar hall is also found in the building F in the square D6, we may venture to restore similar halls behind A and B. It is unfortunately no longer possible to establish how far the building E extended to the south-east. On the plan I have made it symmetrical with the building B, but I wish to emphasise that this reconstruction is by no means certain.

A larger building D, which consisted of several rooms lying one behind the other, was erected to the south-west of the building E during the third period. As only foundations and no vertical walls have been preserved, the position of the doors and the whole ground-plan cannot be ascertained. The main front of the building probably faced south-east, and was thus turned towards the small court in front of the south-west gate (FM).

Several buildings join on to B on the north-east side. They consist of one large room with a vestibule, *i.e.* they have the ordinary ground-plan of a temple. The foundations of the building K are the

[1] Cf. above, p. 51.　　　　[2] Cf. p. 50.

best preserved (in F3 and F4).   The door still shows traces of a wooden sill that has been charred.   Another somewhat larger building H (in E4) was at one time altered.   This is shown on the plan by different hatchings.

The big foundations M and N, which have been discovered farther to the east in the squares G3-G5, are very remarkable.   In N only the solid foundations, consisting of quarry-stones, with narrow partition-like corridors, have been preserved, while in M the walls are still standing to a height of about 3 feet.   These walls are of sun-dried bricks, which have been burnt red on one side of the building, and have remained unbaked elsewhere.   This phenomenon, which seems to accord ill with the great conflagration, the traces of which are to be found in the other buildings of the third period and even in the citadel walls, can be explained by the simple fact that this brick wall had no horizontal wooden beams, and therefore the fire found food only in the roof and in the doors.

Both buildings are now divided by a trench about 8 feet broad. This remarkable trench, which is marked P on Plan III, cannot be earlier than Macedonian times, for it has been cut from above through all the layers of earth and older buildings.   It is filled with fine river sand to a height of some metres.   One can clearly see that this sand was deposited by means of water.   We may venture to suppose that a building stood here in Macedonian or Roman times, and was built on a sand foundation in a manner still common nowadays.   Its dimensions of the rectangle formed by the trench are approximately 115 feet by 52 feet, and would therefore do very well for a temple. For instance, the temple of Athena built by Lysimachos, the site of which is still unknown, must have been about 52 feet broad to judge from the existing triglyphs and metopes.   It may very well have stood on this sand foundation.   No squared stones have been preserved above the sand, they were probably all removed in the middle ages to serve for some other building.

Before the making of the sand trench the two buildings M N formed a continuous line of wall, the purport of which is unfortunately not yet clear to us.   It might occur to one that this was another citadel wall, especially as N looks like a gate, were it not that the citadel walls of the third period are preserved on the outside.   Perhaps we have here a citadel wall belonging to an older period, or else a considerable addition made to strengthen the citadel wall.   Further excavation in the square G3 will perhaps solve this question.

The buildings of the third period described up to now are chiefly distinguished by the presence of parastades—bases of stone which supported wooden uprights.   These stones, which are figured in *Troja*. p. 80,[1] only occur in the buildings of this period ; they are not found either in the buildings of the older periods of the second stratum, or

[1] Cf. p. 52.

in those of the upper strata. Accordingly the wooden uprights can only have existed in the buildings of the last period of the second stratum.

A few words will suffice concerning the older buildings of the second stratum. They are naturally not so well known as the buildings of the third period, for they are often concealed beneath them, and could therefore only be examined where the later buildings admitted of a shaft being sunk. They are marked on Plan III with broad cross-hatchings (for the second period) and with dots (for the first period).

There is a great building belonging to the second period on the western side of the citadel. On the one hand it had been partially built over the west door (FL), and on the other it had already been destroyed when the south-west gate (FM) received its present form. The south-west gate must therefore have had a simpler plan when this building was still standing (cf. page 48). We may recognise in this building a row of rooms lying one behind the other. Its ground-plan accordingly agrees completely with that of the later building D. Several walls belonging to this period have also been discovered in the eastern half of the citadel. In addition we also have here walls of the first period over which the others were built. The plans of these buildings show in both periods points of resemblance to the megaron A and B; for instance, the building R in F3 seems also to have been a megaron.

(3) The Upper Strata

When the extensive buildings of the second stratum were destroyed and burnt, numerous small houses were built above its ruins. These are not indicated in our plan, with the exception of the largest (formerly known as that of the City Chieftain) in C5 and a few of the later walls in F4 and F5, which are given on the plan without any hatchings. I intend to publish later a plan of the other houses, as far as I have seen them myself. It appears that the standing portions of the citadel wall of the second stratum were repaired during this period of petty settlements and still used as fortifications. Some of the later buildings outside the south-east gate (FO) probably also belong to this time.

Dr. Schliemann had already shown in his books *Ilios* and *Troja* that all this complex of little houses was several times destroyed and then built over by other settlements. We have obtained further and complete confirmation of this fact by excavating a large complex of buildings which lay in front of the south-west gate, and was included in the citadel later on. I have carefully examined the different layers of houses in this place, and have made plans and photographs of them. Dr. A. Brueckner, who spent some weeks at the excavations, has collected and restored with great skill the numerous fragments of

pottery found in the different layers. I do not propose to give a full
description of the buildings, but merely to add a few remarks to the
short account given above (see p. 329) by Dr. Schliemann.

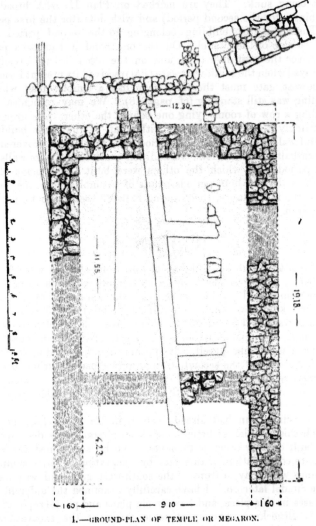

1.—GROUND-PLAN OF TEMPLE OR MEGARON.

Above the ground-level of the second stratum, which is unmistakably fixed by the great ramp in front of the south-west gate, we
found seven other settlements which had been built here one
above the other in the course of centuries. The highest of them

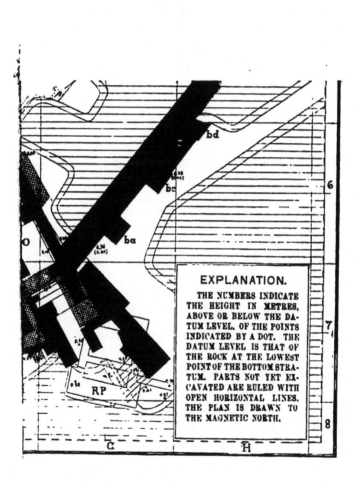

EXPLANATION.

THE NUMBERS INDICATE THE HEIGHT IN METRES, ABOVE OR BELOW THE DATUM LEVEL, OF THE POINTS INDICATED BY A DOT. THE DATUM LEVEL IS THAT OF THE ROCK AT THE LOWEST POINT OF THE BOTTOM STRATUM. PARTS NOT YET EXCAVATED ARE RULED WITH OPEN HORIZONTAL LINES. THE PLAN IS DRAWN TO THE MAGNETIC NORTH.

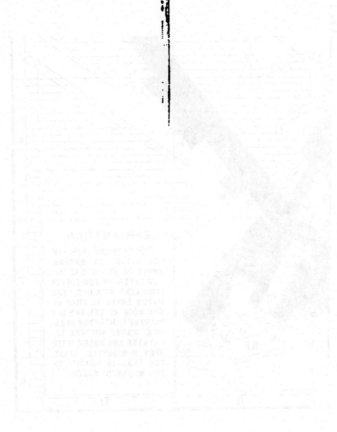

9.

10.

16.

17.

11.

13.

14.

12.

15.

contains Roman buildings of different kinds, some of them small dwelling-houses, and some of them larger buildings. In the second stratum and the one below it were found houses, the walls of which were partly of Greek polygonal masonry. The fourth layer was the most important; in it several buildings constructed of remarkably large blocks of stone were laid bare (p. 332). The ground-plan of one of these buildings can be tolerably well made out, although it has not yet been completely excavated; it resembles a simple Greek temple or the megaron of the royal palace. The ground-plan is given in Fig 4. A vestibule 29 feet 9 inches in breadth and 14 feet in depth gives access to a hall of the same breadth and 37 feet 11 inches in length, which was possibly divided in three by two rows of columns inside. In fact the remains of a foundation have been found which possibly formed the stylobate of an inner row of columns, but this conjecture is quite uncertain. It is impossible to say whether these are the foundations of a temple or a dwelling-house, and the question will probably never be decided. Still the building is of great importance for the history of Trojan antiquities, for in it and in its *débris* several Mycenæan vases and fragments of vases have been found, which have been described above (p. 331).

This circumstance not only dates this layer approximately, but allows us to draw the further conclusion that the second stratum, the citadel of which we have described, must be older than this stratum with the Mycenæan vases. How much older it is impossible to say, but the interval cannot have been a short one, as between the two lie three other strata of poor settlements.

We cannot get any further than these relative dates, as we have as yet no *terminus ante quem* by which to date the Mycenæan vases, and especially the jugs with stirrup handles. It is certain that the jugs with stirrup handles appear as early as the fourteenth century B.C., but whether precisely similar ones were not used much later, *e.g.* in the ninth and eighth centuries, and eventually imported to Troy, must remain uncertain for the present.

In conclusion, it must be mentioned that the small building like a theatre, which was found to the south-east of the Roman Acropolis (see p. 329), will be more carefully described next year among the other Roman and Greek buildings. It was not possible to excavate it completely this year.

ATHENS, 24*th December* 1890.

APPENDIX II

(Chapter iii. 3, pp. 120-122)

THE GOLD CUPS FROM THE VAPHEIO TOMB NEAR AMYCLÆ

THE annexed plate is taken from the beautiful reproduction of these cups in the *Ephemeris* (1889, *pinax* 9). Each cup is about $3\frac{1}{4}$ inches high, the lower diameter is $3\frac{1}{4}$ inches, the upper (including the handle) a little over 4 inches. They are of pure gold, of riveted work, but with designs in *repoussé*, which for originality of design and delicacy of execution are unrivalled, except perhaps by the finest goldsmith's work of the Italian Renaissance. The central design of the first cup is formed by a bull, who has rushed into the toils of a great hunting-net, and appears to be roaring in agony as he strains his head to the skies. The net and the two trees to which it is tied are naturally all in the same plane; the farthest of the trees, which seems suspended in mid air, betrays the artist's naïve effort at rendering the distant perspective.[1] In like manner the curious irregular objects which appear suspended from the edge of both cups are doubtless intended for the landscape on the other side. It is probable that the irregular masses on the gold signet rings (Figs. 220 and 221), which have up to now proved so puzzling, must be explained in the same way. To the left of the central design comes the group of a bull and two men already described in the text (p. 121). On the right a third bull is rushing away furiously in terror at the fate of his companion. A tall palm-tree frames the composition on each side. In spite of the spirited movement of the whole composition, certain crudenesses of design cannot escape observation. For instance, the hind legs of the first bull disappear in a clumsy manner behind the bull entangled in the net, while this second bull is himself twisted round in a manner altogether unnatural and impossible, and the bull who is running away raises his hind legs with a stretch, possible perhaps to the feline race, but much too great for a bull. It is evident that the artist has been influenced by the familiar running lion scheme, which was so thoroughly schematised

---

[1] Cf. Winter, *Arch. Anzeiger*, 1890, p. 102.

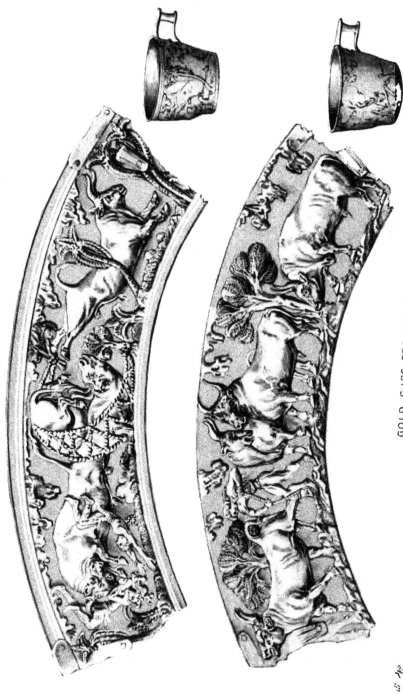

GOLD CUPS FROM VAPHEIO

that it probably influenced all representations of running animals; anyhow it is noticeable that all the Mycenæan animals, whatever their species, have this remarkable action of the hind legs when running at full speed.

On the second cup we have the wild cattle reduced to domesticity; three bulls are grouped peacefully in a pasture, while a herdsman is leading away a fourth bull by a rope tied round one of his hind feet, a scheme familiar on Attic vases, representing Theseus binding the Marathonian bull. The animal apparently shows his reluctance to leave the herd by lowing, and M. Tsountas in the Greek publication aptly quotes the Homeric lines:

> But he breathed forth his spirit with a roar, as when a dragged bull roareth that the young men drag to the altar of the Lord of Helike; for in such hath the earth-shaker his delight.—*Il.* xx. 403.

The second cup is not quite so rich in accessories of landscape as the other. Two trees, resembling those to which the net is fastened on the first cup, help to pleasantly break up the composition, but we see neither palm-trees nor small shrubs. On the other hand, the design of this cup is somewhat the more careful of the two; the cattle are given with more truthfulness to nature, and from the more peaceful nature of the subject, the artist has not been led into any of the exaggerations of drawing noted on the first cup. In other respects the two are so closely connected, both in technical execution and in choice of subject, that there can be no doubt that they were intended as *pendants*. Their artist, like the artist of the shield of Achilles, seems to have delighted in strongly-contrasted scenes borrowed from the same sphere; the stormy cattle-hunting is balanced by the peaceful scene of pasturing, in the same way as the "city at peace" is contrasted on the shield by the "city at war."

Since the discussion raised by Dr. Marx's paper two more Mycenæan gems have been made known, which practically repeat the *motif* of the Tiryns fresco. One is quoted and published by Dr. Herdemann in the *Arch. Anzeiger*, 1889, p. 190. The other is in the British Museum, and is published by Mr. A. S. Murray in *Anzeiger*, 1890, p. 69. It is still difficult to say whether the curious position of the man on the back of the bull is due to lack of skill on the part of the artist, who, unable to depict two objects side by side, places the one above the other, or whether a feature of the hunt was to jump on the back of the bull. As one of the men on the first gold cup has evidently been thrown off the back of the bull, the second view seems the more probable. Even before the discovery of the Vapheio cups Dr. M. Mayer had pointed out that in the Tiryns fresco we probably had a scene of ταυροκαθάψια—a wild-cattle hunt such as Suetonius (*Claud.* 21) says was common in Thessaly. In this sport the huntsman jumped off the back of his horse on to that of the bull. There is no horse on the fresco or the gems, nor is there any reason to suppose that horses were employed in the Mycenæan hunts, but the passage, taken along with the gold cups, is interesting as showing that the leaping of the huntsman on to the back of the bull was a feature common to wild-cattle hunts in all parts of Greece. In Thessalian coin-types, moreover, which undoubtedly refer to this custom (see Head, *Hist. Num.* p. 246), the horse does not appear, and we have only "a Thessalian youth pulling down a raging bull," as in the coin of Larissa given in *H.N.* Fig. 175, p. 254.

Finally, it must be noted that, although Dr. Schuchhardt rejects the notion that the meaning of the Tiryns fresco can be explained by the Catanian coins, he yet admits that they both reproduce the same art type. I cannot help pointing out that on the Sicilian coins the satyr whom Dr. Marx would compare to the "acrobat" seems to have no connection with the bull, but to be merely employed to fill up the space above his back. It will be seen, by looking at Fig. 71 on p. 114 of Head's *Historia Numorum*, that a similar coin to the one given in the text has the space above the man-headed bull filled by a water-fowl instead of by a Silenus. In other coins again a star is found in the same position.

OBJECTS IN FIRST VASE-ROOM OF THE BRITISH MUSEUM ILLUSTRATING THE MYCENÆAN AND GEOMETRIC STYLES

1. Mycenæan Vases.—At the bottom of Case 5 are fragments of vases arranged in order of development; in the first row unglazed ware; in the lower rows fragments of lustrous ware.

2. Gold Mycenæan Work.—On the west side of Table-Case A notice especially gold work in *repoussé*.

3. In Case A (east and south sides) beads of amber, carnelian, crystal, and glass; also objects of ivory.

4. In Case A (south side) weapons, bronze spear-head and arrow-heads.

5. Terra-cotta figurines in Cases 6 and 12.

6. Dipylon Geometric Vases in Cases 14-19.

7. A scarab of Amenophis III, mentioned on p. 316, will be found in Case A.

E. S.

INDEX

ABBREVIATIONS

| H = found at Hissarlik. | M = found at Mycenæ. |
| T = ,, Tiryns. | O = ,, Orchomenos. |

The numerals added to the above give the *strata* at Hissarlik and the graves at Mycenæ.

THE END

Printed by R. & R. CLARK, *Edinburgh.*

MACMILLAN'S CLASSICAL TRANSLATIONS.

Aristotle—The Politics. By Rev. J. E. C. WELLDON, M.A.
10s. 6d.

   THE RHETORIC. By the same. 7s. 6d.

   THE ETHICS. By the same. [In preparation.

Cicero—Select Letters. Translated from Watson's Edition.
By Rev. G. E. JEANS, M.A. 10s. 6d.

   ACADEMICS. Translated by J. S. REID, M.L. 5s. 6d.

Homer—Odyssey. By Professor S. H. BUTCHER, M.A., and
A. LANG, M.A. 6s.

   ILIAD. By A. LANG, M.A., WALTER LEAF, Litt. D., and ERNEST MYERS.
12s. 6d.

   THE ODYSSEY. BOOKS I.-XII. By the EARL OF CARNARVON. 8s. 6d.

Horace—By J. LONSDALE, M.A., and S. LEE, M.A. 3s. 6d.

Herodotus—The History. By G. C. MACAULAY, M.A. 2
vols. 18s.

Juvenal—Thirteen Satires. By A. LEEPER, M.A. 3s. 6d.

Livy. Books XXI.-XXV. By Rev. A. J. CHURCH, M.A.,
and W. J. BRODRIBB, M.A. 7s. 6d.

Longinus—On the Sublime. Translated by H. L. HAVELL,
B.A. With Introduction by ANDREW LANG. Crown 8vo. 4s. 6d.

Meleager: Fifty Poems of. —Translated by WALTER
HEADLAM. Fcap. 4to. 7s. 6d.

Pindar—Odes. By ERNEST MYERS, M.A. Second Edition. 5s.

Plato—Republic. By J. LL. DAVIES, M.A., and D. J.
VAUGHAN, M.A. 4s. 6d.

   EUTHYPHRO, APOLOGY, CRITO, AND PHÆDO. By F. J.
CHURCH. 4s. 6d.

   PHÆDRUS, LYSIS, AND PROTAGORAS. By Rev. J. WRIGHT,
M.A. 4s. 6d.

Polybius—The Histories. By E. S. SHUCKBURGH. 2 vols.
24s.

Sallust—Catiline and Jugurtha. By A. W. POLARD, B.A.
6s. The Catiline, 3s.

Tacitus. By A. J. CHURCH, M.A., and W. J. BRODRIBB, M.A.
History, 6s. Annals, 7s. 6d. Agricola and Germania, 4s. 6d.

Theocritus, Bion, and Moschus. By A. LANG, M.A. 4s. 6d.

Virgil. By J. LONSDALE, M.A., and S. LEE, M.A. 3s. 6d.

   THE ÆNEID. By J. W. MACKAIL, M.A. 7s. 6d.

Xenophon—Complete Works. By H. G. DAKYNS, M.A.
With Introduction and Essays. 4 vols. Vol. I., containing "The
Anabasis" and "The Hellenica." 10s. 6d.

   [Vol. II. in the Press.

MACMILLAN AND CO., LONDON.

MACMILLAN'S CLASSICAL LIBRARY.

Æschylus—The "Seven Against Thebes." (With Translation.) By A. W. VERRALL, Litt.D. 8vo. 7s. 6d.

AGAMEMNON. Edited, with Introduction, Commentary, and Translation, by A. W. VERRALL, Litt.D. 8vo. 12s.

THE SUPPLICES. (With Translation.) By T. G. TUCKER, M.A. 8vo. 10s. 6d.

Babrius. By W. G. RUTHERFORD, M.A., LL.D. 12s. 6d.

Cicero—Academica. By J. S. REID, M.L. 15s.

Euripides—Medea. By A. W. VERRALL, Litt.D. 7s. 6d.

Euripides—Iphigeneia at Aulis. By E. B. ENGLAND, M.A. 7s. 6d.

Herodotus. Books I.–III. By Prof. A. H. SAYCE. 16s.

Homer—Iliad. 2 Vols. Vol. I. Books I.–XII. Vol. II. Books XIII.–XXIV. By WALTER LEAF, Litt.D. 13s. each.

Juvenal—Thirteen Satires. By Prof. J. E. B. MAYOR. Vol. I., Fourth Edition, 10s. 6d. Vol. II. 10s. 6d.

Ktesias—The Fragments of the Persika of Ktesias. Edited, with Introduction and Notes, by JOHN GILMORE, M.A. 8s. 6d.

Pindar—Nemean Odes. By J. B. BURY, M.A. 12s.

Plato—Phædo. By R. D. ARCHER-HIND, M.A. 8s. 6d.

Timæus. By the same Editor. 8vo. 16s.

Pliny—Letters to Trajan. Edited by E. G. HARDY, M.A. 10s. 6d.

Tacitus—Annals. By Prof. G. O. HOLBROOKE. 16s.

THE HISTORIES. Edited, with Introduction and Notes, by Rev. W. A. SPOONER, M.A. 16s.

Thucydides. Book IV. Revised Text, Illustrating the Principal Causes of Corruption in the Manuscripts of this Author. By W. G. RUTHERFORD, M.A. 7s. 6d.

MACMILLAN AND CO., LONDON.

Lightning Source UK Ltd.
Milton Keynes UK
UKOW05f1915050617
302754UK00015B/814/P